YOUR 15-MONTH CANDID,
COMPLETE AND INDIVIDUAL FORECAST

SAGITTARIUS
1986
SUPER HOROSCOPE
NOV. 23—DEC. 20

ARROW BOOKS LIMITED
17-21 Conway Street
London W1P 6JD

CONTENTS

FIRST PUBLISHED IN GREAT BRITAIN BY ARROW BOOKS 1985

PRINTED IN GREAT BRITAIN BY
GUERNSEY PRESS CO. LTD.
GUERNSEY C.I.
ISBN 0 09 941550 X

NOTE TO THE CUSP-BORN

First find the year of your birth, and then find the sign under which you were born according to your day of birth. Thus, you can determine if you are a true Sagittarius (or Scorpio or Capricorn), according to the variations of the dates of the Zodiac. **(See also page7.)**

Are you *really* a Sagittarius? If your birthday falls around the fourth week in November, at the very beginning of Sagittarius, will you still retain the traits of Scorpio, the sign of the Zodiac before Sagittarius? And what if you were born near Christmas—are you more Capricorn than Sagittarius? Many people born at the edge, or cusp, of a sign have great difficulty determining exactly what sign they are. If you are one of these people, here's how you can figure it out once and for all.

Consult the following table. It will tell you the precise days on which the Sun entered and left your sign. If you were born at the beginning or end of Sagittarius, yours is a lifetime reflecting a process of subtle transformation. Your life on Earth will symbolize a significant change in consciousness, for you are about to enter a whole new way of living or are leaving one behind.

If you were born at the beginning of Sagittarius, you may want to read the horoscope for Scorpio as well as Sagittarius, for Scorpio holds the key to many of your hidden weaknesses, sexual uncertainties, wishes, fantasies, and spiritual potentials. You are the symbol of the human mind awakening to its higher capabilities. You are preparing the way for the liberation of your soul into the realms of wisdom and truth. You leave behind greed, blind desire and shallow lust, as you learn to create and understand yourself. You travel, see new places, see how people live, figure yourself out, acquire knowledge.

You may hide a stubborn and dangerous extremism and you may rely too much on luck, but at some crisis point in your life, a change of consciousness will occur to shift your behavior patterns. New worlds open up, as you become aware of immortality and the infinite possiblities of your own mind.

If you were born at the end of Sagittarius, you may want to read the horoscope book for Capricorn as well as Sagittarius, for Capricorn is a deep part of your materialistic values. You were born with the need to bring your dreams into reality and put your talents and ambitions to practical use.

You need to find a balance between believing nothing and believing too much—between cynicism and blind idealism.

DATES SUN ENTERS SAGITTARIUS (LEAVES SCORPIO)

November 22 every year from 1900 to 1990, except the following:

November 23:		November 21:
1902	1923	1976
03	27	80
07	31	84
10	35	88
11	39	
15	43	
19		

DATE SUN LEAVES SAGITTARIUS (ENTERS CAPRICORN)

December 22 every year from 1900 to 1990, except the following:

December 21:

1912	1932	1952	1961	1972	1981
16	36	53	64	73	84
20	40	56	65	76	85
23	44	57	68	77	86
28	48	60	69	80	88
					89

HISTORY AND USES OF ASTROLOGY

Does astrology have a place in the fast-moving, ultra-scientific world we live in today? Can it be justified in a sophisticated society whose outriders are already preparing to step off the moon into the deep space of the planets themselves? Or is it just a hangover of ancient superstition, a psychological dummy for neurotics and dreamers of every historical age?

These are the kind of questions that any inquiring person can be expected to ask when they approach a subject like astrology which goes beyond, but never excludes, the materialistic side of life.

The simple, single answer is that astrology works. It works for tens of millions of people in the western world alone. In the United States there are 10 million followers and in Europe, an estimated 25 million. America has more than 4000 practicing astrologers, Europe nearly three times as many. Even down-under Australia has its hundreds of thousands of adherents. The importance of such vast numbers of people from diverse backgrounds and cultures is recognized by the world's biggest newspapers and magazines who probably devote more of their space to this subject in a year than to any other. In the eastern countries, astrology has enormous followings, again, because it has been proved to work. In countries like India, brides and grooms for centuries have been chosen on the basis of astrological compatibility. The low divorce rate there, despite today's heavy westernizing influence, is attributed largely to this practice.

In the western world, astrology today is more vital than ever before; more practicable because it needs a sophisticated society like ours to understand and develop its contribution to the full; more valid because science itself is confirming the precepts of astrological knowledge with every new exciting step. The ordinary person who daily applies astrology intelligently does not have to wonder whether it is true nor believe in it blindly. He can see it working for himself. And, if he can use it—and this book is designed to help the reader to do just that—he can make living a far richer experience, and become a more developed personality and a better person.

Astrology is the science of relationships. It is not just a study of planetary influences on man and his environment. It is the study of man himself.

We are at the center of our personal universe, of all our relationships. And our happiness or sadness depends on how we act, how we relate to the people and things that surround us. The emotions that we generate have a distinct affect—for better or worse—on the world around us. Our friends and our enemies will confirm this. Just look in the mirror the next time you are angry. In other words, each of us is a kind of sun or planet or star and our influence on our personal universe, whether loving, helpful or destructive, varies with our changing moods, expressed through our individual character.

And to an extent that includes the entire galaxy, this is true of the planetary bodies. Their radiations affect each other, including the earth and all the things on it. And in comparatively recent years, giant constellations called "quasars" have been discovered. These exist far beyond the night stars that we can observe, and science says these quasars are emitting radiating influences more powerful and different than ever recorded on earth. Their effect on man from an astrological point of view is under deep study. Compared with these inter-stellar forces, our personal "radiations" are negligible on the planetary scale. But ours are just as potent in the way they affect our moods, and our ability to control them. To this extent they determine much of the happiness and satisfaction in our lives. For instance, if we were bound and gagged and had to hold some strong emotion within us without being able to move, we would soon start to feel very uncomfortable. We are obviously pretty powerful radiators inside, in our own way. But usually, we are able to throw off our emotion in some sort of action—we have a good cry, walk it off, or tell someone our troubles—before it can build up too far and make us physically ill. Astrology helps us to understand the universal forces working on us, and through this understanding, we can become more properly adjusted to our surroundings and find ourselves coping where others may flounder.

Closely related to our emotions is the "other side" of our personal universe, our physical welfare. Our body, of course, is largely influenced by things around us over which we have very little control. The phone rings, we hear it. The train runs late. We snag our stocking or cut our face shaving. Our body is under a constant bombardment of events that influence our lives to varying degrees.

The question that arises from all this is, what makes each of us act so that we have to involve other people and keep the ball of activity and evolution rolling? This is the question that both science and astrology are involved with. The scientists have attacked it from different angles: anthropology, the study of human evolution as body, mind and response to environment; anatomy, the study of bodily structure; psychology, the science of the human mind; and so on. These studies have produced very impressive classifications and valuable information, but because the approach to the problem is fragmented, so is the result. They remain "branches" of science. Science generally studies effects. It keeps turning up wonderful answers but no lasting solutions. Astrology, on the other hand approaches the question from the broader viewpoint. Astrology began its inquiry with the totality of human experience and saw it as an effect. It then looked to find the cause, or at least the prime movers, and during thousands of years of observation of man and his *universal* environment, came up with the extraordinary principle of planetary influence—or astrology, which, from the Greek, means the science of the stars.

Modern science, as we shall see, has confirmed much of astrology's foundations—most of it unintentionally, some of it reluctantly, but still, indisputably.

It is not difficult to imagine that there must be a connection between outer space and the earth. Even today, scientists are not too sure how our earth was created, but it is generally agreed that it is only a tiny part of the universe. And as a part of the universe, people on earth see and feel the influence of heavenly bodies in almost every aspect of our existence. There is no doubt that the sun has the greatest influence on life on this planet. Without it there would be no life, for without it there would be no warmth, no division into day and night, no cycles of time or season at all. This is clear and easy to see. The influence of the moon, on the other hand, is more subtle, though no less definite.

There are many ways in which the influence of the moon manifests itself here on earth, both on human and animal life. It is a well-known fact, for instance, that the large movements of water on our planet—that is the ebb and flow of the tides—are caused by the moon's gravitational pull. Since this is so, it follows that these water movements do not occur only in the oceans, but that all bodies of water are affected, even down to the tiniest puddle.

The human body, too, which consists of about 70 percent water, falls within the scope of this lunar influence. For example the menstrual cycle of most women corresponds to the lunar month; the period of pregnancy in humans is 273 days, or equal to nine lunar months. Similarly, many illnesses reach a crisis at the change of the moon, and statistics in many countries have shown that the crime rate is highest at the time of the full moon. Even human sexual desire has been associated with the phases of the moon. But, it is in the movement of the tides that we get the clearest demonstration of planetary influence, and the irresistible correspondence between the so-called metaphysical and the physical.

Tide tables are prepared years in advance by calculating the future positions of the moon. Science has known for a long time that the moon is the main cause of tidal action. But only in the last few years has it begun to realize the possible extent of this influence on mankind. To begin with, the ocean tides do not rise and fall as we might imagine from our personal observations of them. The moon as it orbits around the earth, sets up a circular wave of attraction which pulls the oceans of the world after it, broadly in an east to west direction. This influence is like a phantom wave crest, a loop of power stretching from pole to pole which passes over and around the earth like an invisible shadow. It travels with equal effect across the land masses and, as scientists were recently amazed to observe, caused oysters placed in the dark in the middle of the United States where there is no sea, to open their shells to receive the non-existent tide. If the land-locked oysters react to this invisible signal, what effect does it have on us who not so long ago in evolutionary time, came out of the sea and still have its salt in our blood and sweat?

Less well known is the fact that the moon is also the primary force behind the circulation of blood in human beings and animals, and the movement of sap in trees and plants. Agriculturists have established that the moon has a distinct influence on crops, which explains why for centuries people have planted according to moon cycles. The habits of many animals, too, are directed by the movement of the moon. Migratory birds, for instance, depart only at or near the time of the full moon. Just as certain fish, eels in particular, move only in accordance with certain phases of the moon.

Know Thyself—Why?

In today's fast-changing world, everyone still longs to know what the future holds. It is the one thing that everyone has in common: rich and poor, famous and infamous, all are deeply concerned about tomorrow.

But the key to the future, as every historian knows, lies in the past. This is as true of individual people as it is of nations. You cannot understand your future without first understanding your past, which is simply another way of saying that you must first of all know yourself.

The motto "know thyself" seems obvious enough nowadays, but it was originally put forward as the foundation of wisdom by the ancient Greek philosophers. It was then adopted by the "mystery religions" of the ancient Middle East, Greece and Rome, and is still used in all genuine schools of mind training or mystical discipline, both in those of the East, based on yoga, and those of the West. So it is universally accepted now, and has been through the ages.

But how do you go about discovering what sort of person you are? The first step is usually classification into some sort of system of types. Astrology did this long before the birth of Christ. Psychology has also done it. So has modern medicine, in its way.

One system classifies men according to the source of the impulses they respond to most readily: the muscles, leading to direct bodily action; the digestive organs, resulting in emotion, or the brain and nerves. Another such system says that character is determined by the endocrine glands, and gives us labels like "pituitary," "thyroid" and "hyperthyroid" types. These different systems are neither contradictory nor mutually exclusive. In fact, they are very often different ways of saying the same thing.

Very popular and useful classifications were devised by Dr. C. G. Jung, the eminent disciple of Freud. Jung observed among the different faculties of the mind, four which have a predominant influence on character. These four faculties exist in all of us without exception, but not in perfect balance. So when we say, for instance, that a man is a "thinking type," it means that in any situation he tries to be rational. It follows that emotion, which some say is the opposite of thinking, will be his weakest function. This type can be sensible and reasonable, or calculating and unsympathetic. The emotional type, on the other hand, can often be recognized by exaggerated language—everything is either marvelous or terrible—and in extreme cases they even invent dramas and quarrels out of nothing just to make life more interesting.

The other two faculties are intuition and physical sensation. The sensation type does not only care for food and drink, nice clothes and furniture; he is also interested in all forms of physical experience. Many scientists are sensation types as are athletes and nature-lovers. Like sensation, intuition is a form of perception and we all possess it. But it works through that part of the mind which is not under conscious control—consequently it sees meanings and connections which are not obvious to thought or emotion. Inventors and original thinkers are always intuitive, but so, too, are superstitious people who see meanings where none exist.

Thus, sensation tells us what is going on in the world, feeling (that is, emotion) tells us how important it is to ourselves, thinking enables us to interpret it and work out what we should do about it, and intuition tells us what it means to ourselves and others. All four faculties are essential, and all are present in every one of us. But some people are guided chiefly by one, others by another.

Besides these four types, Jung observed a division into extrovert and introvert, which cuts across them. By and large, the introvert is one who finds truth inside himself rather than outside. He is not, therefore, ideally suited to a religion or a political party which tells him what to believe. Original thinkers are almost necessarily introverts. The extrovert, on the other hand, finds truth coming to him from outside. He believes in experts and authorities, and wants to think that nature and the laws of nature really exists, that they are what they appear to be and not just generalities made by men.

A disadvantage of all these systems of classification, is that one cannot tell very easily where to place oneself. Some people are reluctant to admit that they act to please their emotions. So they deceive themselves for years by trying to belong to whichever type they think is the "best." Of course, there is no best; each has its faults and each has its good points.

The advantage of the signs of the Zodiac is that they simplify classification. Not only that, but your date of birth is personal—it is unarguably yours. What better way to know yourself than by going back as far as possible to the very moment of your birth? And this is precisely what your horoscope is all about.

What Is a Horoscope?

If you had been able to take a picture of the heavens at the moment of your birth, that photograph would be your horoscope. Lacking such a snapshot, it is still possible to recreate the picture—and this is at the basis of the astrologer's art. In other words, your horoscope is a representation of the skies with the planets in the exact positions they occupied at the time you were born.

This information, of course, is not enough for the astrologer. He has to have a background of significance to put the photograph on. You will get the idea if you imagine two balls—one inside the other. The inner one is transparent. In the center of both is the astrologer, able to look up, down and around in all directions. The outer sphere is the Zodiac which is divided into twelve approximately equal segments, like the segments of an orange. The inner ball is our photograph. It is transparent except for the images of the planets. Looking out from the center, the astrologer sees the planets in various segments of the Zodiac. These twelve segments are known as the signs or houses.

The position of the planets when each of us is born is always different. So the photograph is always different. But the Zodiac and its signs are fixed.

Now, where in all this are you, the subject of the horoscope?

You, or your character, is largely determined by the sign the sun is in. So that is where the astrologer looks first in your horoscope.

There are twelve signs in the Zodiac and the sun spends approximately one month in each. As the sun's motion is almost perfectly regular, the astrologers have been able to fix the dates governing each sign. There are not many people who do not know which sign of the Zodiac they were born under or who have not been amazed at some time or other at the accuracy of the description of their own character. Here are the twelve signs, the ancient zodiacal symbol, and their dates for the year 1986.*

ARIES	Ram	March 20–April 20
TAURUS	Bull	April 20–May 21
GEMINI	Twins	May 21–June 21
CANCER	Crab	June 21–July 22
LEO	Lion	July 22–August 23
VIRGO	Virgin	August 23–September 23
LIBRA	Scales	September 23–October 23
SCORPIO	Scorpion	October 23–November 22
SAGITTARIUS	Archer	November 22–December 21
CAPRICORN	Sea-Goat	December 21–January 20
AQUARIUS	Water-Bearer	January 20–February 18
PISCES	Fish	February 18–March 20

The time of birth—apart from the date—is important in advanced astrology because the planets travel at such great speed that the patterns they form change from minute to minute. For this reason, each person's horoscope is his and his alone. Further on we will see that the practicing astrologer has ways of determining and reading these minute time changes which dictate the finger character differences in us all.

However, it is still possible to draw significant conclusions and make meaningful predictions based simply on the sign of the Zodiac a person is born under. In a horoscope, the signs do not necessarily correspond with the divisions of the houses. It could be that a house begins half way across a sign. It is the interpretation of such combinations of different influences that distinguishes the professional astrologer from the student and the follower.

However, to gain a workable understanding of astrology, it is not necessary to go into great detail. In fact, the beginner is likely to find himself confused if he attempts to absorb too much too quickly. It should be remembered that this is a science and to become proficient at it, and especially to grasp the tremendous scope of possibilites in man and his affairs and direct them into a worthwhile reading, takes a great deal of study and experience.

*These dates are fluid and change with the motion of the Sun from year to year.

If you do intend to pursue it seriously you will have to learn to figure the exact moment of birth against the degrees of longitude and latitude of the planets at that precise time. This involves adapting local time to Greenwich Mean Time (G.M.T.), reference to tables of houses to establish the Ascendant, as well as making calculations from Ephemeris—the tables of the planets' positions.

After reading this introduction, try drawing up a rough horoscope to get the "feel" of reading some elementary characteristics and natal influences.

Draw a circle with twelve equal segments. Write in counterclockwise the names of the signs—Aries, Taurus, Gemini etc.—one for each segment. Look up an ephemeris for the year of the person's birth and note down the sign each planet was in on the birthday. Do not worry about the number of degrees (although if a planet is on the edge of a sign its position obviously should be considered). Write the name of the planet in the segment/sign on your chart. Write the number 1 in the sign where the sun is. This is the first house. Number the rest of the houses, counterclockwise till you finish at 12. Now you can investigate the probable basic expectation of experience of the person concerned. This is done first of all by seeing what planet or planets is/are in what sign and house. (See also page 72.)

The 12 houses control these functions:

1st.	Individuality, body appearance, general outlook on life	(Personality house)
2nd.	Finance, business	(Money house)
3rd.	Relatives, education, correspondence	(Relatives house)
4th.	Family, neighbors	(Home house)
5th.	Pleasure, children, attempts, entertainment	(Pleasure house)
6th.	Health, employees	(Health house)
7th.	Marriage, partnerships	(Marriage house)
8th.	Death, secret deals, difficulties	(Death house)
9th.	Travel, intellectual affairs	(Travel house)
10th.	Ambition, social standing	(Business and Honor house)
11th.	Friendship, social life, luck	(Friends house)
12th.	Troubles, illness, loss	(Trouble house)

The characteristics of the planets modify the influence of the Sun according to their natures and strengths.

Sun: Source of life. Basic temperament according to sun sign. The will.
Moon: Superficial nature. Moods. Changeable. Adaptive. Mother.
Mercury: Communication. Intellect. Reasoning power. Curiosity. Short travels.
Venus: Love. Delight. Art. Beautiful possessions.
Mars: Energy. Initiative. War. Anger. Destruction. Impulse.
Jupiter: Good. Generous. Expansive. Opportunities. Protection.
Saturn: Jupiter's opposite. Contraction. Servant. Delay. Hardwork. Cold. Privation. Research. Lasting rewards after long struggle.
Uranus: Fashion. Electricity. Revolution. Sudden changes. Modern science.
Neptune: Sensationalism. Mass emotion. Devastation. Delusion.
Pluto: Creates and destroys. Lust for power. Strong obsessions.

Superimpose the characteristics of the planets on the functions of the house in which they appear. Express the result through the character of the birth (sun) sign, and you will get the basic idea of how astrology works.

Of course, many other considerations have been taken into account in producing the carefully worked out predictions in this book: The aspects of the planets to each other; their strength according to position and sign; whether they are in a house of exaltation or decline; whether they are natural enemies or not; whether a planet occupies his own sign; the position of a planet in relation to its own house or sign; whether the planet is male, female or neuter; whether the sign is a fire, earth, water or air sign. These are only a few of the colors on the astrologer's pallet which he must mix with the inspiration of the artist and the accuracy of the mathematician.

The Problem of Love

Love, of course, is never a problem. The problem lies in recognizing the difference between infatuation, emotion, sex and, sometimes, the downright deceit of the other person. Mankind, with its record of broken marriages, despair and disillusionment, is obviously not very good at making these distinctions.

Can astrology help?

Yes. In the same way that advance knowledge can usually help in any human situation. And there is probably no situation as human, as poignant, as pathetic and universal, as the failure of man's love.

Love, of course, is not just between man and woman. It involves love of children, parents, home and so on. But the big problems usually involve the choice of partner.

Astrology has established degrees of compatibility that exist between people born under the various signs of the Zodiac. Because people are individuals, there are numerous variations and modifications and the astrologer, when approached on mate and marriage matters makes allowances for them. But the fact remains that some groups of people are suited for each other and some are not and astrology has expressed this in terms of characteristics which all can study and use as a personal guide.

No matter how much enjoyment and pleasure we find in the different aspects of each other's character, if it is not an overall compatibility, the chances of our finding fulfillment or enduring happiness in each other are pretty hopeless. And astrology can help us to find someone compatible.

History of Astrology

The origins of astrology have been lost far back in history, but we do know that reference is made to it as far back as the first written records of the human race. It is not hard to see why. Even in primitive times, people must have looked for an explanation for the various happenings in their lives. They must have wanted to know why people were different from one to another. And in their search they turned to the regular movements of the sun, moon and stars to see if they could provide an answer.

It is interesting to note that as soon as man learned to use his tools in any type of design, or his mind in any kind of calculation, he turned his attention to the heavens. Ancient cave dwellings reveal dim crescents and circles representative of the sun and moon, rulers of day and night. Mesopotamia and the civilization of Chaldea, in itself the foundation of those of Babylonia and Assyria, show a complete picture of astronomical observation and well-developed astrological interpretation.

Humanity has a natural instinct for order. The study of anthropology reveals that primitive people—even as far back as prehistoric times—were striving to achieve a certain order in their lives. They tried to organize the apparent chaos of the universe. They had the desire to attach meaning to things. This demand for order has persisted throughout the history of man. So that observing the regularity of the heavenly bodies made it logical that primitive peoples should turn heavenwards in their search for an understanding of the world in which they found themselves so random and alone.

And they did find a significance in the movements of the stars. Shepherds tending their flocks, for instance, observed that when the cluster of stars now known as the constellation Aries was in sight, it was the time of fertility and they associated it with the Ram. And they noticed that the growth of plants and plant life corresponded with different phases of the moon, so that certain times were favorable for the planting of crops, and other times were not. In this way, there grew up a tradition of seasons and causes connected with the passage of the sun through the twelve signs of the Zodiac.

Astrology was valued so highly that the king was kept informed of the daily and monthly changes in the heavenly bodies, and the results of astrological studies regarding events of the future. Head astrologers were clearly men of great rank and position, and the office was said to be a hereditary one.

Omens were taken, not only from eclipses and conjunctions of the moon or sun with one of the planets, but also from storms and earthquakes. In the eastern civilizations, particularly, the reverence inspired by astrology appears to have remained unbroken since the very earliest days. In ancient China, astrology, astronomy and religion went hand in hand. The astrologer, who was also an astronomer, was part of the official government service and had his own corner in the Imperial Palace. The duties of the Imperial astrologer, whose office was one of the most important in the land, were clearly defined, as this extract from early records shows:

> "This exalted gentleman must concern himself with the stars in the heavens, keeping a record of the changes and movements of the Planets, the Sun and the Moon, in order to examine the movements of the terrestial world with the object of prognosticating good and bad fortune. He divides the territories of the nine regions of the empire in accordance with their dependence on particular celestial bodies. All the fiefs and principalities are connected with the stars and from this their prosperity or misfortune should be ascertained. He makes prognostications according to the twelve years of the Jupiter cycle of good and evil of the terrestial world. From the colors of the five kinds of clouds, he determines the coming of floods or droughts, abundance or famine. From the twelve winds, he draws conclusions about the state of harmony of heaven and earth, and takes note of good and bad signs that result from their accord or disaccord. In general, he concerns himself with five kinds of phenomena so as to warn the Emperor to come to the aid of the government and to allow for variations in the ceremonies according to their circumstances."

The Chinese were also keen observers of the fixed stars, giving them such unusual names as Ghost Vehicle, Sun of Imperial Concubine, Imperial Prince, Pivot of Heaven, Twinkling Brilliance or Weaving Girl. But, great astrologers though they may have been, the Chinese lacked one aspect of mathematics that the Greeks applied to astrology—deductive geometry. Deductive geometry was the basis of much classical astrology in and after the time of the Greeks, and this explains the different methods of prognostication used in the East and West.

Down through the ages the astrologer's art has depended, not so much on the uncovering of new facts, though this is important, as on the interpretation of the facts already known. This is the essence of his skill. Obviously one cannot always tell how people will react (and this underlines the very important difference between astrology and predestination which will be discussed later on) but one can be prepared, be forewarned, to know what to expect.

But why should the signs of the zodiac have any effect at all on the formation of human character? It is easy to see why people thought they did, and even now we constantly use astrological expressions in our everyday speech. The thoughts of "lucky star," "ill-fated," "star-crossed," "mooning around," are interwoven into the very structure of our language.

In the same way that the earth has been created by influences from outside, there remains an indisputable togetherness in the working of the universe. The world, after all, is a coherent structure, for if it were not, it would be quite without order and we would never know what to expect. A dog could turn into an apple, or an elephant sprout wings and fly at any moment without so much as a by your leave. But nature, as we know, functions according to laws, not whims, and the laws of nature are certainly not subject to capricious exceptions.

This means that no part of the universe is ever arbitrarily cut off from any other part. Everything is therefore to some extent linked with everything else. The moon draws an imperceptible tide on every puddle; tiny and trivial events can be effected by outside forces (such as the fall of a feather by the faintest puff of wind). And so it is fair to think that the local events at any moment reflect to a very small extent the evolution of the world as a whole.

From this principle follows the possibility of divination, and also knowledge of events at a distance, provided one's mind were always as perfectly undisturbed, as ideally smooth, as a mirror or unruffled lake. Provided, in other words, that one did not confuse the picture with hopes, guesses, and expectations. When people try to foretell the future by cards or crystal ball gazing they find it much easier to confuse the picture with expectations than to reflect it clearly.

But the present does contain a good deal of the future to which it leads—not all, but a good deal. The diver halfway between bridge and water is going to make a splash; the train whizzing towards the station will pass through it unless interfered with; the burglar breaking a pane of glass has exposed himself to the possibility of a prison sentence. Yet this is not a doctrine of determinism, as was emphasized earlier. Clearly, there are forces already at work in the present, and any one of them could alter the situation in some way. Equally, a change of decision could alter the whole situation as well. So the future depends, not on an irresistible force, but on a small act of free will.

An individual's age, physique, and position on the earth's surface are remote consequences of his birth. Birth counts as the original cause for all that happens subsequently. The horoscope, in this case, means "this person represents the further evolution of the state of the universe pictured in this chart." Such a chart can apply equally to man or woman, dog, ship or even limited company.

If the evolution of an idea, or of a person, is to be understood as a totality, it must continue to evolve from its own beginnings, which is to say, in the terms in which it began. The brown-eyed person will be faithful to brown eyes all his life; the traitor is being faithful to some complex of ideas which has long been evolving in him; and the person born at sunset will always express, as he evolves, the psychological implications or analogies of the moment when the sun sinks out of sight.

This is the doctrine that an idea must continue to evolve in terms of its origin. It is a completely non-materialist doctrine, though it never fails to apply to material objects. And it implies, too, that the individual will continue to evolve in terms of his moment of origin, and therefore possibly of the sign of the Zodiac rising on the eastern horizon at his birth. It also implies that the signs of the Zodiac themselves will evolve in the collective mind of the human race in the same terms that they were first devised and not in the terms in which modern astrologers consciously think they ought to work.

For the human race, like every other kind of animal, has a collective mind, as Professor Jung discovered in his investigation of dreams. If no such collective mind existed, no infant could ever learn anything, for communication would be impossible. Furthermore, it is absurd to suggest that the conscious mind could be older than the "unconscious," for an infant's nervous system functions correctly before it has discovered the difference between "myself" and "something else" or discovered what eyes and hands are for. Indeed, the involuntary muscles function correctly even before birth, and will never be under conscious control. They are part of what we call the "unconscious" which is not really "unconscious" at all. To the contrary, it is totally aware of itself and everything else; it is merely that part of the mind that cannot be controlled by conscious effort.

And human experience, though it varies in detail with every individual, is basically the same for each one of us, consisting of sky and earth, day and night, waking and sleeping, man and woman, birth and death. So there is bound to be in the mind of the human race a very large number of inescapable ideas, which are called our natural archetypes.

There are also, however, artificial or cultural archetypes which are not universal or applicable to everyone, but are nevertheless inescapable within the limits of a given culture. Examples of these are the cross in Christianity, and the notion of "escape from the wheel of rebirth" in India. There was a time when these ideas did not exist. And there was a time, too, when the scheme of the Zodiac did not exist. One would not expect the Zodiac to have any influence on remote and primitive peoples, for example, who have never heard of it. If the Zodiac is only an archetype, their horoscopes probably would not work and it would not matter which sign they were born under.

But where the Zodiac is known, and the idea of it has become worked into the collective mind, then there it could well appear to have an influence, even if it has no physical existence. For ideas do not have a physical existence, anyway. No physical basis has yet been discovered for the telepathy that controls an anthill; young swallows migrate before, not after, their parents; and the weaver-bird builds its intricate nest without being taught. Materialists suppose, but cannot prove, that "instinct" (as it is called, for no one knows how it works) is controlled by nucleic acid in the chromosomes. This is not a genuine explanation, though, for it only pushes the mystery one stage further back.

Does this mean, then, that the human race, in whose civilization the idea of the twelve signs of the Zodiac has long been embedded, is divided into only twelve types? Can we honestly believe that it is really as simple as that? If so, there must be pretty wide ranges of variation within each type. And if, to explain the variation, we call in heredity and environment, experiences in early childhood, the thyroid and other glands, and also the four functions of the mind mentioned at the beginning of this introduction, and extroversion and introversion, then one begins to wonder if the original classification was worth making at all. No sensible person believes that his favorite system explains everything. But even so, he will not find it much use at all if it does not even save him the trouble of bothering with the others.

Under the Jungian system, everyone has not only a dominant or principal function, but also a secondary or subsidiary one, so that the four can be arranged in order of potency. In the intuitive type, sensation is always the most inefficient function, but the second most inefficient function can be either thinking (which tends to make original thinkers such as Jung himself) or else feeling (which tends to make artistic people). Therefore, allowing for introversion and extroversion, there are at least four kinds of intuitive types, and sixteen types in all. Furthermore, one can see how the sixteen types merge into each other, so that there are no unrealistic or unconvincingly rigid divisions.

In the same way, if we were to put every person under only one sign of the Zodiac, the system becomes too rigid and unlike life. Besides, it was never intended to be used like that. It may be convenient to have only twelve types, but we know that in practice there is every possible gradation between aggressiveness and timidity, or between conscientiousness and laziness. How, then, do we account for this?

The Tyrant and the Saint

Just as the thinking type of man is also influenced to some extent by sensation and intuition, but not very much by emotion, so a person born under Leo can be influenced to some extent by one or two (but not more) of the other signs. For instance, famous persons born under the sign of Gemini include Henry VIII, whom nothing and no-one could have induced to abdicate, and Edward VIII, who did just that. Obviously, then, the sign Gemini does not fully explain the complete character of either of them.

Again, under the opposite sign, Sagittarius, were both Stalin, who was totally consumed with the notion of power, and Charles V, who freely gave up an empire because he preferred to go into a monastery. And we find under Scorpio, many uncompromising characters such as Luther, de Gaulle, Indira Gandhi and Montgomery, but also Petain, a successful commander whose name later became synonymous with collaboration.

A single sign is therefore obviously inadequate to explain the differences between people; it can only explain resemblances, such as the combativeness of the Scorpio group, or the far-reaching devotion of Charles V and Stalin to their respective ideals—the Christian heaven and the Communist utopia.

But very few people are born under one sign only. As well as the month of birth, as was mentioned earlier, the day matters, and, even more, the hour, which ought, if possible, to be noted to the nearest minute. Without this, it is impossible to have an actual horoscope, for the word horoscope means literally, "a consideration of the hour."

The month of birth tells you only which sign of the Zodiac was occupied by the sun. The day and hour tell you what sign was occupied by the moon. And the minute tells you which sign was rising on the eastern horizon. This is called the Ascendant, and it is supposed to be the most important thing in the whole horoscope.

If you were born at midnight, the sun is then in an important position, although invisible. But at one o'clock in the morning the sun is not important, so the moment of birth will not matter much. The important thing then will be the Ascendant, and possibly one or two of the planets. At a given day and hour, say, dawn on January 1st, or 9:00 p.m. on the longest day, the Ascendant will always be the same at any given place. But the moon and planets alter from day to day, at different speeds and have to be looked up in an astronomical table.

The sun is said to signify one's heart, that is to say, one's deepest desires and inmost nature. This is quite different from the moon, which, as we have seen, signifies one's superficial way of behaving. When the ancient Romans referred to the Emperor Augustus as a Capricornian, they meant that he had the moon in Capricorn; they did not pay much attention to the sun, although he was born at sunrise. Or, to take another example, a modern astrologer would call Disraeli a Scorpion because he had Scorpio rising, but most people would call him Sagittarian because he had the sun there. The Romans would have called him Leo because his moon was in Leo.

The sun, as has already been pointed out, is important if one is born near sunrise, sunset, noon or midnight, but is otherwise not reckoned as the principal influence. So if one does not seem to fit one's birth month, it is always worthwhile reading the other signs, for one may have been born at a time when any of them were rising or occupied by the moon. It also seems to be the case that the influence of the sun develops as life goes on, so that the month of birth is easier to guess in people over the age of forty. The young are supposed to be influenced mainly by their Ascendant which characterizes the body and physical personality as a whole.

It should be clearly understood that it is nonsense to assume that all people born at a certain time will exhibit the same characteristics, or that they will even behave in the same manner. It is quite obvious that, from the very moment of its birth, a child is subject to the effects of its environment, and that this in turn will influence its character and heritage to a decisive extent. Also to be taken into account are education and economic conditions, which play a very important part in the formation of one's character as well.

However, it is clearly established that people born under one sign of the Zodiac do have certain basic traits in their character which are different from those born under other signs. It is obvious to every thinking person that certain events produce different reactions in various people. For instance, if a man slips on a banana skin and falls heavily on the pavement, one passer-by may laugh and find this extremely amusing, while another may just walk on, thinking: "What a fool falling down like that. He should look where he is going." A third might also walk away saying to himself: "It's none of my business—I'm glad it wasn't me." A fourth might walk past and think: "I'm sorry for that man, but I haven't the time to be bothered with helping him." And a fifth might stop to help the fallen man to his feet, comfort him and take him home. Here is just one event which could produce entirely different reactions in different people. And, obviously, there are many more. One that comes to mind immediately is the violently opposed views to events such as wars, industrial strikes, and so on. The fact that people have different attitudes to the same event is simply another way of saying that they have different characters. And this is not something that can be put down to background, for people of the same race, religion, or class, very often express quite different reactions to happenings or events. Similarly, it is often the case that members of the same family, where there is clearly uniform background of economic and social standing, education, race and religion, often argue bitterly among themselves over political and social issues.

People have, in general, certain character traits and qualities which, according to their environment, develop in either a positive or a negative manner. Therefore, selfishness (inherent selfishness, that is) might emerge as unselfishness; kindness and consideration as cruelty and lack of consideration towards others. In the same way, a naturally constructive person, may, through frustration, become destructive, and so on. The latent characteristics with which people are born can, therefore, through environment and good or bad training, become something that would appear to be its opposite, and so give the lie to the astrologer's description of their character. But this is not the case. The true character is still there, but it is buried deep beneath these external superficialities.

Careful study of the character traits of different signs can be immeasurable help, and can render beneficial service to the intelligent person. Undoubtedly, the reader will already have discovered that, while he is able to get on very well with some people, he just "cannot stand" others. The causes sometimes seem inexplicable. At times there is intense dislike, at other times immediate sympathy. And there is, too, the phenomenon of love at first sight, which is also apparently inexplicable. People appear to be either sympathetic or unsympathetic towards each other for no apparent reason.

Now if we look at this in the light of the Zodiac, we find that people born under different signs are either compatible or incompatible with each other. In other words, there are good and bad interrelating factors among the various signs. This does not, of course, mean that humanity can be divided into groups of hostile camps. It would be quite wrong to be hostile or indifferent toward people who happen to be born under an incompatible sign. There is no reason why everybody should not, or cannot, learn to control and adjust their feelings and actions, especially after they are aware of the positive qualities of other people by studying their character analyses, among other things.

Every person born under a certain sign has both positive and negative qualities, which are developed more or less according to his free will. Nobody is entirely good or entirely bad, and it is up to each one of us to learn to control himself on the one hand, and at the same time to endeavor to learn about himself and others.

It cannot be repeated often enough that, though the intrinsic nature of man and his basic character traits are born in him, nevertheless it is his own free will that determines whether he will make really good use of his talents and abilities—whether, in other words, he will overcome his vices or allow them to rule him. Most of us are born with at least a streak of laziness, irritability, or some other fault in our nature, and it is up to each one of us to see that we exert sufficient willpower to control our failings so that they do not harm ourselves or others.

Astrology can reveal our inclinations and tendencies. Our weaknesses should not be viewed as shortcomings that are impossible to change. The horoscope of a man may show him to have criminal leanings, for instance, but this does not mean he will definitely become a criminal.

The ordinary man usually finds it difficult to know himself. He is often bewildered. Astrology can frequently tell him more about himself than the different schools of psychology are able to do. Knowing his failings and shortcomings, he will do his best to overcome them, and make himself a better and more useful member of society and a helpmate to his family and friends. It can also save him a great deal of unhappiness and remorse.

And yet it may seem absurd that an ancient philosophy, something that is known as a "pseudo-science," could be a prop to the men and women of the twentieth century. But below the materialistic surface of modern life, there are hidden streams of feeling and thought. Symbology is reappearing as a study worthy of the scholar; the psychosomatic factor in illness has passed from the writings of the crank to those of the specialist; spiritual healing in all its forms is no longer a pious hope but an accepted phenomenon. And it is into this context that we consider astrology, in the sense that it is an analysis of human types.

Astrology and medicine had a long journey together, and only parted company a couple of centuries ago. There still remain in medical language such astrological terms as "saturnine," "choleric," and "mercurial," used in the diagnosis of physical tendencies. The herbalist, for long the handyman of the medical profession, has been dominated by astrology since the days of the Greeks. Certain herbs traditionally respond to certain planetary influences, and diseases must therefore be treated to ensure harmony between the medicine and the disease.

No one expects the most eccentric of modern doctors to go back to the practices of his predecessors. We have come a long way since the time when phases of the moon were studied in illness. Those days were a medical nightmare, with epidemics that were beyond control, and an explanation of the Black Death sought in conjunction with the planets. Nowadays, astrological diagnosis of disease has literally no parallel in modern life. And yet, age-old symbols of types and of the vulnerability of, say, the Saturnian to chronic diseases or the choleric to apoplexy and blood pressure and so on, are still applicable.

But the stars are expected to foretell and not only to diagnose. The astrological forecaster has a counterpart on a highly conventional level in the shape of the weather prophet, racing tipster and stock market forecaster, to name just three examples. All in their own way are aiming at the same result. They attempt to look a little further into the pattern of life and also try to determine future patterns accurately.

Astrological forecasting has been remarkably accurate, but often it is wide of the mark. The brave man who cares to predict world events takes dangerous chances. Individual forecasting is less clear cut; it can be a help or a disillusionment. Then welcome to the nagging question: if it is possible to foreknow, is it right to foretell? A complex point of ethics on which it is hard to pronounce judgment. The doctor faces the same dilemma if he finds that symptoms of a mortal disease are present in his patient and that he can only prognosticate a steady decline. How much to tell an individual in a crisis is a problem that has perplexed many distinguished scholars. Honest and conscientious astrologers in this modern world, where so many people are seeking guidance, face the same problem.

The ancient cults, the symbols of old religions, are eclipsed for the moment. They may return with their old force within a decade or two. But at present the outlook is dark. Human beings badly need assurance, as they did in the past, that all is not chaos. Somewhere, somehow, there is a pattern that must be worked out. As to the why and wherefore, the astrologer is not expected to give judgment. He is just someone who, by dint of talent and training, can gaze into the future.

Five hundred years ago it was customary to call in a learned man who was an astrologer who was probably also a doctor and a philosopher. By his knowledge of astrology, his study of planetary influences, he felt himself qualified to guide those in distress. The world has moved forward at a fantastic rate since then, and in this twentieth century speed has been the keyword everywhere. Tensions have increased, the spur of ambition has been applied indiscriminately. People are uncertain of themselves. At first sight it seems fantastic in the light of modern thinking that they turn to the most ancient of all studies, and get someone to calculate a horoscope for them. But is it *really* so fantastic if you take a second look? For astrology is concerned with tomorrow, with survival. And in a world such as ours, those two things are the keywords of the time in which we live.

HOW TO USE THESE PREDICTIONS

A person reading the predictions in this book should understand that they are produced from the daily position of the planets for a group of people and are not, of course, individually specialized. To get the full benefit of them he should relate the predictions to his own character and circumstances, co-ordinate them, and draw his own conclusions from them.

If he is a serious observer of his own life he should find a definite pattern emerge that will be a helpful and reliable guide.

The point is that we always retain our free will. The stars indicate certain directional tendencies but we are not compelled to follow. We can do or not do, and wisdom must make the choice.

We all have our good and bad days. Sometimes they extend into cycles of weeks. It is therefore advisable to study daily predictions in a span ranging from the day before to several days ahead; also to re-read the monthly predictions for similar cycles.

Daily predictions should be taken very generally. The word "difficult" does not necessarily indicate a whole day of obstruction or inconvenience. It is a warning to you to be cautious. Your caution will often see you around the difficulty before you are involved. This is the correct use of astrology.

In another section, detailed information is given about the influence of the moon as it passes through the various signs of the Zodiac. It includes instructions on how to use the Moon Tables. This information should be used in conjunction with the daily forecasts to give a fuller picture of the astrological trends.

THE MOON

Moon is the nearest planet to the earth. It exerts more observable influence on us from day to day than any other planet. The effect is very personal, very intimate, and if we are not aware of how it works it can make us quite unstable in our ideas. And the annoying thing is that at these times we often see our own instability but can do nothing about it. A knowledge of what can be expected may help considerably. We can then be prepared to stand strong against the moon's negative influences and use its positive ones to help us to get ahead. Who has not heard of going with the tide?

Moon reflects, has no light of its own. It reflects the sun—the life giver—in the form of vital movement. Moon controls the tides, the blood rhythm, the movement of sap in trees and plants. Its nature is inconstancy and change so it signifies our moods, our superficial behavior—walking, talking and especially thinking. Being a true reflector of other forces, moon is cold, watery like the surface of a still lake, brilliant and scintillating at times, but easily ruffled and disturbed by the winds of change.

The moon takes 28½ days to circle the earth and the Zodiac. It spends just over 2¼ days in each sign. During that time it reflects the qualities, energies and characteristics of the sign and, to a degree, the planet which rules the sign. While the moon in its transit occupies a sign incompatible with our own birth sign, we can expect to feel a vague uneasiness, perhaps a touch of irritableness. We should not be discouraged nor let the feeling get us down, or, worse still, allow ourselves to take the discomfort out on others. Try to remember that the moon has to change signs within 55 hours and, provided you are not physically ill, your mood will probably change with it. It is amazing how frequently depression lifts with the shift in the moon's position. And, of course, when the moon is transiting a sign compatible or sympathetic to yours you will probably feel some sort of stimulation or just plain happy to be alive.

In the horoscope, the moon is such a powerful indicator that competent astrologers often use the sign it occupied at birth as the birth sign of the person. This is done particularly when the sun is on the cusp, or edge, of two signs. Most experienced astrologers, however, coordinate both sun and moon signs by reading and confirming from one to the other and secure a far more accurate and personalized analysis.

For these reasons, the moon tables which follow this section (see pages 28–35) are of great importance to the individual. They show the days and the exact times the moon will enter each sign of the Zodiac for the year. Remember, you have to adjust the indicated times to local time. The corrections, already calculated for most of the main cities, are at the beginning of the tables. What follows now is a guide to the influences that will be reflected to the earth by the moon while it transits each of the twelve signs. The influence is at its peak about 26 hours after the moon enters a sign.

MOON IN ARIES

This is a time for action, for reaching out beyond the usual self-imposed limitations and faint-hearted cautions. If you have plans in your head or on your desk, put them into practice. New ventures, applications, new jobs, new starts of any kind—all have a good chance of success. This is the period when original and dynamic impulses are being reflected onto the earth. The energies are extremely vital and favor the pursuit of pleasure and adventure in practically every form. Sick people should feel an improvement. Those who are well will probably find themselves exuding confidence and optimism. People fond of physical exercise should find their bodies growing with tone and well-being. Boldness, strength, determination should characterize most of your activities with a readiness to face up to old challenges. Yesterday's problems may seem petty and exaggerated—so deal with them. Strike out alone. Self-reliance will attract others to you. This is a good time for making friends. Business and marriage partners are more likely to be impressed with the man and woman of action. Opposition will be overcome or thrown aside with much less effort than usual. CAUTION: Be dominant but not domineering.

MOON IN TAURUS

The spontaneous, action-packed person of yesterday gives way to the cautious, diligent, hardworking "thinker." In this period ideas will probably be concentrated on ways of improving finances. A great deal of time may be spent figuring out and going over schemes and plans. It is the right time to be careful with detail. People will find themselves working longer than usual at their desks. Or devoting more time to serious thought about the future. A strong desire to put order into business and financial arrangements may cause extra work. Loved ones may complain of being neglected and may fail to appreciate that your efforts are for their ultimate benefit. Your desire for system may extend to criticism of arrangements in the home and lead to minor upsets. Health may be affected through overwork. Try to secure a reasonable amount of rest and relaxation, although the tendency will be to "keep going" despite good advice. Work done conscientiously in this period should result in a solid contribution to your future security. CAUTION: Try not to be as serious with people as the work you are engaged in.

MOON IN GEMINI

The humdrum of routine and too much work should suddenly end. You are likely to find yourself in an expansive, quicksilver world of change and self-expression. Urges to write, to paint, to experience the freedom of some sort of artistic outpouring, may be very strong. Take full advantage of them. You may find yourself finishing something you began and put aside long ago. Or embarking on something new which could easily be prompted by a chance meeting, a new acquaintance, or even an advertisement. There may be a yearning for a change of scenery, the feeling to visit another country (not too far away), or at least to get away for a few days. This may result in short, quick journeys. Or, if you are planning a single visit, there may be some unexpected changes or detours on the way. Familiar activities will seem to give little satisfaction unless they contain a fresh element of excitement or expectation. The inclination will be towards untried pursuits, particularly those that allow you to express your inner nature. The accent is on new faces, new places. CAUTION: Do not be too quick to commit yourself emotionally.

MOON IN CANCER

Feelings of uncertainty and vague insecurity are likely to cause problems while the moon is in Cancer. Thoughts may turn frequently to the warmth of the home and the comfort of loved ones. Nostalgic impulses could cause you to bring out old photographs and letters and reflect on the days when your life seemed to be much more rewarding and less demanding. The love and understanding of parents and family may be important, and, if it is not forthcoming you may have to fight against a bit of self-pity. The cordiality of friends and the thought of good times with them that are sure to be repeated will help to restore you to a happier frame of mind. The feeling to be alone may follow minor setbacks or rebuffs at this time, but solitude is unlikely to help. Better to get on the telephone or visit someone. This period often causes peculiar dreams and upsurges of imaginative thinking which can be very helpful to authors of occult and mystical works. Preoccupation with the more personal world of simple human needs should overshadow any material strivings. CAUTION: Do not spend too much time thinking—seek the company of loved ones or close friends.

MOON IN LEO

New horizons of exciting and rather extravagant activity open up. This is the time for exhilarating entertainment, glamorous and lavish parties, and expensive shopping sprees. Any merrymaking that relies upon your generosity as a host has every chance of being a spectacular success. You should find yourself right in the center of the fun, either as the life of the party or simply as a person whom happy people like to be with. Romance thrives in this heady atmosphere and friendships are likely to explode unexpectedly into serious attachments. Children and younger people should be attracted to you and you may find yourself organizing a picnic or a visit to a fun-fair, the cinema or the seaside. The sunny company and vitality of youthful companions should help you to find some unsuspected energy. In career, you could find an opening for promotion or advancement. This should be the time to make a direct approach. The period favors those engaged in original research. CAUTION: Bask in popularity but not in flattery.

MOON IN VIRGO

Off comes the party cap and out steps the busy, practical worker. He wants to get his personal affairs straight, to rearrange them, if necessary, for more efficiency, so he will have more time for more work. He clears up his correspondence, pays outstanding bills, makes numerous phone calls. He is likely to make inquiries, or sign up for some new insurance and put money into gilt-edged investment. Thoughts probably revolve around the need for future security—to tie up loose ends and clear the decks. There may be a tendency to be "finicky," to interfere in the routine of others, particularly friends and family members. The motive may be a genuine desire to help with suggestions for updating or streamlining their affairs, but these will probably not be welcomed. Sympathy may be felt for less fortunate sections of the community and a flurry of some sort of voluntary service is likely. This may be accompanied by strong feelings of responsibility on several fronts and health may suffer from extra efforts made. CAUTION: Everyone may not want your help or advice.

MOON IN LIBRA

These are days of harmony and agreement and you should find yourself at peace with most others. Relationships tend to be smooth and sweet-flowing. Friends may become closer and bonds deepen in mutual understanding. Hopes will be shared. Progress by cooperation could be the secret of success in every sphere. In business, established partnerships may flourish and new ones get off to a good start. Acquaintances could discover similar interests that lead to congenial discussions and rewarding exchanges of some sort. Love, as a unifying force, reaches its optimum. Marriage partners should find accord. Those who wed at this time face the prospect of a happy union. Cooperation and tolerance are felt to be stronger than dissension and impatience. The argumentative are not quite so loud in their bellowings, nor as inflexible in their attitudes. In the home, there should be a greater recognition of the other point of view and a readiness to put the wishes of the group before selfish insistence. This is a favorable time to join an art group. CAUTION: Do not be too independent—let others help you if they want to.

MOON IN SCORPIO

Driving impulses to make money and to economize are likely to cause upsets all round. No area of expenditure is likely to be spared the axe, including the household budget. This is a time when the desire to cut down on extravagance can become near fanatical. Care must be exercised to try to keep the aim in reasonable perspective. Others may not feel the same urgent need to save and may retaliate. There is a danger that possessions of sentimental value will be sold to realize cash for investment. Buying and selling of stock for quick profit is also likely. The attention may turn to having a good clean up round the home and at the office. Neglected jobs could suddenly be done with great bursts of energy. The desire for solitude may intervene. Self-searching thoughts could disturb. The sense of invisible and mysterious energies at work could cause some excitability. The reassurance of loves ones may help. CAUTION: Be kind to the people you love.

MOON IN SAGITTARIUS

These are days when you are likely to be stirred and elevated by discussions and reflections of a religious and philosophical nature. Ideas of far-away places may cause unusual response and excitement. A decision may be made to visit someone overseas, perhaps a person whose influence was important to your earlier character development. There could be a strong resolution to get away from present intellectual patterns, to learn new subjects and to meet more interesting people. The superficial may be rejected in all its forms. An impatience with old ideas and unimaginative contacts could lead to a change of companions and interests. There may be an upsurge of religious feeling and metaphysical inquiry. Even a new insight into the significance of astrology and other occult studies is likely under the curious stimulus of the moon in Sagittarius. Physically, you may express this need for fundamental change by spending more time outdoors: sports, gardening or going for long walks. CAUTION: Try to channel any restlessness into worthwhile study.

MOON IN CAPRICORN

Life in these hours may seem to pivot around the importance of gaining prestige and honor in the career, as well as maintaining a spotless reputation. Ambitious urges may be excessive and could be accompanied by quite acquisitive drives for money. Effort should be directed along strictly ethical lines where there is no possibility of reproach or scandal. All endeavors are likely to be characterized by great earnestness, and an air of authority and purpose which should impress those who are looking for leadership or reliability. The desire to conform to accepted standards may extend to sharp criticism of family members. Frivolity and unconventional actions are unlikely to amuse while the moon is in Capricorn. Moderation and seriousness are the orders of the day. Achievement and recognition in this period could come through community work or organizing for the benefit of some amateur group. CAUTION: Dignity and esteem are not always self-awarded.

MOON IN AQUARIUS

Moon in Aquarius is in the second last sign of the Zodiac where ideas can become disturbingly fine and subtle. The result is often a mental "no-man's land" where imagination cannot be trusted with the same certitude as other times. The dangers for the individual are the extremes of optimism and pessimism. Unless the imgination is held in check, situations are likely to be misread, and rosy conclusions drawn where they do not exist. Consequences for the unwary can be costly in career and business. Best to think twice and not speak or act until you think again. Pessimism can be a cruel self-inflicted penalty for delusion at this time. Between the two extremes are strange areas of self-deception which, for example, can make the selfish person think he is actually being generous. Eerie dreams which resemble the reality and even seem to continue into the waking state are also possible. CAUTION: Look for the fact and not just for the image in your mind.

MOON IN PISCES

Everything seems to come to the surface now. Memory may be crystal clear, throwing up long-forgotten information which could be valuable in the career or business. Flashes of clairvoyance and intuition are possible along with sudden realizations of one's own nature, which may be used for self-improvement. A talent, never before suspected, may be discovered. Qualities not evident before in friends and marriage partners are likely to be noticed. As this is a period in which the truth seems to emerge, the discovery of false characteristics is likely to lead to disenchantment or a shift in attachments. However, where qualities are realized it should lead to happiness and deeper feeling. Surprise solutions could bob up for old problems. There may be a public announcement of the solving of a crime or mystery. People with secrets may find someone has "guessed" correctly. The secrets of the soul or the inner self also tend to reveal themselves. Religious and philosophical groups may make some interesting discoveries. CAUTION: Not a time for activities that depend on secrecy.

MOON TABLES

TIME CORRECTIONS FOR GREENWICH MOON TABLES

London, Glasgow, Dublin, Dakar	Same time
Vienna, Prague, Rome, Kinshasa, Frankfurt, Stockholm, Brussels, Amsterdam, Warsaw, Zurich	Add 1 hour
Bucharest, Istanbul, Beirut, Cairo, Johannesburg, Athens, Cape Town, Helsinki, Tel Aviv	Add 2 hours
Dhahran, Baghdad, Moscow, Leningrad, Nairobi, Addis Ababa, Zanzibar	Add 3 hours
Delhi, Calcutta, Bombay, Colombo	Add 5½ hours
Rangoon	Add 6½ hours
Saigon, Bangkok, Chungking	Add 7 hours
Canton, Manila, Hong Kong, Shanghai, Peking	Add 8 hours
Tokyo, Pusan, Seoul, Vladivostok, Yokohama	Add 9 hours
Sydney, Melbourne, Guam, Port Moresby	Add 10 hours
Azores, Reykjavik	Deduct 1 hour
Rio de Janeiro, Montevideo, Buenos Aires, Sao Paulo, Recife	Deduct 3 hours
LaPaz, San Juan, Santiago, Bermuda, Caracas, Halifax	Deduct 4 hours
New York, Washington, Boston, Detroit, Lima, Havana, Miami, Bogota	Deduct 5 hours
Mexico, Chicago, New Orleans, Houston	Deduct 6 hours
San Francisco, Seattle, Los Angeles, Hollywood, Ketchikan, Juneau	Deduct 8 hours
Honolulu, Fairbanks, Anchorage, Papeete	Deduct 10 hours

1986 MOON TABLES—GREENWICH TIME

JANUARY		FEBRUARY		MARCH	
Day Moon Enters		**Day Moon Enters**		**Day Moon Enters**	
1. Virgo		1. Scorpio	6:38 am	1. Scorpio	
2. Libra	8:08 pm	2. Scorpio		2. Sagitt.	3:03 pm
3. Libra		3. Sagitt.	9:35 am	3. Sagitt.	
4. Libra		4. Sagitt.		4. Capric.	6:02 pm
5. Scorpio	0:42 am	5. Capric.	11:50 am	5. Capric.	
6. Scorpio		6. Capric.		6. Aquar.	9:59 pm
7. Sagitt.	2:28 am	7. Aquar.	2:44 pm	7. Aquar.	
8. Sagitt.		8. Aquar.		8. Aquar.	
9. Capric.	3:31 am	9. Pisces	6:49 pm	9. Pisces	3:10 am
10. Capric.		10. Pisces		10. Pisces	
11. Aquar.	5:18 am	11. Pisces		11. Aries	10:30 am
12. Aquar.		12. Aries	1:30 am	12. Aries	
13. Pisces	8:36 am	13. Aries		13. Taurus	8:16 pm
14. Pisces		14. Taurus	11:37 am	14. Taurus	
15. Aries	4:19 pm	15. Taurus		15. Taurus	
16. Aries		16. Taurus		16. Gemini	8:10 am
17. Aries		17. Gemini	0:19 am	17. Gemini	
18. Taurus	3:32 am	18. Gemini		18. Cancer	8:57 pm
19. Taurus		19. Cancer	12:36 pm	19. Cancer	
20. Gemini	4:25 pm	20. Cancer		20. Cancer	
21. Gemini		21. Leo	10:24 pm	21. Leo	7:45 am
22. Gemini		22. Leo		22. Leo	
23. Cancer	4:19 am	23. Leo		23. Virgo	2:49 pm
24. Cancer		24. Virgo	5:15 am	24. Virgo	
25. Leo	1:52 pm	25. Virgo		25. Libra	6:16 pm
26. Leo		26. Libra	9:13 am	26. Libra	
27. Virgo	9:04 pm	27. Libra		27. Scorpio	8:07 pm
28. Virgo		28. Scorpio	12:30 pm	28. Scorpio	
29. Virgo				29. Sagitt.	9:32 pm
30. Libra	2:39 am			30. Sagitt.	
31. Libra				31. Capric.	11:34 pm

Summer time to be considered where applicable.

1986 MOON TABLES—GREENWICH TIME

APRIL			MAY			JUNE		
Day	**Moon Enters**		**Day**	**Moon Enters**		**Day**	**Moon Enters**	
1.	Capric.		1.	Aquar.		1.	Aries	5:01 am
2.	Capric.		2.	Pisces	2:49 pm	2.	Aries	
3.	Aquar.	3:39 am	3.	Pisces		3.	Taurus	4:13 pm
4.	Aquar.		4.	Aries	11:36 pm	4.	Taurus	
5.	Pisces	9:39 am	5.	Aries		5.	Taurus	
6.	Pisces		6.	Aries		6.	Gemini	4:37 am
7.	Aries	5:54 pm	7.	Taurus	10:26 am	7.	Gemini	
8.	Aries		8.	Taurus		8.	Cancer	5:12 pm
9.	Aries		9.	Gemini	10:24 pm	9.	Cancer	
10.	Taurus	3:56 am	10.	Gemini		10.	Cancer	
11.	Taurus		11.	Gemini		11.	Leo	5:09 am
12.	Gemini	3:51 pm	12.	Cancer	11:12 am	12.	Leo	
13.	Gemini		13.	Cancer		13.	Virgo	3:35 pm
14.	Gemini		14.	Leo	11:05 pm	14.	Virgo	
15.	Cancer	4:49 am	15.	Leo		15.	Libra	10:51 pm
16.	Cancer		16.	Leo		16.	Libra	
17.	Leo	4:25 pm	17.	Virgo	9:12 am	17.	Libra	
18.	Leo		18.	Virgo		18.	Scorpio	2:36 am
19.	Leo		19.	Libra	2:45 pm	19.	Scorpio	
20.	Virgo	0:37 am	20.	Libra		20.	Sagitt.	3:22 am
21.	Virgo		21.	Scorpio	4:50 pm	21.	Sagitt.	
22.	Libra	4:52 am	22.	Scorpio		22.	Capric.	3:00 am
23.	Libra		23.	Sagitt.	4:38 pm	23.	Capric.	
24.	Scorpio	6:10 am	24.	Sagitt.		24.	Aquar.	3:11 am
25.	Scorpio		25.	Capric.	4:10 pm	25.	Aquar.	
26.	Sagitt.	6:18 am	26.	Capric.		26.	Pisces	5:47 am
27.	Sagitt.		27.	Aquar.	5:18 pm	27.	Pisces	
28.	Capric.	6:54 am	28.	Aquar.		28.	Aries	Noon
29.	Capric.		29.	Pisces	9:23 pm	29.	Aries	
30.	Aquar.	9:33 am	30.	Pisces		30.	Taurus	10:13 pm
			31.	Pisces				

Summer time to be considered where applicable.

1986 MOON TABLES—GREENWICH TIME

JULY Day Moon Enters		AUGUST Day Moon Enters		SEPTEMBER Day Moon Enters	
1. Taurus		1. Gemini		1. Leo	1:21 am
2. Taurus		2. Cancer	6:09 am	2. Leo	
3. Gemini	10:47 am	3. Cancer		3. Virgo	10:30 am
4. Gemini		4. Leo	5:19 pm	4. Virgo	
5. Cancer	11:13 pm	5. Leo		5. Libra	4:27 pm
6. Cancer		6. Leo		6. Libra	
7. Cancer		7. Virgo	2:44 am	7. Scorpio	9:12 pm
8. Leo	10:50 am	8. Virgo		8. Scorpio	
9. Leo		9. Libra	10:12 am	9. Scorpio	
10. Virgo	8:57 pm	10. Libra		10. Sagitt.	4:34 am
11. Virgo		11. Scorpio	3:20 pm	11. Sagitt.	
12. Virgo		12. Scorpio		12. Capric.	5:41 am
13. Libra	4:44 am	13. Sagitt.	6:53 pm	13. Capric.	
14. Libra		14. Sagitt.		14. Aquar.	5:45 am
15. Scorpio	10:22 am	15. Capric.	9:21 pm	15. Aquar.	
16. Scorpio		16. Capric.		16. Pisces	9:55 am
17. Sagitt.	12:30 pm	17. Aquar.	10:50 pm	17. Pisces	
18. Sagitt.		18. Aquar.		18. Aries	2:55 pm
19. Capric.	1:18 pm	19. Aquar.		19. Aries	
20. Capric.		20. Pisces	1:38 am	20. Taurus	10:30 pm
21. Aquar.	1:39 pm	21. Pisces		21. Taurus	
22. Aquar.		22. Aries	5:47 am	22. Taurus	
23. Pisces	3:39 pm	23. Aries		23. Gemini	8:53 am
24. Pisces		24. Taurus	1:46 pm	24. Gemini	
25. Aries	8:26 pm	25. Taurus		25. Cancer	9:46 pm
26. Aries		26. Taurus		26. Cancer	
27. Aries		27. Gemini	0:55 am	27. Cancer	
28. Taurus	5:30 am	28. Gemini		28. Leo	10:00 am
29. Taurus		29. Cancer	1:49 pm	29. Leo	
30. Gemini	5:27 pm	30. Cancer		30. Virgo	7:25 pm
31. Gemini		31. Cancer			

Summer time to be considered where applicable.

1986 MOON TABLES—GREENWICH TIME

OCTOBER			NOVEMBER			DECEMBER		
Day	**Moon Enters**		**Day**	**Moon Enters**		**Day**	**Moon Enters**	
1.	Virgo		1.	Scorpio	2:21 pm	1.	Sagitt.	2:04 am
2.	Virgo		2.	Scorpio		2.	Sagitt.	
3.	Libra	1:14 am	3.	Sagitt.	3:25 pm	3.	Capric.	1:54 am
4.	Libra		4.	Sagitt.		4.	Capric.	
5.	Scorpio	4:37 am	5.	Capric.	4:05 pm	5.	Aquar.	1:57 am
6.	Scorpio		6.	Capric.		6.	Aquar.	
7.	Sagitt.	6:46 am	7.	Aquar.	5:47 pm	7.	Pisces	4:32 am
8.	Sagitt.		8.	Aquar.		8.	Pisces	
9.	Capric.	8:41 am	9.	Pisces	9:44 pm	9.	Aries	10:00 am
10.	Capric.		10.	Pisces		10.	Aries	
11.	Aquar.	11:49 am	11.	Pisces		11.	Taurus	7:27 pm
12.	Aquar.		12.	Aries	4:35 am	12.	Taurus	
13.	Pisces	4:17 pm	13.	Aries		13.	Taurus	
14.	Pisces		14.	Taurus	1:12 pm	14.	Gemini	6:51 am
15.	Aries	10:38 pm	15.	Taurus		15.	Gemini	
16.	Aries		16.	Taurus		16.	Cancer	7:13 pm
17.	Aries		17.	Gemini	0:30 am	17.	Cancer	
18.	Taurus	6:39 am	18.	Gemini		18.	Cancer	
19.	Taurus		19.	Cancer	12:25 pm	19.	Leo	7:45 am
20.	Gemini	5:00 pm	20.	Cancer		20.	Leo	
21.	Gemini		21.	Cancer		21.	Virgo	7:50 pm
22.	Gemini		22.	Leo	1:13 am	22.	Virgo	
23.	Cancer	5:21 am	23.	Leo		23.	Virgo	
24.	Cancer		24.	Virgo	12:57 pm	24.	Libra	5:11 am
25.	Leo	6:04 pm	25.	Virgo		25.	Libra	
26.	Leo		26.	Libra	9:00 pm	26.	Scorpio	10:51 am
27.	Leo		27.	Libra		27.	Scorpio	
28.	Virgo	4:42 am	28.	Libra		28.	Sagitt.	1:08 pm
29.	Virgo		29.	Scorpio	1:06 am	29.	Sagitt.	
30.	Libra	11:29 am	30.	Scorpio		30.	Capric.	12:47 pm
31.	Libra					31.	Capric.	

Summer time to be considered where applicable.

1986 PHASES OF THE MOON—GREENWICH TIME

New Moon	First Quarter	Full Moon	Last Quarter
(1985)	(1985)	(1985)	Jan. 3
Jan. 10	Jan. 17	Jan. 26	Feb. 2
Feb. 9	Feb. 16	Feb. 24	March 3
March 10	March 18	March 26	April 1
April 9	April 17	April 24	May 1
May 8	May 17	May 23	May 30
June 7	June 15	June 22	June 29
July 7	July 14	July 21	July 28
Aug. 5	Aug. 13	Aug. 19	Aug. 27
Sept. 4	Sept. 11	Sept. 18	Sept. 26
Oct. 3	Oct. 10	Oct. 17	Oct. 25
Nov. 2	Nov. 8	Nov. 16	Nov. 24
Dec. 1	Dec. 8	Dec. 16	Dec. 24
Dec. 31	(1987)	(1987)	(1987)

Summer time to be considered where applicable.

1986 PLANTING GUIDE

	Aboveground Crops	Root Crops	Pruning	Weeds Pests
January	13-14-18-19-23-24	3-4-5-6-9-30-31	5-6	1-7-8-26-27-28-29
February	10-11-15-16-20-21	1-2-6-26-27-28	1-2	3-4-8-25
March	14-15-19-20	1-5-9-26-27-28	1-9-28	3-7-8-30-31
April	10-11-15-16-22-23	1-2-5-6-25-28-29	5-6-25	3-4-8-26-27-30
May	13-14-20-21-22	3-8-26-30-31	3-30-31	1-5-6-24-28
June	9-10-16-17-18-19	4-5-22-23-26-27	26-27	1-2-6-24-25-29-30
July	7-13-14-15-16-20	1-2-6-24-28-29	6-24	4-5-22-26-27-31
August	10-11-12-16-17	2-3-20-21-25-26-30-31	2-3-20-21-30-31	1-22-23-27- 28
September	6-7-8-9-12-13-16-17	21-22-26-27	26-27	1-2-3-19-20-23-24-28-29-30
October	4-5-6-9-10-14-15	18-19-23-24-31	23-24	1-2-21-22-26-27-28-29
November	2-6-10-11-15	1-20-21-27-28-29-30	20-21-29-30	17-18-22-23-24-25
December	3-4-7-8-12-13-31	17-18-24-25-26-27	17-18-27	19-20-21-22-23-29

1986 FISHING GUIDE

	Good	Best
January	7-25-26-27-28-29	3-10-23-24
February	9-21-22-23-24-25	2-16-26-27
March	3-18-23-24-25-29	10-26-27-28
April	9-17-21-26-27	1-22-23-24-25
May	1-17-23-24-25	8-20-21-22-26-30
June	7-15-20-21-24-25-29	19-22-23
July	18-19-21-22-23	7-14-20-24-28
August	5-13-18-19-22-27	16-17-20-21
September	4-11-15-18-19-20	16-17-21-26
October	16-17-20-25	3-10-14-15-18-19
November	8-13-14-17-18-19-24	2-15-16
December	1-14-15-16-19	8-13-17-18-24-31

MOON'S INFLUENCE OVER DAILY AFFAIRS

The Moon makes a complete transit of the Zodiac every 27 days 7 hours and 43 minutes. In making this transit the Moon forms different aspects with the planets and consequently has favorable or unfavorable bearings on affairs and events for persons according to the sign of the Zodiac under which they were born.

Whereas the Sun exclusively represents fire, the Moon rules water. The action of the Moon may be described as fluctuating, variable, absorbent and receptive. It is well known that the attraction to the Moon in combination with the movement of the Earth is responsible for the tides. The Moon has a similar effect on men. A clever navigator will make use of the tides to bring his ship to the intended destination. You also can reach your "destination" better by making use of your tides.

When the Moon is in conjunction with the Sun it is called a New Moon; when the Moon and Sun are in opposition it is called a Full Moon. From New Moon to Full Moon, first and second quarter—which takes about two weeks—the Moon is increasing or waxing. From Full Moon to New Moon, third and fourth quarter, the Moon is said to be decreasing or waning. The Moon Table indicates the New Moon and Full Moon and the quarters.

ACTIVITY	*MOON IN*
Business	
buying and selling	Sagittarius, Aries, Gemini, Virgo
new, requiring public support	1st and 2nd quarter
meant to be kept quiet	3rd and 4th quarter
Investigation	3rd and 4th quarter
Signing documents	1st & 2nd quarter, Cancer, Scorpio, Pisces
Advertising	2nd quarter, Sagittarius
Journeys and trips	1st & 2nd quarter, Gemini, Virgo
Renting offices, etc.	Taurus, Leo, Scorpio, Aquarius
Painting of house/apartment	3rd & 4th quarter, Taurus, Scorpio, Aquarius
Decorating	Gemini, Libra, Aquarius
Buying clothes and accessories	Taurus, Virgo
Beauty salon or barber shop visit	1st & 2nd quarter, Taurus, Leo, Libra, Scorpio, Aquarius
Weddings	1st & 2nd quarter

MOON'S INFLUENCE OVER YOUR HEALTH

ARIES	Head, brain, face, upper jaw
TAURUS	Throat, neck, lower jaw
GEMINI	Hands, arms, lungs, shoulders, nervous system
CANCER	Esophagus, stomach, breasts, womb, liver
LEO	Heart, spine
VIRGO	Intestines, liver
LIBRA	Kidneys, lower back
SCORPIO	Sex and eliminative organs
SAGITTARIUS	Hips, thighs, liver
CAPRICORN	Skin, bones, beeth, knees
AQUARIUS	Circulatory system, lower legs
PISCES	Feet, tone of being

Try to avoid work being done on that part of the body when the Moon is in the sign governing that part.

MOON'S INFLUENCE OVER PLANTS

Centuries ago it was established that seeds planted when the Moon is in certain signs and phases called "fruitful" will produce more than seeds planted when the Moon is in a Barren sign.

FRUITFUL SIGNS	*BARREN SIGNS*	*DRY SIGNS*
Taurus	Aries	Aries
Cancer	Gemini	Gemini
Libra	Leo	Sagittarius
Scorpio	Virgo	Aquarius
Capricorn	Sagittarius	
Pisces	Aquarius	

ACTIVITY	MOON IN
Mow lawn, trim plans	Fruitful sign, 1st & 2nd quarter
Plant flowers	Fruitful sign, 2nd quarter; best in Cancer and Libra
Prune	Fruitful sign, 3rd & 4th quarter
Destroy pests; spray	Barren sign, 4th quarter
Harvest potatoes, root crops	Dry sign, 3rd & 4th quarter; Taurus, Leo, and Aquarius

THE SIGNS: DOMINANT CHARACTERISTICS

March 21–April 20

The Positive Side of Aries

The Arien has many positive points to his character. People born under this first sign of the Zodiac are often quite strong and enthusiastic. On the whole, they are forward-looking people who are not easily discouraged by temporary setbacks. They know what they want out of life and they go out after it. Their personalities are strong. Others are usually quite impressed by the Arien's way of doing things. Quite often they are sources of inspiration for others traveling the same route. Aries men and women have a special zest for life that is often contagious; for others, they are often the example of how life should be lived.

The Aries person usually has a quick and active mind. He is imaginative and inventive. He enjoys keeping busy and active. He generally gets along well with all kinds of people. He is interested in mankind, as a whole. He likes to be challenged. Some would say he thrives on opposition, for it is when he is set against that he often does his best. Getting over or around obstacles is a challenge he generally enjoys. All in all, the Arien is quite positive and young-thinking. He likes to keep abreast of new things that are happening in the world. Ariens are often fond of speed. They like things to be done quickly and this sometimes aggravates their slower colleagues and associates.

The Aries man or woman always seems to remain young. Their whole approach to life is youthful and optimistic. They never say die, no matter what the odds. They may have an occasional setback, but it is not long before they are back on their feet again.

The Negative Side of Aries

Everybody has his less positive qualities—and Aries is no exception. Sometimes the Aries man or woman is not very tactful in communicating with others; in his hurry to get things done he is apt to

be a little callous or inconsiderate. Sensitive people are likely to find him somewhat sharp-tongued in some situations. Often in his eagerness to achieve his aims, he misses the mark altogether. At times the Arien is too impulsive. He can occasionally be stubborn and refuse to listen to reason. If things do not move quickly enough to suit the Aries man or woman, he or she is apt to become rather nervous or irritable. The uncultivated Arien is not unfamiliar with moments of doubt and fear. He is capable of being destructive if he does not get his way. He can overcome some of his emotional problems by steadily trying to express himself as he really is, but this requires effort.

April 21–May 20

The Positive Side of Taurus

The Taurus person is known for his ability to concentrate and for his tenacity. These are perhaps his strongest qualities. The Taurus man or woman generally has very little trouble in getting along with others; it's his nature to be helpful toward people in need. He can always be depended on by his friends, especially those in trouble.

The Taurean generally achieves what he wants through his ability to persevere. He never leaves anything unfinished but works on something until it has been completed. People can usually take him at his word; he is honest and forthright in most of his dealings. The Taurus person has a good chance to make a success of his life because of his many positive qualities. The Taurean who aims high seldom falls short of his mark. He learns well by experience. He is thorough and does not believe in short-cuts of any kind. The Taurean's thoroughness pays off in the end, for through his deliberateness he learns how to rely on himself and what he has learned. The Taurus person tries to get along with others, as a rule. He is not overly critical and likes people to be themselves. He is a tolerant person and enjoys peace and harmony—especially in his home life.

The Taurean is usually cautious in all that he does. He is not a person who believes in taking unnecessary risks. Before adopting any one line of action, he will weigh all of the pros and cons. The

Taurus person is steadfast. Once his mind is made up it seldom changes. The person born under this sign usually is a good family person—reliable and loving.

The Negative Side of Taurus

Sometimes the Taurus man or woman is a bit too stubborn. He won't listen to other points of view if his mind is set on something. To others, this can be quite annoying. The Taurean also does not like to be told what to do. He becomes rather angry if others think him not too bright. He does not like to be told he is wrong, even when he is. He dislikes being contradicted.

Some people who are born under this sign are very suspicious of others—even of those persons close to them. They find it difficult to trust people fully. They are often afraid of being deceived or taken advantage of. The Taurean often finds it difficult to forget or forgive. His love of material things sometimes makes him rather avaricious and petty.

May 21–June 20

The Positive Side of Gemini

The person born under this sign of the Heavenly Twins is usually quite bright and quick-witted. Some of them are capable of doing many different things. The Gemini person very often has many different interests. He keeps an open mind and is always anxious to learn new things.

The Geminian is often an analytical person. He is a person who enjoys making use of his intellect. He is governed more by his mind than by his emotions. He is a person who is not confined to one view; he can often understand both sides to a problem or question. He knows how to reason; how to make rapid decisions if need be.

He is an adaptable person and can make himself at home almost anywhere. There are all kinds of situations he can adapt to. He is a person who seldom doubts himself; he is sure of his talents and his

ability to think and reason. The Geminian is generally most satisfied when he is in a situation where he can make use of his intellect. Never short of imagination, he often has strong talents for invention. He is rather a modern person when it comes to life; the Geminian almost always moves along with the times—perhaps that is why he remains so youthful throughout most of his life.

Literature and art appeal to the person born under this sign. Creativity in almost any form will interest and intrigue the Gemini man or woman.

The Geminian is often quite charming. A good talker, he often is the center of attraction at any gathering. People find it easy to like a person born under this sign because he can appear easygoing and usually has a good sense of humor.

The Negative Side of Gemini

Sometimes the Gemini person tries to do too many things at one time—and as a result, winds up finishing nothing. Some Geminians are easily distracted and find it rather difficult to concentrate on one thing for too long a time. Sometimes they give in to trifling fancies and find it rather boring to become too serious about any one thing. Some of them are never dependable, no matter what they promise.

Although the Gemini man or woman often appears to be well-versed on many subjects, this is sometimes just a veneer. His knowledge may be only superficial, but because he speaks so well he gives people the impression of erudition. Some Geminians are sharp-tongued and inconsiderate; they think only of themselves and their own pleasure.

June 21–July 20

The Positive Side of Cancer

The Cancerians's most positive point is his understanding nature. On the whole, he is a loving and sympathetic person. He would never go out of his way to hurt anyone. The Cancer man or woman

is often very kind and tender; they give what they can to others. They hate to see others suffering and will do what they can to help someone in less fortunate circumstances than themselves. They are often very concerned about the world. Their interest in people generally goes beyond that of just their own families and close friends; they have a deep sense of brotherhood and respect humanitarian values. The Cancerian means what he says, as a rule; he is honest about his feelings.

The Cancer man or woman is a person who knows the art of patience. When something seems difficult, he is willing to wait until the situation becomes manageable again. He is a person who knows how to bide his time. The Cancerian knows how to concentrate on one thing at a time. When he has made his mind up he generally sticks with what he does, seeing it through to the end.

The Cancerian is a person who loves his home. He enjoys being surrounded by familiar things and the people he loves. Of all the signs, Cancer is the most maternal. Even the men born under this sign often have a motherly or protective quality about them. They like to take care of people in their family—to see that they are well loved and well provided for. They are usually loyal and faithful. Family ties mean a lot to the Cancer man or woman. Parents and in-laws are respected and loved. The Cancerian has a strong sense of tradition. He is very sensitive to the moods of others.

The Negative Side of Cancer

Sometimes the Cancerian finds it rather hard to face life. It becomes too much for him. He can be a little timid and retiring, when things don't go too well. When unfortunate things happen, he is apt to just shrug and say, "Whatever will be will be." He can be fatalistic to a fault. The uncultivated Cancerian is a bit lazy. He doesn't have very much ambition. Anything that seems a bit difficult he'll gladly leave to others. He may be lacking in initiative. Too sensitive, when he feels he's been injured, he'll crawl back into his shell and nurse his imaginary wounds. The Cancer woman often is given to crying when the smallest thing goes wrong.

Some Cancerians find it difficult to enjoy themselves in environments outside their homes. They make heavy demands on others, and need to be constantly reassured that they are loved.

July 21–August 21

The Positive Side of Leo

Often Leos make good leaders. They seem to be good organizers and administrators. Usually they are quite popular with others. Whatever group it is that he belongs to, the Leo man is almost sure to be or become the leader.

The Leo person is generous most of the time. It is his best characteristic. He or she likes to give gifts and presents. In making others happy, the Leo person becomes happy himself. He likes to splurge when spending money on others. In some instances it may seem that the Leo's generosity knows no boundaries. A hospitable person, the Leo man or woman is very fond of welcoming people to his house and entertaining them. He is never short of company.

The Leo person has plenty of energy and drive. He enjoys working toward some specific goal. When he applies himself correctly, he gets what he wants most often. The Leo person is almost never unsure of himself. He has plenty of confidence and aplomb. He is a person who is direct in almost everything he does. He has a quick mind and can make a decision in a very short time.

He usually sets a good example for others because of his ambitious manner and positive ways. He knows how to stick to something once he's started. Although the Leo person may be good at making a joke, he is not superficial or glib. He is a loving person, kind and thoughtful.

There is generally nothing small or petty about the Leo man or woman. He does what he can for those who are deserving. He is a person others can rely upon at all times. He means what he says. An honest person, generally speaking, he is a friend that others value.

The Negative Side of Leo

Leo, however, does have his faults. At times, he can be just a bit too arrogant. He thinks that no one deserves a leadership position except him. Only he is capable of doing things well. His opinion of himself is often much too high. Because of his conceit, he is sometimes rather unpopular with a good many people. Some Leos are too materialistic; they can only think in terms of money and profit.

Some Leos enjoy lording it over others—at home or at their place of business. What is more, they feel they have the right to. Egocentric to an impossible degree, this sort of Leo cares little about how others think or feel. He can be rude and cutting.

August 22–September 22

The Positive Side of Virgo

The person born under the sign of Virgo is generally a busy person. He knows how to arrange and organize things. He is a good planner. Above all, he is practical and is not afraid of hard work.

The person born under this sign, Virgo, knows how to attain what he desires. He sticks with something until it is finished. He never shirks his duties, and can always be depended upon. The Virgo person can be thoroughly trusted at all times.

The man or woman born under this sign tries to do everything to perfection. He doesn't believe in doing anything half-way. He always aims for the top. He is the sort of a person who is constantly striving to better himself—not because he wants more money or glory, but because it gives him a feeling of accomplishment.

The Virgo man or woman is a very observant person. He is sensitive to how others feel, and can see things below the surface of a situation. He usually puts this talent to constructive use.

It is not difficult for the Virgoan to be open and earnest. He believes in putting his cards on the table. He is never secretive or under-handed. He's as good as his word. The Virgo person is generally plain-spoken and down-to-earth. He has no trouble in expressing himself.

The Virgo person likes to keep up to date on new developments in his particular field. Well-informed, generally, he sometimes has a keen interest in the arts or literature. What he knows, he knows well. His ability to use his critical faculties is well-developed and sometimes startles others because of its accuracy.

The Virgoan adheres to a moderate way of life; he avoids excesses. He is a responsible person and enjoys being of service.

The Negative Side of Virgo

Sometimes a Virgo person is too critical. He thinks that only he can do something the way it should be done. Whatever anyone else does is inferior. He can be rather annoying in the way he quibbles over insignificant details. In telling others how things should be done, he can be rather tactless and mean.

Some Virgos seem rather emotionless and cool. They feel emo-

tional involvement is beneath them. They are sometimes too tidy, too neat. With money they can be rather miserly. Some try to force their opinions and ideas on others.

September 23–October 22

The Positive Side of Libra

Librans love harmony. It is one of their most outstanding character traits. They are interested in achieving balance; they admire beauty and grace in things as well as in people. Generally speaking, they are kind and considerate people. Librans are usually very sympathetic. They go out of their way not to hurt another person's feelings. They are outgoing and do what they can to help those in need.

People born under the sign of Libra almost always make good friends. They are loyal and amiable. They enjoy the company of others. Many of them are rather moderate in their views; they believe in keeping an open mind, however, and weighing both sides of an issue fairly before making a decision.

Alert and often intelligent, the Libran, always fair-minded, tries to put himself in the position of the other person. They are against injustice; quite often they take up for the underdog. In most of their social dealings, they try to be tactful and kind. They dislike discord and bickering, and most Libras strive for peace and harmony in all their relationships.

The Libra man or woman has a keen sense of beauty. They appreciate handsome furnishings and clothes. Many of them are artistically inclined. Their taste is usually impeccable. They know how to use color. Their homes are almost always attractively arranged and inviting. They enjoy entertaining people and see to it that their guests always feel at home and welcome.

The Libran gets along with almost everyone. He is well-liked and socially much in demand.

The Negative Side of Libra

Some people born under this sign tend to be rather insincere. So eager are they to achieve harmony in all relationships that they will even go so far as to lie. Many of them are escapists. They find facing

the truth an ordeal and prefer living in a world of make-believe.

In a serious argument, some Librans give in rather easily even when they know they are right. Arguing, even about something they believe in, is too unsettling for some of them.

Librans sometimes care too much for material things. They enjoy possessions and luxuries. Some are vain and tend to be jealous.

October 23–November 22

The Positive Side of Scorpio

The Scorpio man or woman generally knows what he or she wants out of life. He is a determined person. He sees something through to the end. The Scorpion is quite sincere, and seldom says anything he doesn't mean. When he sets a goal for himself he tries to go about achieving it in a very direct way.

The Scorpion is brave and courageous. They are not afraid of hard work. Obstacles do not frighten them. They forge ahead until they achieve what they set out for. The Scorpio man or woman has a strong will.

Although the Scorpion may seem rather fixed and determined, inside he is often quite tender and loving. He can care very much for others. He believes in sincerity in all relationships. His feelings about someone tend to last; they are profound and not superficial.

The Scorpio person is someone who adheres to his principles no matter what happens. He will not be deterred from a path he believes to be right.

Because of his many positive strengths, the Scorpion can often achieve happiness for himself and for those that he loves.

He is a constructive person by nature. He often has a deep understanding of people and of life, in general. He is perceptive and unafraid. Obstacles often seem to spur him on. He is a positive person who enjoys winning. He has many strengths and resources; challenge of any sort often brings out the best in him.

The Negative Side of Scorpio

The Scorpio person is sometimes hypersensitive. Often he imagines injury when there is none. He feels that others do not bother to

recognize him for his true worth. Sometimes he is given to excessive boasting in order to compensate for what he feels is neglect

The Scorpio person can be rather proud and arrogant. They can be rather sly when they put their minds to it and they enjoy outwitting persons or institutions noted for their cleverness.

Their tactics for getting what they want are sometimes devious and ruthless. They don't care too much about what others may think. If they feel others have done them an injustice, they will do their best to seek revenge. The Scorpion often has a sudden, violent temper; and this person's interest in sex is sometimes quite unbalanced or excessive.

November 23–December 20

The Positive Side of Sagittarius

People born under this sign are often honest and forthright. Their approach to life is earnest and open. The Sagittarian is often quite adult in his way of seeing things. They are broadminded and tolerant people. When dealing with others the person born under the sign of Sagittarius is almost always open and forthright. He doesn't believe in deceit or pretension. His standards are high. People who associate with the Sagittarian, generally admire and respect him.

The Sagittarian trusts others easily and expects them to trust him. He is never suspicious or envious and almost always thinks well of others. People always enjoy his company because he is so friendly and easy-going. The Sagittarius man or woman is often good-humored. He can always be depended upon by his friends, family, and co-workers.

The person born under this sign of the Zodiac likes a good joke every now and then; he is keen on fun and this makes him very popular with others.

A lively person, he enjoys sports and outdoor life. The Sagittarian is fond of animals. Intelligent and interesting, he can begin an animated conversation with ease. He likes exchanging ideas and discussing various views.

He is not selfish or proud. If someone proposes an idea or plan that is better than his, he will immediately adopt it. Imaginative yet practical, he knows how to put ideas into practice.

He enjoys sport and game, and it doesn't matter if he wins or loses. He is a forgiving person, and never sulks over something that has not worked out in his favor.

He is seldom critical, and is almost always generous.

The Negative Side of Sagittarius

Some Sagittarians are restless. They take foolish risks and seldom learn from the mistakes they make. They don't have heads for money and are often mismanaging their finances. Some of them devote much of their time to gambling.

Some are too outspoken and tactless, always putting their feet in their mouths. They hurt others carelessly by being honest at the wrong time. Sometimes they make promises which they don't keep. They don't stick close enough to their plans and go from one failure to another. They are undisciplined and waste a lot of energy.

December 21–January 19

The Positive Side of Capricorn

The person born under the sign of Capricorn is usually very stable and patient. He sticks to whatever tasks he has and sees them through. He can always be relied upon and he is not averse to work.

An honest person, the Capricornian is generally serious about whatever he does. He does not take his duties lightly. He is a practical person and believes in keeping his feet on the ground.

Quite often the person born under this sign is ambitious and knows how to get what he wants out of life. He forges ahead and never gives up his goal. When he is determined about something, he almost always wins. He is a good worker—a hard worker. Although things may not come easy to him, he will not complain, but continue working until his chores are finished.

He is usually good at business matters and knows the value of money. He is not a spendthrift and knows how to put something away for a rainy day; he dislikes waste and unnecessary loss.

The Capricornian knows how to make use of his self-control. He

can apply himself to almost anything once he puts his mind to it. His ability to concentrate sometimes astounds others. He is diligent and does well when involved in detail work.

The Capricorn man or woman is charitable, generally speaking, and will do what is possible to help others less fortunate. As a friend, he is loyal and trustworthy. He never shirks his duties or responsibilities. He is self-reliant and never expects too much of the other fellow. He does what he can on his own. If someone does him a good turn, then he will do his best to return the favor.

The Negative Side of Capricorn

Like everyone, the Capricornian, too, has his faults. At times, he can be over-critical of others. He expects others to live up to his own high standards. He thinks highly of himself and tends to look down on others.

His interest in material things may be exaggerated. The Capricorn man or woman thinks too much about getting on in the world and having something to show for it. He may even be a little greedy.

He sometimes thinks he knows what's best for everyone. He is too bossy. He is always trying to organize and correct others. He may be a little narrow in his thinking.

January 20–February 18

The Positive Side of Aquarius

The Aquarius man or woman is usually very honest and forthright. These are his two greatest qualities. His standards for himself are generally very high. He can always be relied upon by others. His word is his bond.

The Aquarian is perhaps the most tolerant of all the Zodiac personalities. He respects other people's beliefs and feels that everyone is entitled to his own approach to life.

He would never do anything to injure another's feelings. He is never unkind or cruel. Always considerate of others, the Aquarian is always willing to help a person in need. He feels a very strong tie between himself and all the other members of mankind.

The person born under this sign is almost always an individualist. He does not believe in teaming up with the masses, but prefers going his own way. His ideas about life and mankind are often quite advanced. There is a saying to the effect that the average Aquarian is fifty years ahead of his time.

He is broadminded. The problems of the world concern him greatly. He is interested in helping others no matter what part of the globe they live in. He is truly a humanitarian sort. He likes to be of service to others.

Giving, considerate, and without prejudice, Aquarians have no trouble getting along with others.

The Negative Side of Aquarius

The Aquarian may be too much of a dreamer. He makes plans but seldom carries them out. He is rather unrealistic. His imagination has a tendency to run away with him. Because many of his plans are impractical, he is always in some sort of a dither.

Others may not approve of him at all times because of his unconventional behavior. He may be a bit eccentric. Sometimes he is so busy with his own thoughts, that he loses touch with the realities of existence.

Some Aquarians feel they are more clever and intelligent than others. They seldom admit to their own faults, even when they are quite apparent. Some become rather fanatic in their views. Their criticism of others is sometimes destructive and negative.

February 19–March 20

The Positive Side of Pisces

The Piscean can often understand the problems of others quite easily. He has a sympathetic nature. Kindly, he is often dedicated in the way he goes about helping others. The sick and the troubled often turn to him for advice and assistance.

He is very broadminded and does not criticize others for their faults. He knows how to accept people for what they are. On the whole, he is a trustworthy and earnest person. He is loyal to his

friends and will do what he can to help them in time of need. Generous and good-natured, he is a lover of peace; he is often willing to help others solve their differences. People who have taken a wrong turn in life often interest him and he will do what he can to persuade them to rehabilitate themselves.

He has a strong intuitive sense and most of the time he knows how to make it work for him; the Piscean is unusually perceptive and often knows what is bothering someone before that person, himself, is aware of it. The Pisces man or woman is an idealistic person, basically, and is interested in making the world a better place in which to live. The Piscean believes that everyone should help each other. He is willing to do more than his share in order to achieve cooperation with others.

The person born under this sign often is talented in music or art. He is a receptive person; he is able to take the ups and downs of life with philosophic calm.

The Negative Side of Pisces

Some Pisceans are often depressed; their outlook on life is rather glum. They may feel that they have been given a bad deal in life and that others are always taking unfair advantage of them. The Piscean sometimes feel that the world is a cold and cruel place. He is easily discouraged. He may even withdraw from the harshness of reality into a secret shell of his own where he dreams and idles away a good deal of his time.

The Piscean can be rather lazy. He lets things happen without giving the least bit of resistance. He drifts along, whether on the high road or on the low. He is rather short on willpower.

Some Pisces people seek escape through drugs or alcohol. When temptation comes along they find it hard to resist. In matters of sex, they can be rather permissive.

THE SIGNS AND THEIR KEY WORDS

		POSITIVE	NEGATIVE
ARIES	self	courage, initiative, pioneer instinct	brash rudeness, selfish impetuosity
TAURUS	money	endurance, loyalty, wealth	obstinacy, gluttony
GEMINI	mind	versatility	capriciousness, unreliability
CANCER	family	sympathy, homing instinct	clannishness, childishness
LEO	children	love, authority, integrity	egotism, force
VIRGO	work	purity, industry, analysis	fault-finding, cynicism
LIBRA	marriage	harmony, justice	vacillation, superficiality
SCORPIO	sex	survival, regeneration	vengeance, discord
SAGITTARIUS	travel	optimism, higher learning	lawlessness
CAPRICORN	career	depth	narrowness, gloom
AQUARIUS	friends	human fellowship, genius	perverse unpredictability
PISCES	confine-ment	spiritual love, universality	diffusion, escapism

THE ELEMENTS AND QUALITIES OF THE SIGNS

ELEMENT	SIGN
FIRE	ARIES
	LEO
	SAGITTARIUS
EARTH	TAURUS
	VIRGO
	CAPRICORN
AIR	GEMINI
	LIBRA
	AQUARIUS
WATER	CANCER
	SCORPIO
	PISCES

QUALITY	SIGN
CARDINAL	ARIES
	LIBRA
	CANCER
	CAPRICORN
FIXED	TAURUS
	LEO
	SCORPIO
	AQUARIUS
MUTABLE	GEMINI
	VIRGO
	SAGITTARIUS
	PISCES

Every sign has both an element and a quality associated with it. The element indicates the basic makeup of the sign, and the quality describes the kind of activity associated with each.

Signs can be grouped together according to their *element* and *quality.* Signs of the same element share many basic traits in common. They tend to form stable configurations and ultimately harmonious relationships. Signs of the same quality are often less harmonious, but they share many dynamic potentials for growth as well as profound fulfillment.

THE FIRE SIGNS

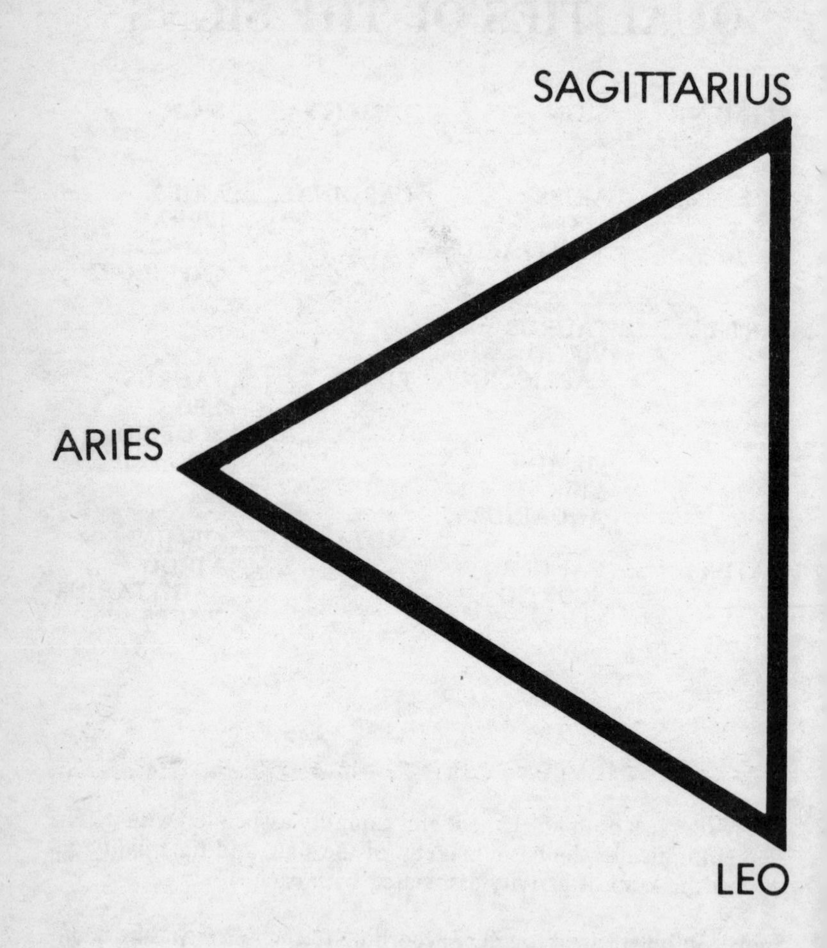

This is the fire group. On the whole these are emotional, volatile types, quick to anger, quick to forgive. They are adventurous, powerful people and act as a source of inspiration for everyone. They spark into action with immediate exuberant impulses. They are intelligent, self-involved, creative and idealistic. They all share a certain vibrancy and glow that outwardly reflects an inner flame and passion for living.

THE EARTH SIGNS

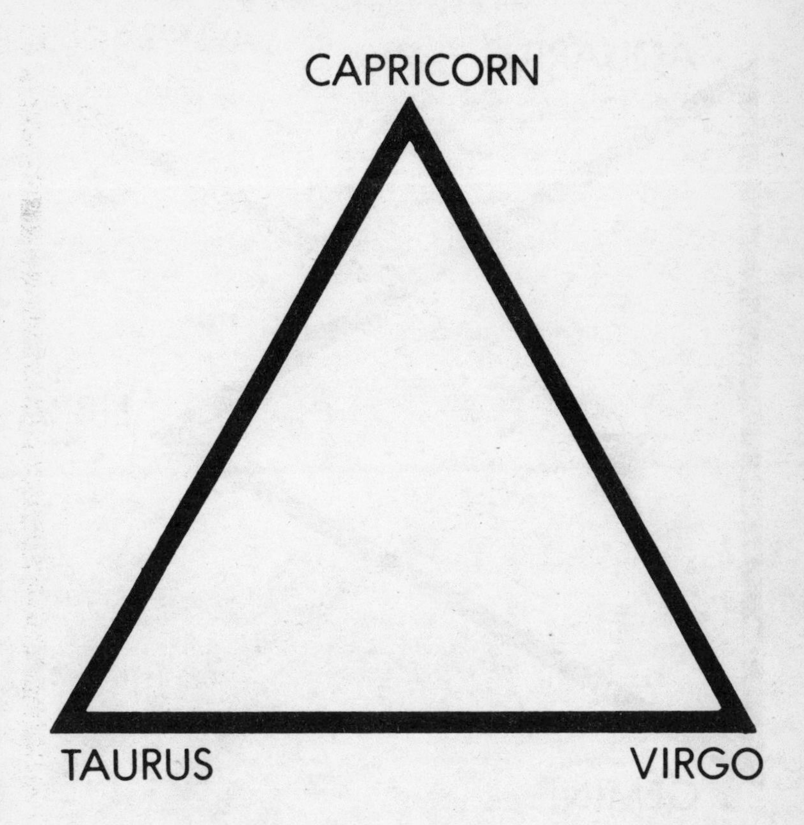

This is the earth group. They are in constant touch with the material world and tend to be conservative. Although they are all capable of spartan self-discipline, they are earthy, sensual people who are stimulated by the tangible, elegant and luxurious. The thread of their lives is always practical, but they do fantasize and are often attracted to dark, mysterious, emotional people. They are like great cliffs overhanging the sea, forever married to the ocean but always resisting erosion from the dark, emotional forces that thunder at their feet.

THE AIR SIGNS

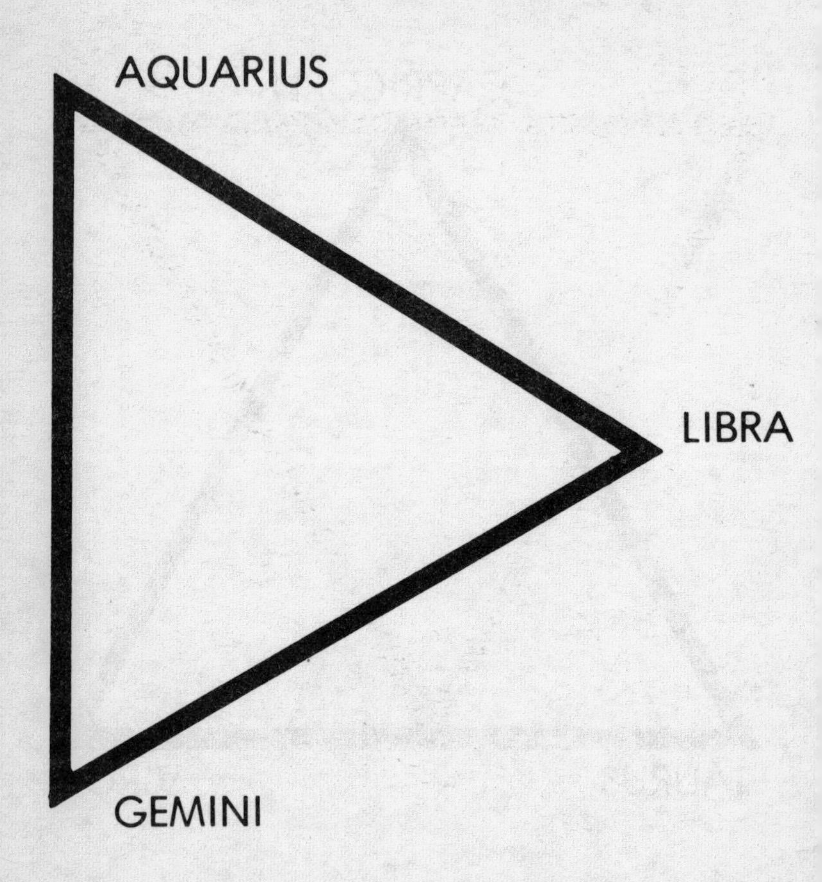

This is the air group. They are light, mental creatures desirous of contact, communication and relationship. They are involved with people and the forming of ties on many levels. Original thinkers, they are the bearers of human news. Their language is their sense of word, color, style and beauty. They provide an atmosphere suitable and pleasant for living. They add change and versatility to the scene, and it is through them that we can explore new territory of human intelligence and experience.

THE WATER SIGNS

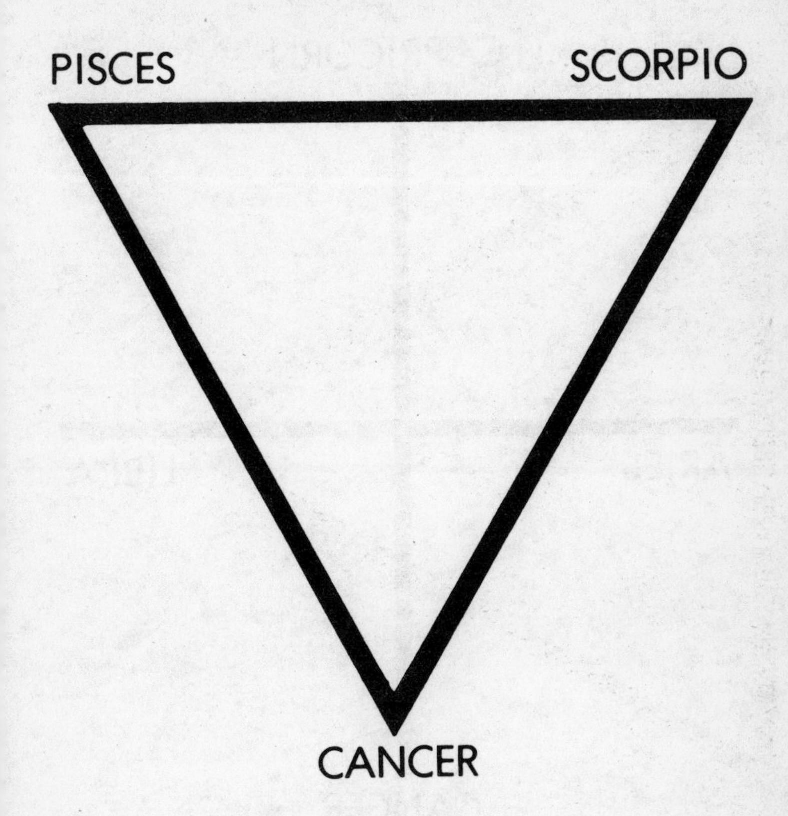

This is the water group. Through the water people, we are all joined together on emotional, non-verbal levels. They are silent, mysterious types whose magic hypnotizes even the most determined realist. They have uncanny perceptions about people and are as rich as the oceans when it comes to feeling, emotion or imagination. They are sensitive, mystical creatures with memories that go back beyond time. Through water, life is sustained. These people have the potential for the depths of darkness or the heights of mysticism and art.

THE CARDINAL SIGNS

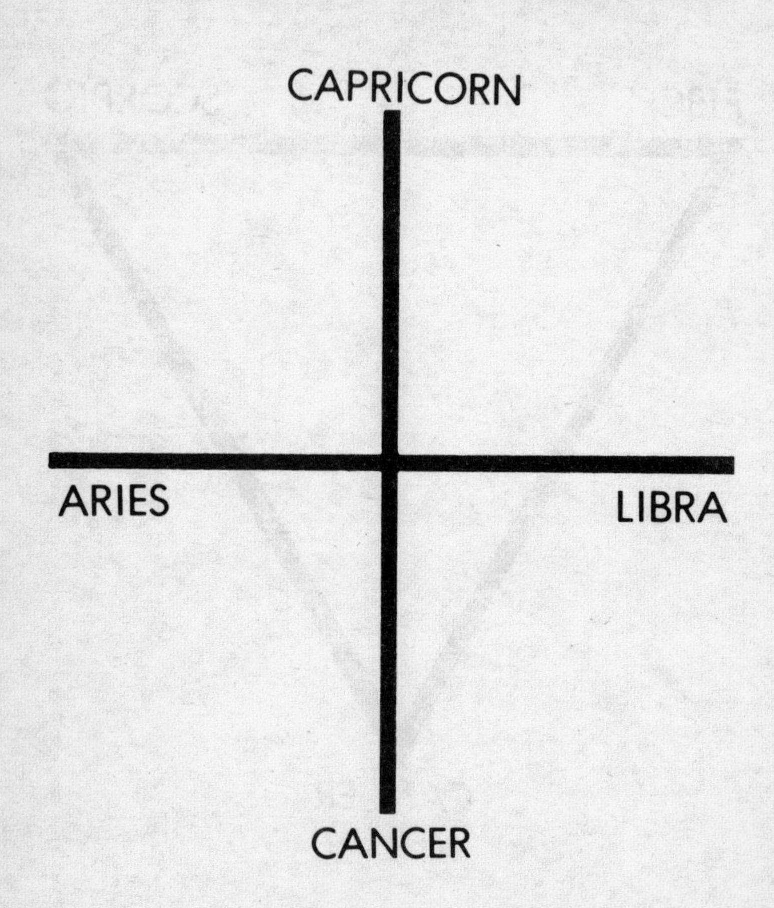

Put together, this is a clear-cut picture of dynamism, activity, tremendous stress and remarkable achievement. These people know the meaning of great change since their lives are often characterized by significant crises and major successes. This combination is like a simultaneous storm of summer, fall, winter and spring. The danger is chaotic diffusion of energy; the potential is irrepressible growth and victory.

THE FIXED SIGNS

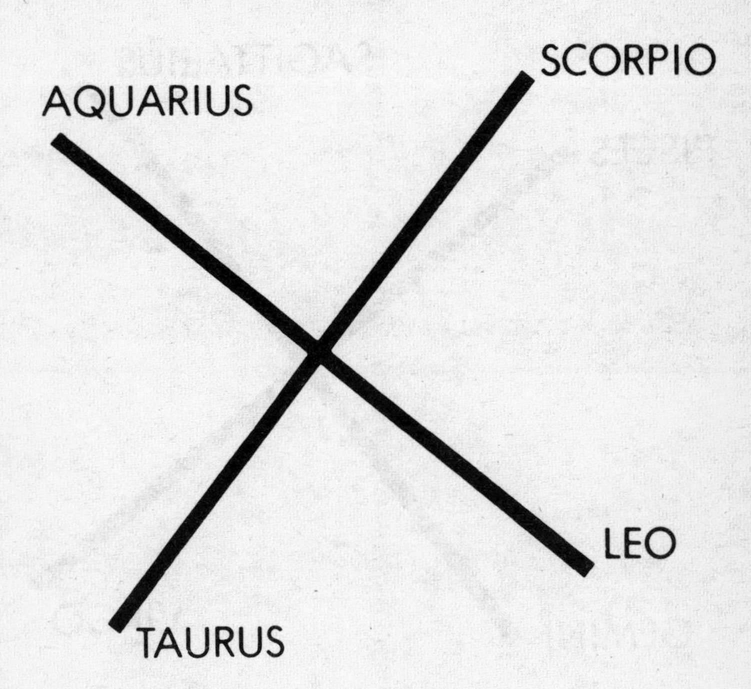

Fixed signs are always establishing themselves in a given place or area of experience. Like explorers who arrive and plant a flag, these people claim a position from which they do not enjoy being deposed. They are staunch, stalwart, upright, trusty, honorable people, although their obstinacy is well-known. Their contribution is fixity, and they are the angels who support our visible world.

THE MUTABLE SIGNS

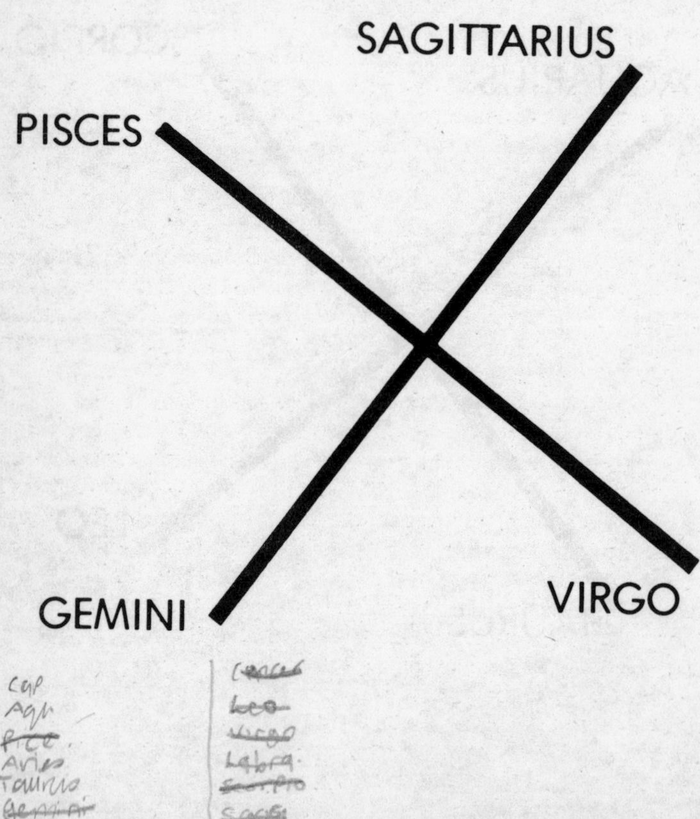

Mutable people are versatile, sensitive, intelligent, nervous and deeply curious about life. They are the translators of all energy. They often carry out or complete tasks initiated by others. Combinations of these signs have highly developed minds; they are imaginative and jumpy and think and talk a lot. At worst their lives are a Tower of Babel. At best they are adaptable and ready creatures who can assimilate one kind of experience and enjoy it while anticipating coming changes.

HOW TO APPROXIMATE YOUR RISING SIGN

Apart from the month and day of birth, the exact *time* of birth is another vital factor in the determination of an accurate horoscope. Not only do the planets move with great speed, but one must know how far the Earth has turned during the day. That way you can determine exactly where the planets are located with respect to the precise birthplace of an individual. This makes *your* horoscope *your* horoscope. In addition to these factors, another grid is laid upon that of the Zodiac and the planets: the houses. After all three have been considered, specific planetary relationships can be measured and analyzed in accordance with certain ordered procedures. It is the skillful translation of all this complex astrological language that a serious astrologer strives for in his attempt at coherent astrological synthesis. Keep this in mind.

The horoscope sets up a kind of framework around which the life of an individual grows like wild ivy, this way and that, weaving its way around the trellis of the natal positions of the planets. The year of birth tells us the positions of the distant, slow-moving planets like Jupiter, Saturn, Uranus and Pluto. The month of birth indicates the Sun sign, or birth sign as it is commonly called, as well as indicating the positions of the rapidly moving planets like Venus, Mercury and Mars. The day of birth locates the position of our Moon, and the moment of birth determines the houses through what is called the Ascendant, or Rising Sign.

As the Earth rotates on its axis once every 24 hours, each one of the twelve signs of the Zodiac appears to be "rising" on the horizon, with a new one appearing about every two hours. Actually it is the turning of the Earth that exposes each sign to view, but you will remember that in much of our astrological work we are discussing "apparent" motion. This *Rising Sign* marks the Ascendant and it colors the whole orientation of a horoscope. It indicates the sign governing the first house of the chart, and will thus determine which signs will govern all the other houses. The idea is a bit complicated at first, and we needn't dwell on complications in this introduction, but if you can imagine two color wheels with twelve divisions superimposed upon each other, one moving slowly and the other remaining still, you will have some idea of how the signs keep shifting the "color" of the houses as the Rising Sign continues to change every two hours.

The important point is that the birth chart, or horoscope, actually does define specific factors of a person's makeup. It contains a picture of being, much the way the nucleus of a tiny cell contains the potential for an entire elephant, or a packet of seeds contains a rosebush. If there were no order or continuity to the world, we could plant roses and get elephants. This same order that gives continuous flow to our lives often annoys people if it threatens to determine too much of their lives. We must grow from what we were planted, and there's no reason why we can't do that magnificently. It's all there in the horoscope. Where there is limitation, there is breakthrough; where there is crisis, there is transformation. Accurate analysis of a horoscope can help you find these points of breakthrough and transformation, and it requires knowledge of subtleties and distinctions that demand skillful judgment in order to solve even the simplest kind of personal question.

It is still quite possible, however, to draw some conclusions based upon the sign occupied by the Sun alone. In fact, if you're just being introduced to this vast subject, you're better off keeping it simple. Otherwise it seems like an impossible jumble, much like trying to read a novel in a foreign language without knowing the basic vocabulary. As with anything else, you can progress in your appreciation and understanding of astrology in direct proportion to your interest. To become really good at it requires study, experience, patience and above all—and maybe simplest of all—a fundamental understanding of what is actually going on right up there in the sky over your head. It is a vital living process you can observe, contemplate and ultimately understand. You can start by observing sunrise, or sunset, or even the full Moon.

In fact you can do a simple experiment after reading this introduction. You can erect a rough chart by following the simple procedure below:

1. Draw a circle with twelve equal segments.
2. Starting at what would be the nine o'clock position on a clock, number the segments, or houses, from 1 to 12 in a *counterclockwise direction.*
3. Label house number 1 in the following way: 4 A.M.-6 A.M.
4. In a counterclockwise direction, label the rest of the houses: 2 A.M.-4 A.M., MIDNIGHT-2 A.M., 10 P.M-MIDNIGHT, 8 P.M.-10 P.M., 6 P.M.-8 P.M., 4 P.M.-6 P.M., 2 P.M.-4 P.M., NOON-2 P.M., 10 A.M.-NOON, 8 A.M.-10 A.M., and6 A.M.-8 A.M.
5. Now find out what time you were born and place the sun in the appropriate house.

6. Label the edge of that house with your Sun sign. You now have a description of your basic character and your fundamental drives. You can also see in what areas of life on Earth you will be most likely to focus your constant energy and center your activity.

7. If you are really feeling ambitious, label the rest of the houses with the signs, starting with your Sun sign, in order, still in a *counterclockwise direction.* When you get to Pisces, start over with Aries and keep going until you reach the house behind the Sun.

8. Look to house number 1. The sign that you have now labeled and attached to house number 1 is your Rising sign. It will color your self-image, outlook, physical constitution, early life and whole orientation to life. Of course this is a mere approximation, since there are many complicated calculations that must be made with respect to adjustments for birth time, but if you read descriptions of the sign preceding and the sign following the one you have calculated in the above manner, you may be able to identify yourself better. In any case, when you get through labeling all the houses, your drawing should look something like this:

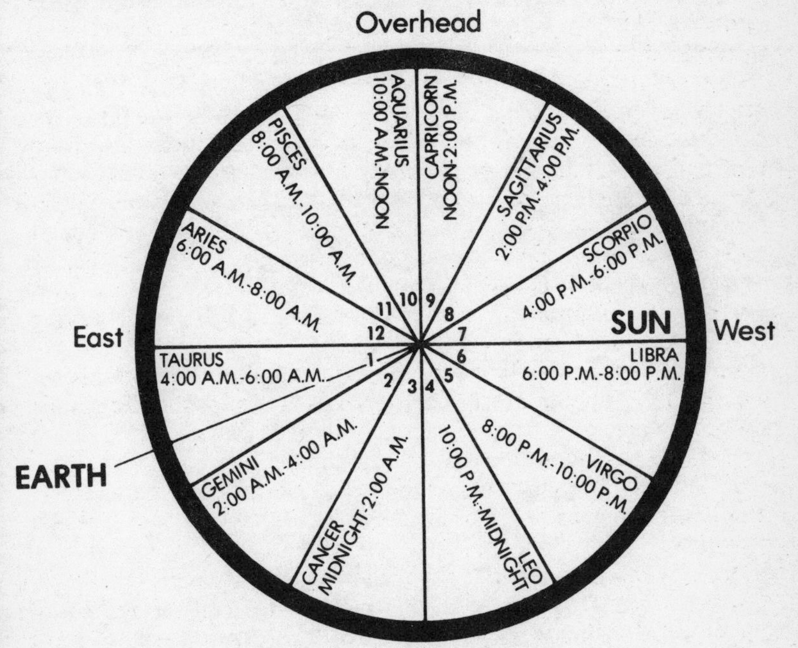

Basic chart illustrating the position of the Sun in Scorpio, with the Ascendant Taurus as the Rising Sign.'

This individual was born at 5:15 P.M. on October 31 in New York City. The Sun is in Scorpio and is found in the 7th house. The Rising sign, or the sign governing house number 1, is Taurus, so this person is a blend of Scorpio and Taurus.

Any further calculation would necessitate that you look in an ephemeris, or table of planetary motion, for the positions of the rest of the planets for your particular birth year. But we will take the time to define briefly all the known planets of our Solar System and the Sun to acquaint you with some more of the astrological vocabulary that you will be meeting again and again. (See page 21 for a full explanation of the Moon in all the Signs.)

THE PLANETS AND SIGNS THEY RULE

The signs of the Zodiac are linked to the planets in the following way. Each sign is governed or ruled by one or more planets. No matter where the planets are located in the sky at any given moment, they still rule their respective signs, and when they travel through the signs they rule, they have special dignity and their effects are stronger.

Following is a list of the planets and the signs they rule. After looking at the list, go back over the definitions of the planets and see if you can determine how the planet ruling *your* Sun sign has affected your life.

SIGNS	RULING PLANETS
Aries	Mars, Pluto
Taurus	Venus
Gemini	Mercury
Cancer	Moon
Leo	Sun
Virgo	Mercury
Libra	Venus
Scorpio	Mars, Pluto
Sagittarius	Jupiter
Capricorn	Saturn
Aquarius	Saturn, Uranus
Pisces	Jupiter, Neptune

THE PLANETS OF THE SOLAR SYSTEM

Here are the planets of the Solar System. They all travel around the Sun at different speeds and different distances. Taken with the Sun, they all distribute individual intelligence and ability throughout the entire chart.

The planets modify the influence of the Sun in a chart according to their own particular natures, strengths and positions. Their positions must be calculated for each year and day, and their function and expression in a horoscope will change as they move from one area of the Zodiac to another.

Following, you will find brief statements of their pure meanings.

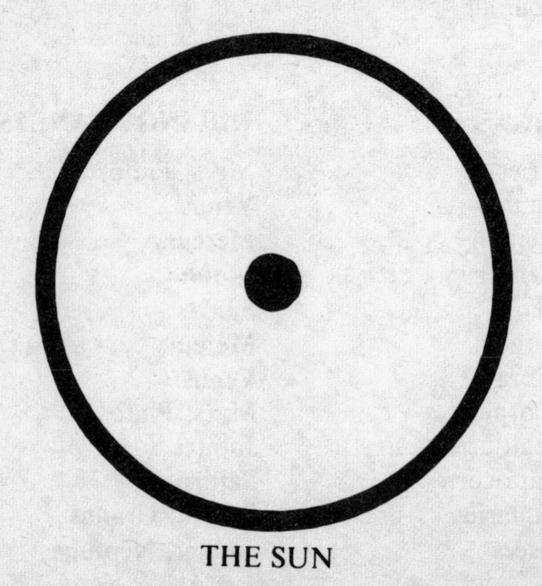

THE SUN

SUN

This is the center of existence. Around this flaming sphere all the planets revolve in endless orbits. Our star is constantly sending out its beams of light and energy without which no life on Earth would be possible. In astrology it symbolizes everything we are trying to become, the center around which all of our activity in life will always revolve. It is the symbol of our basic nature and describes the natural and constant thread that runs through everything that we do from birth to death on this planet.

To early astrologers, the sun seemed to be another planet because it crossed the heavens every day, just like the rest of the bodies in the sky.

It is the only star near enough to be seen well—it is, in fact, a dwarf star. Approximately 860,000 miles in diameter, it is about ten times as wide as the giant planet Jupiter. The next nearest star is nearly 300,000 times as far away, and if the Sun were located as far away as most of the bright stars, it would be too faint to be seen without a telescope.

Everything in the horoscope ultimately revolves around this singular body. Although other forces may be prominent in the charts of some individuals, still the Sun is the total nucleus of being and symbolizes the complete potential of every human being alive. It is vitality and the life force. Your whole essence comes from the position of the Sun.

You are always trying to express the Sun according to its position by house and sign. Possibility for all development is found in the Sun, and it marks the fundamental character of your personal radiations all around you.

It is the symbol of strength, vigor, wisdom, dignity, ardor and generosity, and the ability for a person to function as a mature individual. It is also a creative force in society. It is consciousness of the gift of life.

The underdeveloped solar nature is arrogant, pushy, undependable and proud, and is constantly using force.

MERCURY

Mercury is the planet closest to the Sun. It races around our star, gathering information and translating it to the rest of the system. Mercury represents your capacity to understand the desires of your own will and to translate those desires into action.

In other words it is the planet of Mind and the power of communication. Through Mercury we develop an ability to think, write, speak and observe—to become aware of the world around us. It colors our attitudes and vision of the world, as well as our capacity to communicate our inner responses to the outside world. Some people who have serious disabilities in their power of verbal communication have often wrongly been described as people lacking intelligence.

Although this planet (and its position in the horoscope) indicates your power to communicate your thoughts and perceptions to the world, intelligence is something deeper. Intelligence is distributed throughout all the planets. It is the relationship of the planets to each other that truly describes what we call intelligence. Mercury rules speaking, language, mathematics, draft and design, students, messengers, young people, offices, teachers and any pursuits where the mind of man has wings.

VENUS

Venus is beauty. It symbolizes the harmony and radiance of a rare and elusive quality: beauty itself. It is refinement and delicacy, softness and charm. In astrology it indicates grace, balance and the aesthetic sense. Where Venus is we see beauty, a gentle drawing in of energy and the need for satisfaction and completion. It is a special touch that finishes off rough edges. It is sensitivity, and affection, and it is always the place for that other elusive phenomenon: love. Venus describes our sense of what is beautiful and loving. Poorly developed, it is vulgar, tasteless and self-indulgent. But its ideal is the flame of spiritual love—Aphrodite, goddess of love, and the sweetness and power of personal beauty.

MARS

This is raw, crude energy. The planet next to Earth but outward from the Sun is a fiery red sphere that charges through the horoscope with force and fury. It represents the way you reach out for new adventure and new experience. It is energy and drive, initiative, courage and daring. The power to start something and see it through. It can be thoughtless, cruel and wild, angry and hostile, causing cuts, burns, scalds and wounds. It can stab its way through a chart, or it can be the symbol of healthy spirited adventure, well-channeled constructive power to begin and keep up the drive. If you have trouble starting things, if you lack the get-up-and-go to start the ball rolling, if you lack aggressiveness and self-confidence, chances are there's another planet influencing your Mars. Mars rules soldiers, butchers, surgeons, salesmen—any field that requires daring, bold skill, operational technique or self-promotion.

JUPITER

This is the largest planet of the Solar System. Scientists have recently learned that Jupiter reflects more light than it receives from the Sun. In a sense it is like a star itself. In astrology it rules good luck and good cheer, health, wealth, optimism, happiness, success and joy. It is the symbol of opportunity and always opens the way for new possibilities in your life. It rules exuberance, enthusiasm, wisdom, knowledge, generosity and all forms of expansion in general. It rules actors, statesmen, clerics, professional people, religion, publishing and the distribution of many people over large areas.

Sometimes Jupiter makes you think you deserve everything, and you become sloppy, wasteful, careless and rude, prodigal and lawless, in the illusion that nothing can ever go wrong. Then there is the danger of over-confidence, exaggeration, undependability and over-indulgence.

Jupiter is the minimization of limitation and the emphasis on spirituality and potential. It is the thirst for knowledge and higher learning.

SATURN

Saturn circles our system in dark splendor with its mysterious rings, forcing us to be awakened to whatever we have neglected in the past. It will present real puzzles and problems to be solved, causing delays, obstacles and hindrances. By doing so, Saturn stirs our own sensitivity to those areas where we are laziest.

Here we must patiently develop *method,* and only through painstaking effort can our ends be achieved. It brings order to a horoscope and imposes reason just where we are feeling least reasonable. By creating limitations and boundary, Saturn shows the consequences of being human and demands that we accept the changing cycles inevitable in human life. Saturn rules time, old age and sobriety. It can bring depression, gloom, jealousy and greed, or serious acceptance of responsibilities out of which success will develop. With Saturn there is nothing to do but face facts. It rules laborers, stones, granite, rocks and crystals of all kinds.

The Outer Planets

The following three are the outer planets. They liberate human beings from cultural conditioning, and in that sense are the law breakers. In early times it was thought that Saturn was the last planet of the system—the outer limit beyond which we could never go. The discovery of the next three planets ushered in new phases of human history, revolution and technology.

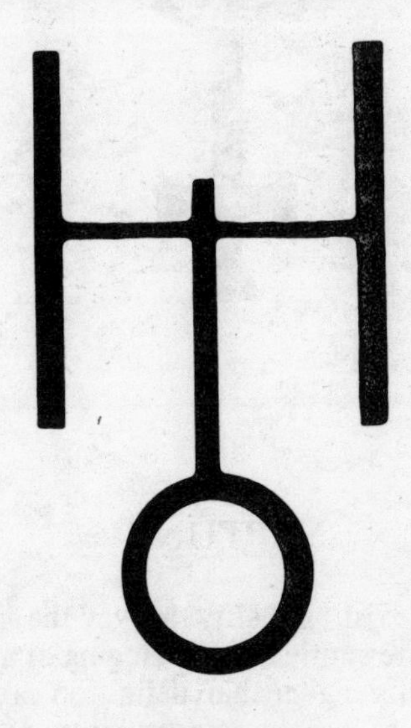

URANUS

Uranus rules unexpected change, upheaval, revolution. It is the symbol of total independence and asserts the freedom of an individual from all restriction and restraint. It is a breakthrough planet and indicates talent, originality and genius in a horoscope. It usually causes last-minute reversals and changes of plan, unwanted separations, accidents, catastrophes and eccentric behavior. It can add irrational rebelliousness and perverse bohemianism to a personality or a streak of unaffected brilliance in science and art. It rules technology, aviation and all forms of electrical and electronic advancement. It governs great leaps forward and topsy-turvy situations, and *always* turns things around at the last minute. Its effects are difficult to ever really predict, since it rules sudden last-minute decisions and events that come like lightning out of the blue.

NEPTUNE

Neptune dissolves existing reality the way the sea erodes the cliffs beside it. Its effects are subtle like the ringing of a buoy's bell in the fog. It suggests a reality higher than definition can usually describe. It awakens a sense of higher responsibility often causing guilt, worry, anxieties or delusions. Neptune is associated with all forms of escape and can make things seem a certain way so convincingly that you are absolutely sure of something that eventually turns out to be quite different.

It is the planet of illusion and therefore governs the invisible realms that lie beyond our ordinary minds, beyond our simple factual ability to prove what is "real." Treachery, deceit, disillusionment and disappointment are linked to Neptune. It describes a vague reality that promises eternity and the divine, yet in a manner so complex that we cannot really fathom it at all. At its worst Neptune is a cheap intoxicant; at its best it is the poetry, music and inspiration of the higher planes of spiritual love. It has dominion over movies, photographs and much of the arts.

PLUTO

Pluto lies at the outpost of our system and therefore rules finality in a horoscope—the final closing of chapters in your life, the passing of major milestones and points of development from which there is no return. It is a final wipeout, a closeout, an evacuation. It is a distant, subtle but powerful catalyst in all transformations that occur. It creates, destroys, then recreates. Sometimes Pluto starts its influence with a minor event or insignificant incident that might even go unnoticed. Slowly but surely, little by little, everything changes, until at last there has been a total transformation in the area of your life where Pluto has been operating. It rules mass thinking and the trends that society first rejects, then adopts and finally outgrows.

Pluto rules the dead and the underworld—all the powerful forces of creation and destruction that go on all the time beneath, around and above us. It can bring a lust for power with strong obsessions.

It is the planet that rules the metamorphoses of the caterpillar into a butterfly, for it symbolizes the capacity to change totally and forever a person's life style, way of thought and behavior.

FAMOUS PERSONALITIES

ARIES: Dean Acheson, Edie Adams, Pearl Bailey, Baudelaire, Marlon Brando, Wernher von Braun, McGeorge Bundy, Clifford Case, Charlie Chaplin, Franco Corelli, Bette Davis, Doris Day, Thomas E. Dewey, J. William Fulbright, James Gavin, Alec Guinness, Gil Hodges, Adolf Hitler, Thomas Jefferson, Nikita Khrushchev, Clare Booth Luce, Eugene McCarthy, Edmund Muskie, Paul Robeson, Lowell Thomas, William Westmoreland, Tennessee Williams

TAURUS: Carol Burnett, Lucius D. Clay, Perry Como, Bing Crosby, Salvador Dali, Moshe Dayan, Elizabeth II, Duke Ellington, Ella Fitzgerald, Henry Fonda, Pancho Gonzalez, Hirohito, Karl Marx, Robespierre, Ray Robinson, Bertrand Russell, Shakespeare, Fulton J. Sheen, Kate Smith, Benjamin Spock, Barbara Streisand, Shirley Temple, Harry Truman, Mike Wallace, Orson Welles

GEMINI: Raymond Burr, Carlos Chavez, Constantine II of Greece, Tony Curtis, Bob Dylan, Sir Anthony Eden, Maurice Evans, Allan Ginsberg, George V, Bob Hope, Burl Ives, John F. Kennedy, Laurence Olivier, Rosalind Russell, Tito of Yugoslavia, Queen Victoria, John Wayne

CANCER: David Brinkley, Yul Brynner, Pearl S. Buck, Marc Chagall, Van Cliburn, Jack Dempsey, Erle Stanley Gardner, John H. Glenn, Carl Hubbell, Thurgood Marshall, George McGovern, Nelson Rockefeller, Richard Rodgers, George W. Romney, Jane Russell, Jean-Paul Sartre, O.J. Simpson, Andrew Wyeth

LEO: Neil Armstrong, Russell Baker, James Baldwin, Wilt Chamberlain, Leo Durocher, Arthur Goldberg, Alfred Hitchcock, Ben Hogan, Princess Margaret, George Meany, Mussolini, Napoleon, Jacqueline Onassis, Haile Selassie, Casey Stengel, Mae West

VIRGO: Warren Burger, Maurice Chevalier, Sean Connery, Milton Eisenhower, Peter Falk, Henry Ford II, Greta Garbo, Arthur Godfrey, Goethe, John Gunther, Buddy Hackett, Lyndon Johnson, Arnold Palmer, Walter Reuther, Peter Sellers, George Wallace

LIBRA: Art Buchwald, Dwight Eisenhower, Gandhi, Glenn Gould, Eamon De Valera, John Galbraith, Dizzy Gillespie, Vladimir Horowitz, Pope Paul VI, Eddie Rickenbacker, Ed Sullivan, Pierre Trudeau, Gore Vidal

SCORPIO: Richard Burton, Roy Campanella, Art Carney, Johnny Carson, Chiang Kai-shek, Aaron Copland, Walter Cronkite, Charles de Gaulle, Indira Gandhi, George Gallup, Billy Graham, Averell Harriman, Mahalia Jackson, Martin Luther, James Reston, Alan Shepard Jr., Sargent Shriver, Ted Williams

SAGITTARIUS: Beethoven, Berlioz, Willy Brandt, Leonid Brezhnev, William F. Buckley, Maria Callas, Shirley Chisholm, Winston Churchill, Noel Coward, Sammy Davis, Joe DiMaggio, Disraeli, Walt Disney, James Doolittle, Kirk Douglas, Chet Huntley, Charles Schulz, Eric Sevareid, Vincent Sheean, Frank Sinatra, Andy Williams

CAPRICORN: The Emperor Augustus, Pablo Casals, Cassius Clay, Dizzy Dean, Marlene Dietrich, James Farmer, Gladstone, Barry M. Goldwater, Cary Grant, J. Edgar Hoover, Joan of Arc, Mrs. Lyndon Johnson, Martin Luther King, Richard Nixon, J.D. Salinger, Danny Thomas

AQUARIUS: Charles Dickens, Jimmy Durante, Dame Edith Evans, Jules Feiffer, Federico Fellini, John Ford, Tennessee Ernie Ford, Frederick the Great of Prussia, Jascha Heifetz, Abraham Lincoln, Harold Macmillan, Yehudi Menuhin, Ronald Reagan, Jackie Robinson, Norman Rockwell, Dean Rusk, Cesare Siepi, U Thant, Margaret Truman

PISCES: Ralph Abernathy, Edward Albee, Harry Belafonte, Frank Borman, Chopin, "Buffalo Bill" Cody, Cardinal Terence Cooke, Albert Einstein, Jackie Gleason, Robert Lowell, Edward M. Kennedy, Mike Mansfield, Ralph Nader, Mrs. Richard Nixon, Linus Pauling, Irwin Shaw, Svetlana Alliluyeva Stalina, Elizabeth Taylor, George Washington

On the preceding pages you found some general information about all the signs of the zodiac. If you want to have more information about a certain sign please consult the individual volume of the sign.

Aries . . . . March 21st-April 20th
Taurus . . . . April 21st-May 20th
Gemini . . . . May 21st-June 20th
Cancer . . . . June 21st-July 20th
Leo . . . . July 21st-August 21st
Virgo . . . . August 22nd-September 22nd
Libra . . . . September 23rd-October 22nd
Scorpio . . . . October 23rd-November 22nd
Sagittarius . . . . November 23rd-December 20th
Capricorn . . . . December 21st-January 19th
Aquarius . . . . January 20th-February 18th
Pisces . . . . February 19th-March 20th

SAGITTARIUS

CHARACTER ANALYSIS

People born under this ninth sign of the Zodiac are quite often self-reliant and intelligent. Generally, they are quite philosophical in their outlook on life. They know how to make practical use of their imagination.

There is seldom anything narrow about a Sagittarian. He is generally very tolerant and considerate. He would never consciously do anything that would hurt another's feelings. He is gifted with a good sense of humor and believes in being honest in his relationships with others. At times he is a little short of tact. He is so intent on telling the truth that sometimes he is a bit blunt. At any rate, he means well, and people who enjoy their relationship with him are often willing to overlook this flaw. He may even tell people true things about themselves that they do not wish to hear. At times this can cause a strain in the relationship. The Sagittarian often wishes that others were as forthright and honest as he is—no matter what the consequences.

The person born under this sign is often positive and optimistic. He likes life. He often helps others to snap out of an ill mood. His joie de vivre is often infectious. People enjoy being around the Sagittarian because he is almost always in a good mood. Quite often people born under the sign of Sagittarius are fond of the outdoors. They enjoy sporting events and often excel in them. Many of them are fond of animals—especially horses. Generally speaking they are healthy—in mind and limb. They have pluck; they enjoy the simple things of life. Fresh air and good comradeship are important to them. On the other hand, they are fond of developing their minds. Many Sagittarians cannot read or study enough. They like to keep abreast of things. They are interested in theater and the arts in general. Some of them are rather religious. Some choose a religious life.

Because they are outgoing for the most part, they sometimes come in touch with situations that others are never confronted with. In the long run this tends to make their life experiences quite rich and varied. They are well-balanced. They like to be active; they enjoy using their intellects.

It is important to the person born under this sign that justice prevails. They dislike seeing anyone treated unfairly. If the Sagittarian feels that the old laws are out-of-date or unrealistic he will fight to have them changed. At times he can be quite a rebel. It is important to him that law is carried out impartially. In matters of law, he often excels.

Sagittarians are almost always fond of travel. It seems to be imbedded in their natures. At times, they feel impelled to get away from familiar surroundings and people. Far away places have a magical attraction for someone born under this sign. They enjoy reading about foreign lands and strange customs. Many people who are Sagittarians are not terribly fond of living in big cities; they prefer the quiet and greenery of the countryside. Of all the signs of the Zodiac the Sign of Sagittarius is closest to mother nature. They can usually build a trusting relationship with animals.

The Sagittarian is quite clever in conversation. He has a definite way with words. He is fond of a good argument. He knows how to phrase things exactly; his sense of humor often has a cheerful effect on his manner of speech. He is seldom without a joke of some sort. At times he is apt to hurt others with his wit, but this is never done intentionally. A slip of the tongue sometimes gets him into social difficulties. The person born under this sign often angers quite easily; however, they cool down quickly and are not given to holding grudges. They are willing to forgive and forget.

On the whole, the Sagittarian is good-natured and fun-loving. He finds it easy to take up with people of all sorts. In most cases, his social circle is rather large. People enjoy his company. Many of his friends share his interest in outdoor life and intellectual pursuits.

At times, he can be rather impulsive. He is not afraid of risk; on the contrary, at times he can be rather foolhardy in the way he courts danger. However, he is very sporting in all that he does, and if he should wind up the loser, he is not apt to waste much time grieving about it. He can be fairly optimistic—he believes in good luck.

Health

Often people born under the sign of Sagittarius are quite athletic. They are healthy-looking—quite striking in a robust way. Often they are rather tall and well-built. They are enthusiastic people and like being active or involved. Exercise may interest them a great deal. The Sagittarian cannot stand not being active. He has to be on the go. As he grows older, he seems to increase his strength and physical ability. At times he may have worries, but he never allows them to affect his humor or health.

It is important to the Sagittarian to remain physically sound. He is usually very physically fit, but his nervous system may be somewhat sensitive. Too much activity—even while he finds action attractive—may put a severe strain upon him after a time. The Sagittarian should try to concentrate his energies on as few objects as possible. However, usually he has his projects scattered here and there, and as a result he is easily exhausted. At times illnesses fall upon him rather suddenly. Some Sagittarians are accident-prone. They are not afraid of taking risks and as a result are sometimes careless in the way they do things. Injuries often come to them by way of sports or other vigorous activities.

At times, people of this sign try to ignore signs of illness —especially if they are engaged in some activity that has captured their interest. This results in a severe setback at times.

In later life, the Sagittarian sometimes suffers from stomach disorders. High blood pressure is another ailment that might affect him; he should also be on guard for signs of arthritis and sciatica. In spite of these possible dangers, the average Sagittarian manages to stay quite youthful and alert through his interest in life.

Occupation

The Sagittarian is someone who can be relied upon in a work situation. He is loyal and dependable. He is an energetic worker, anxious to please his superiors. He is forward-looking by nature and enjoys working in modern surroundings and toward progressive goals. Challenges do not frighten him. He is rather flexible and can work in confining situations even though he may not enjoy it. Work which gives him a chance to move about and meet new people is well suited to his character. If he has to stay in one locale he is apt to become sad and ill-humored. He can take orders but he would rather be in a situation where he does not have to. He is difficult to please at times, and may hop from job to job before feeling that it is really time to settle down. He does his best work when he is allowed to work on his own.

The Sagittarian is interested in expressing himself in the work he does. If he occupies a position which does not allow him to do this, he will seek outside activities that give him a chance to develop in a direction which interests him.

Some Sagittarians do well in the field of journalism; others make good teachers and public speakers. They are generally quite flexible and would do well in many different positions. Some excel as foreign ministers or in music; others do well in government work or in publishing.

The person born under this sign is often more intelligent than the average man. The cultivated Sagittarian knows how to employ his intellectual gifts to their best advantage. In politics and religion, the Sagittarian often displays considerable brilliance.

He is generally pleasant to work with; he is considerate of his colleagues and would do nothing that might upset their working relationship. Because he is so self-reliant he often inspires others. He likes to work with detail. His ideas are often quite practical and intelligent. The Sagittarian is curious by nature and is always looking for ways of increasing his knowledge.

The people born under this sign are almost always generous. They rarely refuse someone in need, but are always willing to share what they have. Whether he is up or down, the Sagittarian can always be relied upon to help someone in dire straits. His attitude toward life may be happy-go-lucky in general. He is difficult to depress no matter what his situation. He is optimistic and forward-looking. Money always seems to fall into his hands; it's seldom a problem for him.

The average Sagittarian is interested in expansion and promotion. Sometimes these concerns weaken his projects rather than strengthen them.

He is interested in large profit and is sometimes willing to take risks to secure it. In the long run he is successful. He has a flair for carrying off business deals well. It is the cultivated Sagittarian who prepares himself well in business matters so that he is well-supported in his interests by knowledge, as well as by experience.

The average person born under this sign is more interested in contentment and joy than in material gain. However he will do his best to make the most of profit when it comes his way.

Home and Family

Not all Sagittarians are very interested in home life. Many of them set great store in being mobile. Their activities outside the home may attract them more than those inside the home. Not exactly homebodies, Sagittarians, however, can adjust themselves to a stable domestic life if they put their minds to it.

People born under this sign are not keen on luxuries and other displays of wealth. They prefer the simple things. Anyone entering their home should be able to discern this. They are generally neat; they like a place that has plenty of space—not too cluttered with imposing furniture.

Even when he settles down, the Sagittarian likes to keep a small corner of his life just for himself; independence is important to him. If necessary, he'll insist upon it, no matter what the situation. He likes a certain amount of beauty in his home, but he may not be too interested in keeping things looking nice—his interests lead him elsewhere. Housekeeping may bore him to distraction. If he is forced to stick to a domestic routine he is liable to become somewhat disagreeable.

Children bring him a great deal of happiness. He is fond of family life. Friends generally drop in any old time to visit a Sagittarian for they know they will always be welcomed and properly entertained. The Sagittarian's love of his fellow man is well known.

When children are small, he may not understand them too well, even though he tries. He may feel he is a bit too clumsy to handle them properly—although this may be far from the case. As they begin to grow up and develop definite personalities, the Sagittarian's interest grows. There is always a strong tie between children and the Sagittarian parent.

Children are especially drawn to Sagittarians because they seem to understand them better than other adults.

One is apt to find children born under this sign a little restless and disorganized at times. They are usually quite independent in their ways and may ask for quite a bit of freedom while still young. They don't like being fussed over by adults. They like to feel that their parents believe in them and trust them on their own.

Social Relationships

The Sagittarian enjoys having people around. It is not difficult for him to make friends. He is very sociable by nature. Most of the friends he makes, he keeps for life. As a rule, the person born under this sign is rather broadminded; he is apt to have all sorts of friends. He appreciates people for their good qualities, however few they may have. He is not quick to judge and is often very forgiving. He is not impressed by what a friend has in the way of material goods.

The Sagittarian is generally quite popular. He is much in demand socially; people like him for his easy disposition and his good humor. His friendship is valued by others. Quite often in spite of his chumminess, the Sagittarian is rather serious; light conversation may be somewhat difficult for him.

He believes in speaking his mind—in saying what he feels—yet at times, he can appear rather quiet and retiring. It all depends on his mood. Others may feel that there are two sides to his personality because of this quirk in his nature; for this reason it may be difficult for some people to get to know him. In some instances, he employs his silence as a sort of protection. When people pierce through however and don't leave him in peace, he can become rather angry.

On the whole, he is a kind and considerate person. His nature is gentle and unassuming. With the wrong people though, he can become somewhat disagreeable. He can become angry quite easily at times; however, he cools down quickly and is willing to let bygones be bygones. He never holds a grudge against anyone. Companionship and harmony in all social relationships is quite necessary for the Sagittarian; he is willing to make some sacrifices for it. The partner for someone born under this sign must be a good listener. There are times when the Sagittarian feels it is necessary to pour his heart out. He is willing to listen to another's problems, too. His mate or loved one should be able to take an interest in his hobbies and such. If not, the Sagittarian may be tempted to go his own way even more.

The Sagittarian says what he means; he doesn't beat around the bush. Being direct is one of his strongest qualities. Sometimes it pays off; sometimes it doesn't. He is often forgetful that the one he loves may be more sensitive than she allows herself to appear—even to him. He has a tendency to put his foot in his mouth at times. However, his mate should be able to overlook this flaw in his character or else try to correct it in some subtle way. At times, when joking broadly he has the ability to strike a sensitive chord in his loved one and this may result in a serious misunderstanding. The cultivated Sagittarian learns his boundaries; he knows when not to go too far. Understanding his partner's viewpoint is also an important thing for someone born under this sign to learn.

LOVE AND MARRIAGE

Sagittarians are faithful to their loved ones. They are affectionate in nature and not at all possessive. Love is important for them spiritually as well as physically. For some people born under this sign, romance is a chance to escape reality—it is a chance for adventure. Quite often, the Sagittarian's mate finds it difficult to keep up with him—he is so active and energetic. When Sagittarians fall in love, however, they are quite easy to handle.

Sagittarians do like having freedom. They will make concessions in a steady relationship; still there will be a part of themselves that they keep from others. He or she is very keen on preserving his individual rights, no matter what sort of relationship he is engaged in. The Sagittarian's ideals are generally high and they are important to him. He is looking for someone with similar standards, not someone too lax or conventional.

In love, the Sagittarian may be a bit childlike at times. As a result of this he is apt to encounter various disappointments before he has found the one meant for him. At times he or she says things he really shouldn't and this causes the end of a romantic relationship. The person born under this sign may have many love affairs before he feels he is ready to settle down with just one person. If the person he loves does not exactly measure up to his standards, the Sagittarian is apt to overlook this—depending on how strong his love is—and accept the person for what that person is.

On the whole, the Sagittarian is not an envious person. He is willing to allow his or her partner needed freedoms—within reason. The Sagittarian does this so that he will not have to jeopardize his own liberties. Live and let live could easily be his motto. If his ideals and freedom are threatened, the Sagittarian fights hard to protect what he believes is just and fair.

He does not want to make any mistakes in love, so he takes his time when choosing someone to settle down with. He is direct and positive when he meets the right one; he does not waste time.

The average Sagittarian may be a bit altar-shy. It may take a bit of convincing before Sagittarians agree that married life is right for them. This is generally because they do not want to lose their freedom. The Sagittarian is an active person who enjoys being around a lot of other people. Sitting quietly at home does not interest him at all. At times it may seem that he or she wants to have things his own way, even in marriage. It may take some doing to get him to realize that in marriage, as in other things, give and take plays a great role.

Romance and the Sagittarius Woman

The Sagittarian woman is often kind and gentle. Most of the time she is very considerate of others and enjoys being of help in some way to her friends. She can be quite active and, as a result, be rather difficult to catch. On the whole, she is optimistic and friendly. She believes in looking on the bright side of things. She knows how to make the best of situations that others feel are not worth salvaging. She has plenty of pluck.

Men generally like her because of her easy-going manner. Quite often she becomes friends with a man before venturing on to romance. There is something about her that makes her more of a companion than a lover. She can best be described as sporting and broad-minded.

She is almost never possessive; she enjoys her own freedom too much to want to make demands on that of another person.

She is always youthful in her disposition. She may seem rather guileless at times. Generally it takes her longer really to mature than it does others. She tends to be impulsive and may easily jump from one thing to another. If she has an unfortunate experience in love early in life, she may shy away from fast or intimate contacts for a while. She is usually very popular. Not all the men who are attracted to her see her as a possible lover, but more as a friend or companion.

The woman born under this sign generally believes in true love. She may have several romances before she decides to settle down. For her there is no particular rush. She is willing to have a long romantic relationship with the man she loves before making marriage plans.

The Sagittarius woman is often the outdoors type and has a strong liking for animals—especially dogs and horses. Quite often she excels in sports. She is not generally someone who is content to stay at home and cook and take care of the house. She would rather be out attending to her other interests. When she does household work, however, she does it well.

She makes a good companion as well as a wife. She usually enjoys participating with her husband in his various interests and affairs. Her sunny disposition often brightens up the dull moments of a love affair.

At times her temper may flare, but she is herself again after a few moments. She would never butt into her husband's business affairs, but she does enjoy being asked for her opinion from time to time. Generally she is up to date on all that her husband is doing and can offer him some pretty sound advice.

The Sagittarius woman is seldom jealous of her husband's interest in other people—even if some of them are of the opposite sex. If she has no reason to doubt his love, she never questions it.

She makes a loving and sympathetic mother. Quite often she will play with her children. Her cheerful manner makes her an invaluable playmate.

Romance and the Sagittarius Man

The Sagittarius man is often an adventurer. He likes taking chances in love as well as in life. He may hop around quite a bit—from one romance to another—before really thinking about settling down. Many men born under this sign feel that marriage would mean the end of their freedom—so they avoid it as much as possible. Whenever a romance becomes too serious, they move on. Many Sagittarians are rather impulsive in love. Early marriages for some often end unpleasantly. The Sagittarian is not a very mature person—even at an age when most others are. He takes a bit more time. He may not always make a wise choice in a love partner.

He is affectionate and loving but not at all possessive. Because he is rather lighthearted in love, he sometimes gets into trouble.

Most Sagittarius men find romance an exciting adventure. They make attentive lovers and are never cool or indifferent. Love should also have a bit of fun in it for him too. He likes to keep things light and gay. Romance without humor—at times—is difficult for him to accept. The woman he loves should also be a good sport. She should have as open and fun-loving a disposition as he has—if she is to understand him properly.

He wants his mate to share his interest in the outdoor life and animals. If she is good at sports, she is likely to win his heart, for the average Sagittarian generally has an interest in athletics of various sorts—from bicycling to baseball.

His mate must also be a good intellectual companion; someone who can easily discuss those matters which interest her Sagittarian. Physical love is important to him—but so is spiritual love. A good romance will contain these in balance.

His sense of humor may sometimes seem a little unkind to someone who is not used to being laughed at. He enjoys playing jokes now and again; it is the child in his nature that remains a part of his character even when he grows old and gray.

He is not a homebody. He is responsible, however, and will do what is necessary to keep a home together. Still and all, the best wife for him is one who can manage household matters single-handedly if need be.

He loves children—especially as they grow older and begin to take on definite personalities.

Woman—Man

SAGITTARIUS WOMAN
ARIES MAN

In some ways, the Aries man resembles an intellectual mountain goat leaping from crag to crag. He has an insatiable thirst for knowledge. He's ambitious and is apt to have his finger in many pies. He can do with a woman like you—someone attractive, quick-witted, and smart.

He is not interested in a clinging vine kind of wife, but someone who is there when he needs her; someone who listens and understands what he says; someone who can give advice if he should ever need it . . . which is not likely to be often. The Aries man wants a woman who will look good on his arm without hanging on it too heavily. He is looking for a woman who has both feet on the ground and yet is mysterious and enticing . . . a kind of domestic Helen of Troy whose face or fine dinner can launch a thousand business deals if need be. That woman he's in search of sounds a little like you, doesn't she? If the shoe fits, put it on. You won't regret it.

The Aries man makes a good husband. He is faithful and attentive. He is an affectionate kind of man. He'll make you feel needed and loved. Love is a serious matter for the Aries man. He does not believe in flirting or playing the field—especially after he's found the woman of his dreams. He'll expect you to be as constant in your affection as he is in his. He'll expect you to be one hundred percent his; he won't put up with any nonsense while romancing you.

The Aries man may be pretty progressive and modern about many things; however, when it comes to pants wearing, he's downright conventional: it's strictly male attire. The best position you can take in the relationship is a supporting one. He's the boss and that's that. Once you have learned to accept that, you'll find the going easy.

The Aries man, with his endless energy and drive, likes to relax in the comfort of his home at the end of the day. The good homemaker can be sure of holding his love. He's keen on slippers and pipe and a comfortable armchair. If you see to it that everything in the house is where he expects to find it, you'll have no difficulty keeping the relationship on an even keel.

Life and love with an Aries man may be just the medicine you need. He'll be a good provider. He'll spoil you if he's financially able.

He's young at heart and can get along with children easily. He'll spoil them every chance he gets.

SAGITTARIUS WOMAN
TAURUS MAN

If you've got your heart set on a man born under the sign of Taurus, you'll have to learn the art of being patient. Taureans take their time about everything—even love.

The steady and deliberate Taurus man is a little slow on the draw; it may take him quite a while before he gets around to popping that question. For the woman who doesn't mind twiddling her thumbs, the waiting and anticipating almost always pays off in the end. Taurus men want to make sure that every step they take is a good one—particularly, if they feel that the path they're on is one that leads to the altar.

If you are in the mood for a whirlwind romance, you had better cast your net in shallower waters. Moreover, most Taureans prefer to do the angling themselves. They are not keen on a woman taking the lead; once she does, they are liable to drop her like a dead fish. If you let yourself get caught on a Taurean's terms, you'll find that he's fallen for you—hook, line, and sinker.

The Taurus man is fond of a comfortable homelife. It is very important to him. If you keep those home fires burning you will have no trouble keeping that flame in your Taurean's heart aglow. You have a talent for homemaking; use it. Your taste in furnishings is excellent. You know how to make a house come to life with colors and decorations.

Taurus, the strong, steady, and protective Bull may not be your idea of a man on the move, still he's reliable. Perhaps he could be the anchor for your dreams and plans. He could help you to acquire a more balanced outlook and approach to your life. If you're given to impulsiveness, he could help you to curb it. He's the man who is always there when you need him.

When you tie the knot with a man born under Taurus, you can put away fears about creditors pounding on the front door. Taureans are practical about everything including bill-paying. When he carries you over that threshold, you can be certain that the entire house is paid for, not only the doorsill.

As a housewife, you won't have to worry about putting aside your many interests for the sake of back-breaking house chores. Your Taurus husband will see to it that you have all the latest time-saving appliances and comforts.

Your children will be obedient and orderly. Your Taurus husband will see to that.

SAGITTARIUS WOMAN GEMINI MAN

The Gemini man is quite a catch. Many a woman has set her cap for him and failed to bag him. Generally, Gemini men are intelligent, witty, and outgoing. Many of them tend to be versatile.

On the other hand, some of them seem to lack that sort of common sense that you set so much store in. Their tendency to start a half-dozen projects, then toss them up in the air out of boredom may do nothing more than exasperate you.

One thing that causes a Twin's mind and affection to wander is a bore, but it is unlikely that an active woman like you would ever allow herself to be accused of dullness. The Gemini man that has caught your heart will admire you for your ideas and intellect—perhaps even more than for your homemaking talents and good looks.

A strong willed woman could easily fill the role of rudder for her Gemini's ship-without-a-sail. The intelligent Gemini is often aware of his shortcomings and doesn't mind if someone with better bearings gives him a shove in the right direction—when it's needed. The average Gemini doesn't have serious ego-hangups and will even accept a well-deserved chewing out from his mate or girlfriend gracefully.

A successful and serious-minded Gemini could make you a very happy woman, perhaps, if you gave him half the chance. Although he may give you the impression that he has a hole in his head, the Gemini man generally has a good head on his shoulders and can make efficient use of it when he wants. Some of them, who have learned the art of being steadfast, have risen to great heights in their professions. President Kennedy was a Gemini as was Thomas Mann and William Butler Yeats.

Once you convince yourself that not all people born under the sign of the Twins are witless grasshoppers, you won't mind dating a few—to test your newborn conviction. If you do wind up walking down the aisle with one, accept the fact that married life with him will mean your taking the bitter with the sweet.

Life with a Gemini man can be more fun than a barrel of clowns. You'll never be allowed to experience a dull moment. But don't leave money matters to him or you'll both wind up behind the eight ball.

Gemini men are always attractive to the opposite sex. You'll perhaps have to allow him an occasional harmless flirt—it will seldom amount to more than that if you're his proper mate.

The Gemini father is a pushover for children. See to it that you keep them in line; otherwise they'll be running the house.

SAGITTARIUS WOMAN CANCER MAN

Chances are you won't hit it off too well with the man born under Cancer if your plans concern love, but then, Cupid has been known to do some pretty unlikely things. The Cancerian is a very sensitive man—thin-skinned and occasionally moody. You've got to keep on your toes—and not step on his—if you're determined to make a go of the relationship.

The Cancer man may be lacking in some of the qualities you seek in a man, but when it comes to being faithful and being a good provider, he's hard to beat.

The perceptive woman will not mistake the Crab's quietness for sullenness or his thriftiness for penny-pinching. In some respects, he is like that wise old owl out on a limb; he may look like he's dozing but actually he hasn't missed a thing. Cancerians often possess a well of knowledge about human behavior; they can come across with some pretty helpful advice to those in trouble or in need. He can certainly guide you in making investments both in time and money. He may not say much, but he's always got his wits about him.

The Crab may not be the match or catch for a woman like you; at times, you are likely to find him downright dull. True to his sign, he can be fairly cranky and crabby when handled the wrong way. He is perhaps more sensitive than he should be.

If you're smarter than your Cancer friend, be smart enough

not to let him know. Never give him the idea that you think he's a little short on brain power. It would send him scurrying back into his shell—and all that ground lost in the relationship will perhaps never be recovered.

The Crab is most content at home. Once settled down for the night or the weekend, wild horses couldn't drag him any farther than the gatepost—that is, unless those wild horses were dispatched by his mother. The Crab is sometimes a Momma's boy. If his mate does not put her foot down, he will see to it that his mother always comes first. No self-respecting wife would ever allow herself to play second fiddle—even if it's to her old gray-haired mother-in-law. With a little bit of tact, however, she'll find that slipping into that number-one position is as easy as pie (that legendary one his mother used to bake).

If you pamper your Cancer man, you'll find that "Mother" turns up increasingly less—at the front door as well as in conversations.

Cancerians make protective, proud, and patient fathers.

SAGITTARIUS WOMAN LEO MAN

For the woman who enjoys being swept off her feet in a romantic whirlwind fashion, Leo is the sign of such love. When the Lion puts his mind to romancing, he doesn't stint. It's all wining and dining and dancing till the wee hours of the morning.

Leo is all heart and knows how to make his woman feel like a woman. The girl in constant search of a man she can look up to need go no farther: Leo is ten-feet tall—in spirit if not in stature. He's a man not only in full control of his faculties but in full control of just about any situation he finds himself in. He's a winner.

The Leo man may not look like Tarzan, but he knows how to roar and beat his chest if he has to. The woman who has had her fill of weak-kneed men finds in a Leo someone she can at last lean upon. He can support you not only physically but spiritually as well. He's good at giving advice that pays off.

Leos are direct people. They don't believe in wasting time or effort. They almost never make unwise investments.

Many Leos rise to the top of their professions; through example, they often prove to be a source of great inspiration to others.

Although he's a ladies' man, the Leo man is very particular about his ladies. His standards are high when it comes to love interests. The idealistic and cultivated woman should have no trouble keeping her balance on the pedestal the Lion sets her on. Leo believes that romance should be played on a fair give-and-take basis. He won't stand for any monkey business in a love relationship. It's all or nothing.

You'll find him a frank, off-the-shoulder person; he generally says what is on his mind.

If you decide upon a Leo man for a mate, you must be prepared to stand behind him full-force. He expects it—and usually deserves it. He's the head of the house and can handle that position without a hitch. He knows how to go about breadwinning and, if he has his way (and most Leos do have their own way), he'll see to it that you'll have all the luxuries you crave and the comforts you need.

It's unlikely that the romance in your marriage will ever die out. Lions need love like flowers need sunshine. They're ever amorous and generally expect similar attention and affection from their mates. Leos are fond of going out on the town; they love to give parties, as well as to go to them.

Leos make strict fathers, generally. They love their children but won't spoil them.

SAGITTARIUS WOMAN
VIRGO MAN

Although the Virgo man may be a bit of a fussbudget at times, his seriousness and dedication to common sense may help you to overlook his tendency to sometimes be overcritical about minor things.

Virgo men are often quiet, respectable types who set great store in conservative behavior and levelheadedness. He'll admire you for your practicality and tenacity . . . perhaps even more than for your good looks. He's seldom bowled over by a glamour-puss. When he gets his courage up, he turns to a serious and reliable girl for romance. He'll be far from a Valentino while dating. In fact, you may wind up making all the passes. Once he does get his motor running, however, he can be a warm and wonderful fellow—to the right girl.

He's gradual about love. Chances are your romance with him will start out looking like an ordinary friendship. Once he's sure you're no fly-by-night flirt and have no plans of taking him for a ride, he'll open up and rain sunshine all over your heart.

Virgo men tend to marry late in life. The Virgo believes in holding out until he's met the right girl. He may not have many names in his little black book; in fact, he may not even have a black book. He's not interested in playing the field; leave that to men of the more flamboyant signs. The Virgo man is so particular that he may remain romantically inactive for a long period. His girl has to be perfect or it's no go. If you find yourself feeling weak-kneed for a Virgo, do your best to convince him that perfect is not so important when it comes to love; help him to realize that he's missing out on a great deal by not considering the near perfect or whatever it is you consider yourself to be. With your surefire perseverance, you will most likely be able to make him listen to reason and he'll wind up reciprocating your romantic interests.

The Virgo man is no block of ice. He'll respond to what he feels to be the right feminine flame. Once your love-life with a Virgo man starts to bubble, don't give it a chance to fall flat. You may never have a second chance at winning his heart.

If you should ever have a falling out with him, forget about patching it up. He'd prefer to let the pieces lie scattered. Once married, though, he'll stay that way—even if it hurts. He's too conscientious to try to back out of a legal deal of any sort.

The Virgo man is as neat as a pin. He's thumbs down on sloppy housekeeping. Keep everything bright, neat, and shiny . . . and that goes for the children, too, at least by the time he gets home from work. Chocolate-coated kisses from Daddy's little girl go over like a lead balloon with him.

SAGITTARIUS WOMAN
LIBRA MAN

If there's a Libran in your life, you are most likely a very happy woman. Men born under this sign have a way with women. You'll always feel at ease in a Libran's company; you can be yourself when you're with him.

The Libra man can be moody at times. His moodiness is often puzzling. One moment he comes on hard and strong with declarations of his love, the next moment you find that he's left you like yesterday's mashed potatoes. He'll come back, though; don't worry. Librans are like that. Deep down inside he really knows what he wants even though he may not appear to.

You'll appreciate his admiration of beauty and harmony. If you're dressed to the teeth and never looked lovelier, you'll get a ready compliment—and one that's really deserved. Librans don't indulge in idle flattery. If they don't like something, they are tactful enough to remain silent.

Librans will go to great lengths to preserve peace and harmony—they will even tell a fat lie if necessary. They don't like showdowns or disagreeable confrontations. The frank woman is all for getting whatever is bothering her off her chest and out into the open, even if it comes out all wrong. To the Libran, making a clean breast of everything seems like sheer folly sometimes.

You may lose your patience while waiting for your Libra friend to make up his mind. It takes him ages sometimes to make a decision. He weighs both sides carefully before comitting himself to anything. You seldom dillydally—at least about small things—and so it's likely that you will find it difficult to see eye to eye with a hesitating Libran when it comes to decision-making methods.

All in all, though, he is kind, considerate, and fair. He is interested in the "real" truth; he'll try to balance everything out until he has all the correct answers. It's not difficult for him to see both sides of a story.

He's a peace-loving man. The sight of blood is apt to turn his stomach.

Librans are not show-offs. Generally, they are well-balanced, modest people. Honest, wholesome, and affectionate, they are serious about every love encounter they have. If one should find that the girl he's dating is not really suited to him, he will end the relationship in such a tactful manner that no hard feelings will come about.

The Libra father is firm, gentle, and patient.

SAGITTARIUS WOMAN SCORPIO MAN

Many find the Scorpio's sting a fate worse than death. When his anger breaks loose, you had better clear out of the vicinity.

The average Scorpio may strike you as a brute. He'll stick pins into the balloons of your plans and dreams if they don't line up with what he thinks is right. If you do anything to irritate him—just anything—you'll wish you hadn't. He'll give you a sounding out that would make you pack your bags and go back to Mother—if you were that kind of a girl.

The Scorpio man hates being tied down to homelife—he would rather be out on the battlefield of life, belting away at whatever he feels is a just and worthy cause, instead of staying home nestled in a comfortable armchair with the evening paper. If you are a girl who has a homemaking streak—don't keep those home fires burning too brightly too long; you may just run out of firewood.

As passionate as he is in business affairs and politics, the Scorpio man still has plenty of pep and ginger stored away for lovemaking.

Most women are easily attracted to him—perhaps you are no exception. Those who allow a man born under this sign to sweep them off their feet, shortly find that they're dealing with a pepper pot of seething excitement. The Scorpio man is passionate with a capital P, you can be sure of that. But he's capable of dishing out as much pain as pleasure. Damsels with fluttering hearts who, when in the embrace of a Scorpio, think "This is it," had better be in a position moments later to realize that "Perhaps this isn't it."

Scorpios are blunt. An insult is likely to whiz out of their mouths quicker than a compliment.

If you're the kind of woman who can keep a stiff upper lip, take it on the chin, turn a deaf ear, and all of that, because you feel you are still under his love spell in spite of everything: lots of luck.

If you have decided to take the bitter with the sweet, prepare yourself for a lot of ups and downs. Chances are you won't have as much time for your own affairs and interests as you'd like. The Scorpio's love of power may cause you to be at his constant beck and call.

Scorpios like fathering large families. They love children but quite often they fail to live up to their responsibilities as a parent.

SAGITTARIUS WOMAN
SAGITTARIUS MAN

The woman who has set her cap for a man born under the sign of Sagittarius may have to apply an awful amount of strategy before she can get him to drop down on bended knee. Although some Sagittarians may be marriage-shy, they're not ones to skitter away from romance. A high-spirited woman may find a relationship with a Sagittarian—whether a fling or "the real thing"—a very enjoyable experience.

As a rule, Sagittarians are bright, happy, and healthy people. They have a strong sense of fair play. Often they're a source of inspiration to others. They're full of ideas and drive.

You'll be taken by the Sagittarian's infectious grin and his lighthearted friendly nature. If you do wind up being the woman in his life, you'll find that he's apt to treat you more like a buddy than the love of his life. It's just his way. Sagittarians are often chummy instead of romantic.

You'll admire his broadmindedness in most matters—including those of the heart. If, while dating you, he claims that he still wants to play the field, he'll expect you to enjoy the same liberty. Once he's promised to love, honor, and obey, however, he does just that. Marriage for him, once he's taken that big step, is very serious business.

A woman who has a keen imagination and a great love of freedom will not be disappointed if she does tie up with a Sagittarian. The Sagittarius man is often quick-witted. Men of this sign have a genuine interest in equality. They hate prejudice and injustice.

If he does insist on a night out with the boys once a week, he won't scowl if you decide to let him shift for himself in the kitchen once a week while you pursue some of your own interests. He believes in fairness.

He's not much of a homebody. Quite often he's occupied with faraway places either in his dreams or in reality. He enjoys—just as you do—being on the go or on the move. He's got ants in his pants and refuses to sit still for long stretches at a time. Humdrum routine—especially at home—bores him. At the drop of a hat, he may ask you to whip off your apron and dine out for a change. He likes surprising people. He'll take great pride in showing you off to his friends. He'll always be a considerate mate; he will never embarrass or disappoint you intentionally.

He's very tolerant when it comes to friends and you'll most likely spend a lot of time entertaining people.

Sagittarians become interested in their children when the children are out of the baby stage.

SAGITTARIUS WOMAN
CAPRICORN MAN

A with-it girl like you is likely to find the average Capricorn man a bit of a drag. The man born under this sign is often a closed up person and difficult to get to know. Even if you do get to know him, you may not find him very interesting.

In romance, Capricorn men are a little on the rusty side. You'll probably have to make all the passes.

You may find his plodding manner irritating and his conservative, traditional ways downright maddening. He's not one to take a chance on anything. "If it was good enough for my father, it's good enough for me" may be his motto. He follows a way that is tried and true.

Whenever adventure rears its tantalizing head, the Goat will turn the other way; he's just not interested.

He may be just as ambitious as you are—perhaps even more so—but his ways of accomplishing his aims are more subterranean or, at least, seem so. He operates from the background a good deal of the time. At a gathering you may never even notice him, but he's there, taking everything in, sizing everyone up, planning his next careful move.

Although Capricorns may be intellectual to a degree, it is not generally the kind of intelligence you appreciate. He may not be as quick or as bright as you; it may take him ages to understand a simple joke.

If you do decide to take up with a man born under this sign of the Goat, you ought to be pretty good in the "Cheering Up" department. The Capricorn man often acts as though he's constantly being followed by a cloud of gloom.

The Capricorn man is most himself when in the comfort and privacy of his own home. The security possible within four walls can make him a happy man. He'll spend as much time as he can at home. If he is loaded down with extra work, he'll bring it home instead of finishing it up at the office.

You'll most likely find yourself frequently confronted by his relatives. Family is very important to the Capricorn—*his* family that is. They had better take an important place in your life, too, if you want to keep your home a happy one.

Although his caution in most matters may all but drive you up the wall, you'll find that his concerned way with money is justified most of the time. He'll plan everything right down to the last penny.

He can be quite a scolder with children. You'll have to step in and smooth things out.

SAGITTARIUS WOMAN
AQUARIUS MAN

Aquarians love everybody—even their worst enemies sometimes. Through your love relationship with an Aquarian you'll find yourself running into all sorts of people, ranging from near-genius to downright insane . . . and they're all friends of his.

As a rule, Aquarians are extremely friendly and open. Of all the signs, they are perhaps the most tolerant. In the thinking department, they are often miles ahead of others.

You'll most likely find your relationship with this man a challenging one. Your high respect for intelligence and imagination may be reason enough for you to set your heart on a Water Bearer. You'll find that you can learn a lot from him.

In the holding-hands phase of your romance, you may find that your Water Bearing friend has cold feet. Aquarians take quite a bit of warming up before they are ready to come across with that first goodnight kiss. More than likely, he'll just want to be your pal in the beginning. For him, that's an important first step in any relationship—love, included. The "poetry and flowers" stage—if it ever comes—will come later. The Aquarian is all heart; still, when it comes to tying himself down to one person and for keeps, he is almost always sure to hesitate. He may even try to get out of it if you breathe down his neck too heavily.

The Aquarius man is no Valentino and wouldn't want to be. The kind of love-life he's looking for is one that's made up mainly of companionship. Although he may not be very romantic, the memory of his first romance will always hold an important position in his heart. Some Aquarians wind up marrying their childhood sweethearts.

You won't find it difficult to look up to a man born under the sign of the Water Bearer, but you may find the challenge of trying to keep up with him dizzying. He can pierce through the most complicated problem as if it were a matter of 2 + 2. You may find him a little too lofty and high-minded—but don't judge him too harshly if that's the case; he's way ahead of his time—your time, too, most likely.

If you marry this man, he'll stay true to you. Don't think that once the honeymoon is over, you'll be chained to the kitchen sink forever. Your Aquarius husband will encourage you to keep active in your own interests and affairs. You'll most likely have a minor tiff now and again but never anything serious.

Kids love him and vice-versa. He'll be as tolerant with them as he is with adults.

SAGITTARIUS WOMAN PISCES MAN

The man born under Pisces is quite a dreamer. Sometimes he's so wrapped up in his dreams that he's difficult to reach. To the average, active woman, he may seem a little sluggish.

He's easygoing most of the time. He seems to take things in his stride. He'll entertain all kinds of views and opinions from just about everyone, nodding or smiling vaguely, giving the impression that he's with them one hundred percent while that may not be the case at all. His attitude may be "why bother" when he's confronted with someone wrong who thinks he's right. The Pisces man will seldom speak his mind if he thinks he'll be rigidly opposed.

The Pisces man is oversensitive at times—he's afraid of getting his feelings hurt. He'll sometimes imagine a personal affront when none's been made. Chances are you'll find this complex of his maddening; at times you may feel like giving him a swift kick where it hurts the most. It wouldn't do any good, though. It would just add fuel to the fire of his complex.

One thing you'll admire about this man is his concern for people who are sickly or troubled. He'll make his shoulder available to anyone in the mood for a good cry. He can listen to one hard-luck story after another without seeming to tire. When his advice is asked, he is capable of coming across with some words of wisdom. He often knows what is bugging someone before that person is aware of it himself. It's almost intuitive with Pisceans, it seems.

Still, at the end of the day, this man will want some peace and quiet. If you've got a problem when he comes home, don't unload it in his lap. If you do, you are liable to find him short-tempered. He's a good listener but he can only take so much.

Pisceans are not aimless although they may seem so at times. The positive sort of Pisces man is quite often successful in his profession and is likely to wind up rich and influential. Material gain, however, is never a direct goal for a man born under this sign.

The weaker Pisces are usually content to stay on the level where they find themselves. They won't complain too much if the roof leaks or if the fence is in need of repair.

Because of their seemingly laissez-faire manner, people under this sign—needless to say—are immensely popular with children. For tots they play the double role of confidant and playmate. It will never enter the mind of a Pisces to discipline a child, no matter how spoiled or incorrigible that child becomes.

Man—Woman

SAGITTARIUS MAN
ARIES WOMAN

The Aries woman is quite a charmer. When she tugs at the strings of your heart, you'll know it. She's a woman who's in search of a knight in shining armor. She is a very particular person with very high ideals. She won't accept anyone but the man of her dreams.

The Aries woman never plays around with passion; she means business when it comes to love.

Don't get the idea that she's a dewy-eyed Miss. She isn't. In fact, she can be pretty practical and to-the-point when she wants. She's a girl with plenty of drive and ambition. With an Aries woman behind you, you are liable to go far in life. She knows how to help her man get ahead. She's full of wise advice; you only have to ask. In some cases, the Aries woman has a keen business sense; many of them become successful career women. There is nothing backward or retiring about her. She is equipped with a good brain and she knows how to use it.

Your union with her could be something strong, secure, and romantic. If both of you have your sights fixed in the same direction, there is almost nothing that you could not accomplish.

The Aries woman is proud and capable of being quite jealous. While you're with her, never cast your eye in another woman's direction. It could spell disaster for your relationship. The Aries woman won't put up with romantic nonsense when her heart is at stake.

If the Aries woman backs you up in your business affairs, you can be sure of succeeding. However, if she only is interested in advancing her own career and puts her interests before yours, she can be sure to rock the boat. It will put a strain on the relationship. The over-ambitious Aries woman can be a pain in the neck and make you forget that you were in love with her once.

The cultivated Aries woman makes a wonderful wife and mother. She has a natural talent for homemaking. With a pot of paint and some wallpaper, she can transform the dreariest domicile into an abode of beauty and snug comfort. The perfect hostess—even when friends just happen by—she knows how to make guests feel at home.

You'll also admire your Arien because she knows how to stand on her own two feet. Hers is an independent nature. She won't break down and cry when things go wrong, but will pick herself up and try to patch up matters.

The Aries woman makes a fine, affectionate mother.

SAGITTARIUS MAN
TAURUS WOMAN

The woman born under the sign of Taurus may lack a little of the sparkle and bubble you often like to find in a woman. The Taurus woman is generally down-to-earth and never flighty. It's important to her that she keep both feet flat on the ground. She is not fond of bounding all over the place, especially if she's under the impression that there's no profit in it.

On the other hand, if you hit it off with a Taurus woman, you won't be disappointed in the romance area. The Taurus woman is all woman and proud of it, too. She can be very devoted and loving once she decides that her relationship with you is no fly-by-night romance. Basically, she's a passionate person. In sex, she's direct and to-the-point. If she really loves you, she'll let you know she's yours—and without reservations.

Better not flirt with other women once you've committed yourself to her. She's capable of being very jealous and possessive.

She'll stick by you through thick and thin. It's almost certain that if the going ever gets rough, she won't go running home to her mother. She can adjust to the hard times just as graciously as she can to the good times.

Taureans are, on the whole, pretty even-tempered. They like to be treated with kindness. Pretty things and soft objects make them purr like kittens.

You may find her a little slow and deliberate. She likes to be safe and sure about everything. Let her plod along if she likes;

don't coax her, but just let her take her own sweet time. Everything she does is done thoroughly and, generally, without mistakes.

Don't deride her for being a slow-poke. It could lead to flying pots and pans and a fireworks display that could put Bastille Day to shame. The Taurus woman doesn't anger readily but when prodded often enough, she's capable of letting loose with a cyclone of ill-will. If you treat her with kindness and consideration, you'll have no cause for complaint.

The Taurean loves doing things for her man. She's a whiz in the kitchen and can whip up feasts fit for a king if she thinks they'll be royally appreciated. She may not fully understand you, but she'll adore you and be faithful to you if she feels you're worthy of it.

The Taurus woman makes a wonderful mother. She knows how to keep her children well-loved, cuddled, and warm. She may have some difficult times with them when they reach adolescence, though.

SAGITTARIUS MAN
GEMINI WOMAN

You may find a romance with a woman born under the sign of the Twins a many splendoured thing. In her you can find the intellectual companionship you often look for in a friend or mate. A Gemini girl friend can appreciate your aims and desires because she travels pretty much the same road as you do intellectually . . . that is, at least part of the way. She may share your interests but she will lack your tenacity.

She suffers from itchy feet. She can be here, there . . . all over the place and at the same time, or so it would seem. Her eagerness to move about may make you dizzy, still you'll enjoy and appreciate her liveliness and mental agility.

Geminians often have sparkling personalities; you'll be attracted by her warmth and grace. While she's on your arm you'll probably notice that many male eyes are drawn to her—she may even return a gaze or two, but don't let that worry you. All women born under this sign have nothing against a harmless flirt once in a while. They enjoy this sort of attention; if the Gemini feels she is already spoken for, however, she will never let such attention get out of hand.

Although she may not be as handy as you'd like in the kitchen, you'll never go hungry for a filling and tasty meal. The Gemini girl is always in a rush; she won't feel like she's cheating by breaking out the instant mashed potatoes or the frozen peas. She may not be much of a good cook but she is clever; with a dash of this and a suggestion of that, she can make an uninteresting TV dinner taste like something out of a Jim Beard cookbook. Then, again, maybe you've struck it rich and have a Gemini girl friend who finds complicated recipes a challenge to her intellect. If so, you'll find every meal a tantalizing and mouth-watering surprise.

When you're beating your brains out over the Sunday crossword puzzle and find yourself stuck, just ask your Gemini girl; she'll give you all the right answers without batting an eyelash.

Like you, she loves all kinds of people. You may even find that you're a bit more particular than she. Often all that a Geminian requires is that her friends be interesting . . . and stay interesting. One thing she's not able to abide is a dullard.

Leave the party-organizing to your Gemini sweetheart or mate and you'll never have a chance to know a dull moment. She'll bring out the swinger in you if you give her half the chance.

A Gemini mother enjoys her children. Like them, she's often restless, adventurous, and easily bored.

SAGITTARIUS MAN
CANCER WOMAN

If you fall in love with a Cancer woman, be prepared for anything. The Cancerian is sometimes difficult to understand when it comes to love. In one hour, she can unravel a whole gamut of emotions that will leave you in a tizzy. She'll undoubtedly keep you guessing.

You may find her a little too uncertain and sensitive for your liking. You'll most likely spend a good deal of time encouraging her—helping her to erase her foolish fears. Tell her she's a living doll a dozen times a day and you'll be well loved in return.

Be careful of the jokes you make when in her company—don't let any of them revolve around her, her personal interests, or her family. If you do, you'll most likely reduce her to tears. She can't stand being made fun of. It will take bushels of roses and tons of chocolates—not to mention the apologies—to get her to come back out of her shell.

In matters of money-managing, she may not easily come around to your way of thinking. Money will never burn a hole in her pocket. You may get the notion that your Cancerian sweetheart or mate is a direct descendent of Scrooge. If she has her way, she'll hang onto that first dollar you earned. She's not only that way with money, but with everything right on up from bakery string to jelly jars. She's a saver; she never throws anything away, no matter how trivial.

Once she returns your "I love you," you'll find you have an affectionate, self-sacrificing, and devoted woman on your hands. Her love for you will never alter unless you want it to. She'll put you high upon a pedestal and will do everything—even if it's against your will—to keep you up there.

Cancer women love homelife. For them, marriage is an easy step. They're domestic with a capital D. The Cancerian will do her best to make your home comfortable and cozy. She, herself, is more at ease at home than anywhere else. She makes an excellent hostess. The best in her comes out when she is in her own environment.

Cancer women make the best mothers. Each will consider every complaint of her child a major catastrophe. With her, children always come first. If you're lucky, you'll run a close second. You'll perhaps see her as too devoted to the children. You may have a hard time convincing her that her apron strings are a little too tight.

SAGITTARIUS MAN
LEO WOMAN

If you can manage a girl who likes to kick up her heels every now and again, then the Leo woman was made for you. You'll have to learn to put away jealous fears when you take up with a woman born under this sign, as she's often the kind that makes heads turn and tongues wag. You don't necessarily have to believe any of what you hear—it's most likely just jealous gossip or wishful thinking.

The Leo girl has more than a fair share of grace and glamour. She knows it, generally, and knows how to put it to good use. Needless to say, other women in her vicinity turn green with envy and will try anything short of shoving her into the nearest lake in order to put her out of the running.

If she's captured your heart and fancy, woo her full-force—if your intention is eventually to win her. Shower her with expensive gifts and promise her the moon—if you're in a position to go that far—then you'll find her resistance beginning to weaken. It's not that she's such a difficult cookie—she'll probably make a lot over you once she's decided you're the man for her—but she does enjoy a lot of attention. What's more, she feels she's entitled to it. Her mild arrogance, however, is becoming. The Leo woman knows how to transform the crime of excessive pride into a very charming misdemeanor. It sweeps most men—or rather, all men—right off their feet. Those who do not succumb to her leonine charm are few and far between.

If you've got an important business deal to clinch and you have doubts as to whether you can bring it off as you should, take your Leo wife along to the business luncheon and it'll be a cinch that you'll have that contract—lock, stock, and barrel—in your pocket before the meeting is over. She won't have to say or do anything . . . just be there at your side. The grouchiest oil magnate can be transformed into a gushing, obedient schoolboy if there's a Leo woman in the room.

If you're rich and want to see to it that you stay that way, don't give your Leo spouse a free hand with the charge accounts and credit cards. When it comes to spending, Leo tend to overdo. If you're poor, you have no worries because the luxury-loving Leo will most likely never recognize your existence—let alone, consent to marry you.

As a mother, she's both strict and easy. She can pal around with her children and still see to it that they know their places. She won't spoil them but she'll be a loving and devoted parent.

SAGITTARIUS MAN
VIRGO WOMAN

The Virgo woman may be a little too difficult for you to understand at first. Her waters run deep. Even when you think you know her, don't take any bets on it. She's capable of keeping things hidden in the deep recesses of her womanly soul—things she'll only release when she's sure that you're the man she's been looking for. It may take her some time to come around to this decision. Virgo girls are finnicky about almost everything; everything has to be letter-perfect before they're satisfied. Many of them have the idea that the only people who can do things right are Virgos.

Nothing offends a Virgo woman more than slovenly dress, sloppy character, or a careless display of affection. Make sure your tie is not crooked and that your shoes sport a bright shine before you go calling on this lady. Keep your off-color jokes for the locker room; she'll have none of that. Take her arm when crossing the street. Don't rush the romance. Trying to corner her in the back of a cab may be one way of striking out. Never criticize the way she looks—in fact, the best policy would be to agree with her as much as possible. Still, there's just so much a man can take; all those dos and don'ts you'll have to observe if you want to get to first base with a Virgo may be just a little too much to ask of you. After a few dates, you may come to the conclusion that she just isn't worth all that trouble. However, the Virgo woman is mysterious enough, generally speaking, to keep her men running back for more. Chances are you'll be intrigued by her airs and graces.

If lovemaking means a lot to you, you'll be disappointed at first in the cool ways of your Virgo girl. However, under her glacial facade there lies a hot cauldron of seething excitement. If you're patient and artful in your romantic approach, you'll find that all that caution was well worth the trouble. When Virgos love, they don't stint. It's all or nothing as far as they're concerned. Once they're convinced that they love you, they go all the way right off the bat—tossing all cares to the wind.

One thing a Virgo woman can't stand in love is hypocrisy. They don't give a hoot about what the neighbors say if their hearts tell them "Go ahead!" They're very concerned with human truths—so much so that if their hearts stumble upon another fancy, they're liable to be true to that new heartthrob and leave you standing in the rain. She's honest to her heart and will be as true to you as you are with her, generally. Do her wrong once, however, and it's farewell.

Both strict and tender, she tries to bring out the best in her children.

SAGITTARIUS MAN
LIBRA WOMAN

You'll probably find that the girl born under the sign of Libra is worth more than her weight in gold. She's a woman after your own heart.

With her, you'll always come first—make no mistake about that. She'll always be behind you 100 percent, no matter what you do. When you ask her advice about almost anything, you are likely to get a very balanced and realistic opinion. She is good at thinking things out and never lets her emotions run away with her when clear logic is called for.

As a homemaker she is hard to beat. She is very concerned with harmony and balance. You can be sure she'll make your house a joy to live in; she'll see to it that the home is tastefully furnished and decorated. A Libran cannot stand filth or disarray—it gives her goose-bumps. Anything that does not radiate harmony, in fact, runs against her orderly grain.

She is chock-full of charm and womanly ways. She can sweep just about any man off his feet with one winning smile. When it comes to using her brains, she can out-think almost anyone and, sometimes, with half the effort. She is diplomatic enough, though, never to let this become glaringly apparent. She may even turn the conversation around so that you think you were the one who did all the brain-work. She couldn't care less, really, just as long as you wind up doing what is right.

The Libra woman will put you up on a pretty high pedestal. You are her man and her idol. She'll leave all the decision-making—large or small—up to you. She's not interested in running things and will only offer her assistance if she feels you really need it.

Some find her approach to reason masculine; however, in the areas of love and affection the Libra woman is *all* woman. She'll literally shower you with love and kisses during your romance with her. She doesn't believe in holding out. You shouldn't, either, if you want to hang onto her.

She is the kind of girl who likes to snuggle up to you in front of the fire on chilly autumn nights . . . the kind of girl who will bring you breakfast in bed on Sunday. She'll be very thoughtful about anything that concerns you. If anyone dares suggest you're not the grandest guy in the world, she'll give that person what-for. She'll defend you till her dying breath. The Libra woman will be everything you want her to be.

She'll be a sensitive and loving mother. Still, you'll always come before the children.

SAGITTARIUS MAN SCORPIO WOMAN

The Scorpio woman can be a whirlwind of passion—perhaps too much passion to really suit you. When her temper flies, you'd better lock up the family heirlooms and take cover. When she chooses to be sweet, you're apt to think that butter wouldn't melt in her mouth . . . but, of course, it would.

The Scorpio woman can be as hot as a *tamale* or as cool as a cucumber, but whatever mood she's in, she's in it for real. She does not believe in posing or putting on airs.

The Scorpio woman is often sultry and seductive—her femme fatale charme can pierce through the hardest of hearts like a laser ray. She may not look like Mata Hari (quite often Scorpios resemble the tomboy next door) but once she's fixed you with her tantalizing eyes, you're a goner.

Life with the Scorpio woman will not be all smiles and smooth-sailing; when prompted, she can unleash a gale of venom. Generally, she'll have the good grace to keep family battles within the walls of your home. When company visits, she's apt to give the impression that married life with you is one great big joy-ride. It's just one of her ways of expressing her loyalty to you—at least in front of others. She may fight you tooth and nail in the confines of your living room, but at a ball or during an evening out, she'll hang onto your arm and have stars in her eyes.

Scorpio women are good at keeping secrets. She may even keep a few buried from you if she feels like it.

Never cross her up on even the smallest thing. When it comes to revenge, she's an eye-for-an-eye woman. She's not too keen on forgiveness—especially if she feels she's been wronged unfairly. You'd be well-advised not to give her any cause to be jealous, either. When the Scorpio woman sees green, your life will be made far from rosy. Once she's put you in the doghouse, you can be sure that you're going to stay there a while.

You may find life with a Scorpio woman too draining. Although she may be full of the old paprika, it's quite likely that she's not the kind of girl you'd like to spend the rest of your natural life with. You'd prefer someone gentler and not so hot-tempered . . . someone who can take the highs with the lows and not complain . . . someone who is flexible and understanding. A woman born under Scorpio can be heavenly, but she can also be the very devil when she chooses.

As a mother, a Scorpio is protective and encouraging.

SAGITTARIUS MAN
SAGITTARIUS WOMAN

You'll most likely never come across a more good-natured girl than the one born under the sign of Sagittarius. Generally, they're full of bounce and good cheer. Their sunny dispositions seem almost permanent and can be relied upon even on the rainiest of days.

Women born under this sign are almost never malicious. If ever they seem to be, it is only seeming. Sagittarians are often a little short on tact and say literally anything that comes into their pretty little heads—no matter what the occasion. Sometimes the words that tumble out of their mouths seem downright cutting and cruel. Still, no matter what the Sagittarian says, she means well. The Sagittarius woman is quite capable of losing some of her friends—and perhaps even some of yours—through a careless slip of the lip.

On the other hand, you are liable to appreciate her honesty and good intentions. To you, qualities of this sort play an important part in life. With a little patience and practice, you can probably help cure your Sagittarian of her loose tongue; in most cases, she'll give in to your better judgement and try to follow your advice to the letter.

Chances are, she'll be the outdoors type of girlfriend. Long hikes, fishing trips, and white-water canoeing will most likely appeal to her. She's a busy person; no one could ever call her a slouch. She sets great store in mobility. She won't sit still for one minute if she doesn't have to.

She is great company most of the time and, generally, lots of fun. Even if your buddies drop by for poker and beer, she won't have any trouble fitting in.

On the whole, she is a very kind and sympathetic woman. If she feels she's made a mistake, she'll be the first to call your attention to it. She's not afraid to own up to her own faults and shortcomings.

You might lose your patience with her once or twice. After she's seen how upset her shortsightedness or tendency to blabbermouth has made you, she'll do her best to straighten up.

The Sagittarius woman is not the kind who will pry into your business affairs. But she'll always be there, ready to offer advice if you need it.

The Sagittarius woman is seldom suspicious. Your word will almost always be good enough for her.

She is a wonderful and loving friend to her children.

SAGITTARIUS MAN
CAPRICORN WOMAN

If you are not a successful businessman or, at least, on your way to success, it's quite possible that a Capricorn woman will have no interest in entering your life. Generally speaking, she is a very security-minded female; she'll see to it that she invests her time only in sure things. Men who whittle away their time with one unsuccessful scheme or another, seldom attract a Capricorn. Men who are interested in getting somewhere in life and keep their noses close to the grindstone quite often have a Capricorn woman behind them, helping them to get ahead.

Although she is a kind of "climber," she is not what you could call cruel or hard-hearted. Beneath that cool, seemingly calculating, exterior, there's a warm and desirable woman. She just happens to think that it is just as easy to fall in love with a rich or ambitious man as it is with a poor or lazy one. She's practical.

The Capricorn woman may be keenly interested in rising to the top, but she'll never be aggressive about it. She'll seldom step on someone's feet or nudge competitors away with her elbows. She's quiet about her desires. She sits, waits, and watches. When an opening or opportunity does appear, she'll latch onto it lickety-split. For an on-the-move man, an ambitious Capricorn wife or girlfriend can be quite an asset. She can probably give you some very good advice about business matters. When you invite the boss and his wife for dinner, she'll charm them both right off the ground.

The Capricorn woman is thorough in whatever she does: cooking, cleaning, making a success out of life . . . Capricorns make excellent hostesses as well as guests. Generally, they are very well-mannered and gracious, no matter what their backgrounds are. They seem to have a built-in sense of what is right. Crude behavior or a careless faux-pas can offend them no end.

If you should marry a woman born under Capricorn, you need never worry about her going on a wild shopping spree. Capricorns are careful with every cent that comes into their hands. They understand the value of money better than most women and have no room in their lives for careless spending.

The Capricorn girl is usually very fond of family—her own, that is. With her, family ties run very deep. Don't make jokes about her relatives; she won't stand for it. You'd better check her family out before you get down on bended knee; after your marriage you'll undoubtedly be seeing a lot of them.

Capricorn mothers train their children to be polite and kind.

SAGITTARIUS MAN
AQUARIUS WOMAN

If you find that you've fallen head over heels for a woman born under the sign of the Water Bearer, you'd better fasten your safety belt. It may take you quite a while actually to discover what this girl is like—and even then, you may have nothing to go on but a string of vague hunches. The Aquarian is like a rainbow, full of bright and shining hues; she's like no other girl you've ever known. There is something elusive about her—something delightfully mysterious. You'll most likely never be able to put your finger on it. It's nothing calculated, either; Aquarians don't believe in phony charm.

There will never be a dull moment in your life with this Water Bearing woman; she seems to radiate adventure and magic. She'll most likely be the most open-minded and tolerant woman you've ever met. She has a strong dislike for injustice and prejudice. Narrow-mindedness runs against her grain.

She is very independent by nature and quite capable of shifting for herself if necessary. She may receive many proposals of marriage from all sorts of people without ever really taking them seriously. Marriage is a very big step for her; she wants to be sure she knows what she's getting into. If she thinks that it will seriously curb her independence and love of freedom, she's liable to shake her head and give the man his engagement ring back—if indeed she's let the romance get that far.

The line between friendship and romance is a pretty fuzzy one for an Aquarian. It's not difficult for her to remain buddy-buddy with an ex-lover. She's tolerant, remember? So, if you should see her on the arm of an old love, don't jump to any hasty conclusions.

She's not a jealous person herself and doesn't expect you to be, either. You'll find her pretty much of a free spirit most of the time. Just when you think you know her inside-out, you'll discover that you don't really know her at all, though.

She's a very sympathetic and warm person; she can be helpful to people in need of assistance and advice.

She'll seldom be suspicious even if she has every right to be. If she loves a man, she'll forgive him just about anything. If he allows himself a little fling, chances are she'll just turn her head the other way. Her tolerance does have its limits, however, and her man should never press his luck at hanky-panky.

She makes a big-hearted mother; her good qualities rub off on her children.

SAGITTARIUS MAN
PISCES WOMAN

Many a man dreams of a Piscean kind of girl. You're perhaps no exception. She's soft and cuddly—and very domestic. She'll let you be the brains of the family; she's contented to just lean on your shoulder and let you be the master of the household.

She can be very ladylike and proper. Your business associates and friends will be dazzled by her warmth and femininity. Although she's a charmer, there is a lot more to her than just a pretty exterior. There is a brain ticking away behind that soft, womanly facade. You may never become aware of it—that is, until you're married to her. It's no cause for alarm, however; she'll most likely never use it against you.

If she feels you're botching up your married life through careless behavior or if she feels you could be earning more money than you do, she'll tell you about it. But any wife would, really. She will never try to usurp your position as head and breadwinner of the family.

No one had better dare say an uncomplimentary word about you in her presence. It's liable to cause her to break into tears. Pisces women are usually very sensitive beings. Their reaction to adversity, frustration, or anger is just a plain, good, old-fashioned cry. They can weep buckets when so inclined.

She'll have an extra-special dinner prepared for you when you make a new conquest in your profession. Don't bother to go into details, though, at the dinner table; she doesn't have much of a head for business matters usually, and is only too happy to leave that up to you.

She can do wonders with a house. She is very fond of soft and beautiful things. There will always be plenty of fresh-cut flowers around the house. She'll see that you always have plenty of socks and underwear in that top drawer of your dresser.

Treat her with tenderness and generosity and your relationship will be an enjoyable one. She's most likely fond of chocolates. A bunch of beautiful flowers will never fail to make her eyes light up. See to it that you never forget her birthday or your anniversary. These things are very important to her. If you let them slip your mind, you'll send her into a crying fit that could last a considerable length of time. If you are patient and kind, you can keep a Pisces woman happy for a lifetime. She, however, is not without her faults. Her "sensitivity" may get on your nerves after a while; you may find her lacking in imagination and zest; you may even feel that she uses her tears as a method of getting her own way.

She makes a strong, self-sacrificing mother.

SAGITTARIUS
YEARLY FORECAST: 1986

Forecast for 1986 Concerning Business and Financial Matters, Job Prospects, Travel, Health, Romance and Marriage for Those Born with the Sun in the Zodiacal Sign of Sagittarius. November 23–December 20

This year ahead should prove to be one of challenge and constructive progress for you of forward-looking Sagittarius, ruled by Jupiter, the planet of wisdom, judgment, and good fortune. You know how valuable it is to look for new horizons in order to develop your knowledge and interests, but are equally aware of the serious side of life, which must be understood if you are to become a wise person as the sign implies. You have, indeed, the capacity to be two persons at once and can be adventurous as well as quiet or considerate according to the needs of the situation. It could be that you need this year to discipline yourself and practice the more responsible qualities of your nature in order to enjoy the full flavor of your life.

This could be a highly adventurous time for you as you accept responsibility, thus being able to stand on your own two feet and do that which is so important for ego and recognition. In consequence there could be some restriction on your opportunity to travel the world, but you will have other, more pressing, interests, no doubt. Health may bring you problems. You are one who can see the signs of any such difficulty, so you can be prepared for trials of strength and cope with them adequately.

Money matters are likely to take up much of your time. You are a wise speculator who is often considered by those who are envious to be a gambler. This year you should be able to impress the timid with your resourcefulness in working for and accumulating resources enough to see you through any bad patch. Property deals could be interesting and rewarding during the year. Your responsible attitude to life will ensure business achievements that can put you in a more secure position than up to now. Cooperative ventures in business could have to be seriously considered.

You will be inclined to get your house in order before expanding or sharing responsibilities. In relationships, generally, you could be obliged to face up to facts. Some will need to consider marriage as a way to stabilize their personal affairs. Others will concentrate on making their own situation viable before committing themselves to a partnership that could presently be restrictive. As ever, there can be periods in the year when a peak of romance can be reached. You are not one to be hidebound by convention, though you are also very considerate of precedent. Employment will be important to those who are either self-employed or hire their services out. As personal finance is likely to mean a great deal to you, it is essential to make the most of your chances in your occupation. You will look for reward through production and promotion.

You are never afraid to put on a show or publicize yourself. It seems your activities, desires, or needs this year could be quite small in this direction. Business prospects are not dependent on the wider world you can reach by advertising. Affairs nearer home will be both more rewarding and more pressing. You will get your priorities sorted out and consolidate your gain accordingly. Attend to publicity you feel to be essential in the first seven weeks of the year. From about March 29 to October 9 you are likely to concentrate a lot of your energy on developing business. You should have scope to use new methods and seek creative enterprise that will make business life exciting. Appreciating the need for some self-discipline need not stifle your enterprise. You will know intuitively when you are onto a good thing, so you can make important progress that will increase your personal resources in the process. Two periods, between August 24 and September 23 and from November 23 to December 22, can be particularly interesting and rewarding. In these periods you could attract recognition of influential people who perceive your talent and ability and will, if necessary, lend practical support.

Personal resources seem to need a great deal of attention. In some ways you may be strengthening your position through hard and determined efforts to make the best use of your money. There may be two sides to this coin. Firstly, you may be unsure of the future as it affects your income and savings. This could make you both overadventurous and undecided according to the feeling of the day. You could have great schemes one day and be full of doubts on the next. From about March 29 to October 9 you are likely to put your courage to the test and do something positive about getting financial affairs really working. In this period you are likely to put your shoulder to the wheel and use your resources to the full. Your bank balance may increase through your efforts and foresight as you use your capital wisely.

Property deals could be beneficial after about February 21. Up till then you could be attending to inquiries or arrangements that can be handled more freely from the last week in February on. Your banker and any other person you respect in financial affairs could be helpful to you in the first three weeks and the last ten days of the year. Taxation should not cause any undue problem. Between June 22 and July 23 you should get good advice, if it is needed, from responsible people who deal in this matter. As you will be treating life quite seriously, you are not likely to be too adventurous with your money, or with that of anyone else who depends on you for guidance and advice. In consequence you can accrue sufficient funds to see you through the year and possibly some time ahead.

You are well known for your individuality. This makes you hard to pin down as a partner or spouse. Once committed, you are sincere and honorable. For many this will be a year to take on marital responsibility. Some will feel lonely and will wonder where the past years have flown. The few weeks between March 10 and April 2 are likely to spark off romantic urges that may end in the unexpected, or perhaps be a turning point for those who need an extra nudge before deciding. Plans could be made between April 27 and May 21. For those who intend to remain footloose and free this could be an emotional year in some ways. You will be concerned with fundamental issues and need to look after your innermost self. You will need to confide and find comfort or support at various times. So you will seek relationships that fill this need, yet allow you freedom to take on your own individual responsibilities without involving others at too intimate a level.

Traveling to the far ends of the world may not, this year, be your greatest need. Responsibilities nearer home are likely to keep you occupied. Your education may be improved by concentration on personal essentials rather than widening of horizons. You will not feel this an undue burden, as you can adjust quite easily when it is necessary and realistic to do so. Up to February 20 you could make the most of your chances, either keeping up with matters in a relatively limited area occasionally traveling overseas. From then on your thoughts of expansion may be more homebound. In the period July 24 to August 23, the urge to hit the trail could be extra strong.

Health and vitality depend a great deal on your spirit to overcome difficulties. Good advice can be ignored if you get the bit between your teeth. It is not that your judgment is in error, but more that you are underestimated by people who look on health as a purely physical matter. Some of you could feel the strain of responsibility to be heavy. You will need to conserve your strength. Where you are burdened by the health problems of those close to you, this could be a worrying and wearing situation. Retain your spirit and always live in hope of better days, which will surely come. You hate to be in a rut. When you are obliged to stick to routine for long periods, take advantage of short breaks. You normally enjoy walking the dog and can commune with nature so easily.

You who have to work for someone else to earn a living may find the year starts as the previous one ended, with work problems. From about February 21 a fresh breeze may sweep through your working life. Wiser counsel may influence employers who should now be more cooperative. Productivity will come from this change of attitude. You could benefit through higher wages and better working conditions. Whatever work you do, whether as an employee or as a self-employed person, will have to be worthwhile. You are most interested in getting your finances working properly, so you must apply yourself to the work in hand. Money does not grow on trees, as you are well aware. Your responsible attitude throughout the year is likely to attract the attention of superiors or those who seek your personal services. Efforts concentrated between March 29 and October 9 will be rewarded. Between April 21 and May 21 your good work could be recognized, which could mean promotion, financial bonus, or added business for the self-employed. Many of you will be self-employed. This could be a great year after February 21 for those who work at home or are involved in handling family real estate business.

Personal security along with the corresponding responsibilites could be the most important facet of the year. Family matters may give added meaning to your daily life. Taking on personal responsibility will allow you to strengthen family ties. The married Sagittarius will probably find more security in close cooperation with a partner. Children born this year will find security that gives them a reliable start in life. Preparations for family developments may be completed by the end of February. From then on a great deal of enthusiasm can be expended on developing domestic harmony and the family good fortune. You may be involved in buying or selling properties for the family. This may be due to wise investment of resources while they are available.

If you feel the pressure on you to be too much, look for support and encouragement from your partner or the one you love. This is a year when joint responsibilities can make light of a heavy personal burden. This could be a landmark in the lives of those who are prepared to share and yet retain that sense of personal freedom so essential to the family man or woman. During the periods February 20 to March 21, you should feel the full value of family support. Parents or older members of the family can add to your hopes for future prosperity.

Provided you are patient, constructive, and prepared to take on any responsibility that is duly yours, you will find 1986 to be a year to remember and a landmark in your lifetime.

DAILY FORECAST

January–December 1986

JANUARY

1. WEDNESDAY. Variable. The year begins quite favorably for you Sagittarius-born people. This is a good day for centering your activities on people in the background. See what you can do to improve your relationship with people who might be able to do you a bit of good in areas that have not been open to you to date. You will have to watch your temper though, especially if your New Year celebrating took a lot out of you. Do not take any action that would alienate loved ones. Impulsive moves must be avoided. Do not do anything that would damage your reputation. Take particular care in making decisions; be sure to consider all the angles.

2. THURSDAY. Disquieting. Do not place too much reliance on hearsay. Rumors that come to you are not likely to be absolutely correct. It would be in your best interests to check out all information before you act upon it. This will be an irritating sort of day in many ways. You will probably have to have meetings with people whom you find it hard to reach agreement with. Much of the time of the Sagittarius businessman could be spent in round table conferences that achieve little or nothing at the end of the day. Personal plans may have to be changed later in order to fall into line with the wishes of family members. Don't insist on having your own way.

3. FRIDAY. Difficult. It could be that you find you have to deal today with quite a lot of irritating chores that were left over from last year. This will be an extremely difficult period for advancing your New Year's plans. People with whom you wish to get in touch will not be immediately available. Changes in your schedule will be unavoidable. Friends are not likely to be the good company that you usually find them to be. Relations may be a little strained with someone with whom you have formerly been on a very good wavelength. People may be looking to you for financial assistance that you would prefer not to supply. You do not like to borrow or lend money.

4. SATURDAY. Good. There is no doubt that this will be the best day of the week so far for you people born under the sign of Sagittarius. You should be able to get ahead with your work early in the day. This will leave you with more spare time later on. It is an excellent period for the Sagittarius sportsperson. You will enjoy yourself whether you are a spectator or a participant. Friendship will be rewarding, and past differences will be easier to forget. Short trips will be helpful for opening up new contacts that will be very useful to you in the future. Take advantage of social opportunities that come your way; this will be a good evening to spend with friends, especially those you don't often see.

5. SUNDAY. Mixed. Power struggles can easily develop with people behind the scenes. This will be a tricky period if you are attempting to mix business with pleasure. You will have some difficulty in reaching agreement with people who you meet under social conditions. It might be best to leave the finishing touches to documents and contracts until the working week gets underway. People born under Sagittarius may feel that their independence is threatened in some way today. This is something that they cannot stand. Today is good for social affairs, however, which provide opportunities for romantic meetings. Relax and enjoy yourself.

6. MONDAY. Quiet. Although this will be a fairly quiet start to the working week, you are not likely to have too many objections on this score. There seem to be quite a lot of odd jobs that you would like to catch up on, and you should have ample opportunity to do so today. Conditions may become a little tedious for those of you who are tied to office or factory work. You will not enjoy it if you have people overseeing you and checking the pace at which you work. It would not be a good idea to make any new starts this Monday. Conditions will be too slow to see them through to a satisfactory conclusion. There is no point risking failure of a project on which you are spending time and money.

7. TUESDAY. Disturbing. Try as you might, it will be difficult for you to settle down to normal work. There are likely to be any number of frustrations that you find hard to overcome. In spite of the optimistic nature of the Sagittarius-born person, this will be an extremely difficult day on which to look at the brighter side of things. You may get the feeling that the world is getting on top of you a bit at the moment. Influential people will not be as helpful as you would have hoped. This is not the best of times for suggesting your ideas for change to them. Health may not be up to snuff. Physical risks must not be taken. Make sure you are getting plenty of sleep, as well as maintaining your proper weight.

8. WEDNESDAY. Fair. As long as you continue to take care of your health, all should be well. If you have been suffering from a minor ailment for quite some time, then it would be advisable for you to see your local doctor. Otherwise, you could go to the Emergency Room of a hospital for a checkup. Although it is against the extraverted nature of Sagittarius native, it would be in your best interests to work as much behind the scenes as possible today. This is especially important when it comes to making financial arrangements. Be very careful if you are dealing with lawyers. Be sure that people who are supposed to be acting on your behalf are doing their very best for you.

9. THURSDAY. Good. It is a favorable day for making moves that you may have been held back from taking for one reason or another. You will find that people whom you have been trying to track down unsuccessfully will become more readily available. The Sagittarius personality will be of enormous help to you when it comes to persuading others to agree to your terms. It will be important to operate away from the public eye when tackling the sensitive details of documents that contain hidden clauses. It is a good period for writers and artists among you. Shoppers should be on the lookout for bargains which may be found if they are attending the January sales today. But it may entail hard work.

10. FRIDAY. Encouraging. Centering your activities in an effort to improve the overall financial situation will be extremely helpful to you. Go over your accounts. You may discover to your alarm that you have been throwing around more cash than you might have been meaning to. You will be able to find useful areas where savings can be made without lowering your life-style to any noticeable degree. Influential people will be more inclined to support your schemes. You will find that superiors will take more than a passing interest in any original ideas that you have. Do not be afraid to present them. If they are accepted, be ready to back them up all the way; make sure of your facts.

11. SATURDAY. Variable. This is an excellent day for all activities that are aimed at improving your health. You should certainly pay more attention than you do to your physical condition. If you have been overindulging in food or drink, then now is the time to exert some discipline over yourself. Short trips may be valuable to you. A change of environment would be likely to do you the world of good. Today is favorable for making serious decisions regarding the future security of you and yours. Make sure that you are up to date with all insurance policies and mortgage payments. The advice of elders may well be worth paying more attention to. After all, they have probably had a great deal more experience than you have had in almost all areas.

12. SUNDAY. Pleasant. The more that you can get out and about, and mix with people from walks of life different from your own, the better it is likely to suit you. You will enjoy variety and challenge today. Short trips will continue to offer you very pleasant experiences. You may be able to learn something under social conditions that will be of advantage to you in your career. Today is favorable for all mental endeavors and especially for the writing of letters. Correspondence may result in your being provided valuable information. Luck can bring unexpected gains and developments. You should not have to spend a lot of cash to have an enjoyable and entertaining day of it. There are lots of free parks and perhaps a pond or rink for ice skating.

13. MONDAY. Changeable. You will have to push yourself a good deal harder today if you are going to achieve the sort of results that you know you are capable of. The day starts with you in a somewhat lethargic mood. You will have to pull yourself up by your bootstraps and get on with what you know has to be done. Disagreements with members of your family are also likely. You and your mate or partner may find it hard to see eye-to-eye on many issues. There are likely to be arguments about the best way to deal with the problems of members of the younger generation. Today is good for real estate activities. These can be made more profitable, but only if you devote time and effort to them.

14. TUESDAY. Variable. The cooperation of family members will be easier than usual to obtain. This will leave you free and clear to attend to more outside matters. This is quite a good day for making short trips in connection with your job. Readers who are traveling salespersons should be able to renew orders from last year that will earn good commissions. Act with confidence. There is no reason why you should not put yourself in line for some sort of promotion through what you achieve now. This is not a day for moving your home or giving up comfortable accommodations on impulse. Stay with what you have and work to improve it; it will increase in value considerably if you make it attractive.

15. WEDNESDAY. Deceptive. This is one of those tricky midweek days when you should not put your trust in the promises that are made to you by other people. Associates at your place of employment may let you down, especially if they promise to take over jobs for you. The more that you can rely on yourself, the better you will do. Caution with all financial matters is also required. Try not to lend or borrow cash. Don't go in for any gambling as you are almost certain to end up the loser if you do. Speculative ventures have to be given short shrift in order to avoid losses. It is best for the moment to stick with the steady, reliable investments that you own.

16. THURSDAY. Disquieting. Early hours will be quieter than normal and this will give you the opportunity to tackle work of a routine nature. Pay up on your bills. Write to people to whom you owe letters, especially those who are residing abroad. Financial pressure is likely to be placed upon you once again. You seem to have a lot to talk over with accountants, bank managers, and other financial advisers. The mail or the telephone may bring you in demands to settle outstanding debts. Short trips could work out to be more expensive than you had realized and turn out to be a complete waste of time into the bargain. Activities around the home can be more satisfying than you would imagine.

17. FRIDAY. Demanding. Other people's problems are likely to be something of a burden for you. Family members could interrupt you at your place of employment. It will be hard to concentrate on matters that require attention to detail. All is not likely to be well between you and your mate or partner. It is going to be tricky reaching agreement on emotional matters. You may feel that the demands that are made on you are most unfair. Sensitive personal problems are likely to be left unresolved. It will be a day in which speculative propositions can appear more attractive than is the case. Losses from gambling could be ruinous, so you would be well advised to stay away from track or tables.

18. SATURDAY. Disappointing. Employment affairs are likely to be tedious. The sort of jobs that are proposed for you are not likely to be attractive, and you will find concentration extremely difficult. Results will be disappointing. You may not be able to earn the amount of cash that you were hoping to bring in today. Rest and the avoidance of strain are vital if your emotional feelings are not going to get the better of you. Try to involve yourself in some pastime that you find relaxing later on in the day. There is no point in fretting over matters that you are powerless to alter at the moment. Remember the prayer about accepting what cannot be changed.

19. SUNDAY. Mixed. As long as all of your usual activities are kept open and aboveboard, there is little that can go wrong for you this Sunday. You do have to be wary about complicated emotional entanglements, though. Be sure that you are straightforward with people close to you. You could get yourself into all sort of complicated situations if you do not make it absolutely clear what your feelings are. This should be a fairly enjoyable period for you and yours. Home life will appeal to you. You are unlikely to be tempted to go anywhere where you would be required to spend a great deal of money. Employment changes should not be contemplated at this time. Opportunities will be quite limited.

20. MONDAY. Variable. The intelligent minds of the Sagittarius native will be helpful to all mental pursuits. You will not have any difficulty in concentrating on desk jobs. This is a first-rate period to set aside time to bring your accounts up to date. This is especially true if there are bills left over from last year that have still been left unpaid. Loved ones will be understanding if you have to spend more time than usual away from home attending to job-related duties. Government officials and those in authority will also be more cooperative. Today is good for handling all important document work and for catching up on family financial matters.

21. TUESDAY. Routine. Partners or spouses will be more congenial than usual. This quiet period will afford you the opportunity to work out domestic problems that have remained unresolved for far too long a time. Greater harmony on the home front will be much to your liking. Recent difficulties can be even more easily smoothed over. You will find that your opposite number is in a much more reasonable mood. Today is useful for furthering cooperative efforts that have already started. But it will not be ideal for beginning new projects or for starting new partnerships. The people with whom you have to work quite closely are likely to blow hot and cold. In cases like this, it is usually wisest to have as little to do with them as possible.

22. WEDNESDAY. Good. You should be feeling in fairly good shape, both mentally and physically. This will enable you to tackle many of the tasks that you have set yourself for this week. Your relationship with superiors will be good. This will strengthen your hand in any deals that you are trying to set up at your place of employment. Seek the cooperation of close associates. Two hands will definitely be better than one when attempting to attend to routine matters. Favorable contracts and agreements can be signed. Today is exactly suited to thinking big and working with others to achieve your aims. Make the most of conditions when they are as bright with opportunity as this one.

23. THURSDAY. Rewarding. You seem to have struck a pretty good period at the moment. This is another excellent day for achieving a lot of your aims. With everything running at home fairly smoothly, you ought to be able to concentrate on your outside interests with some success. Today is an ideal one in which resources and joint financial affairs can be increased by operating behind the scenes. This will not be a busy day from the travel angle. You will thus be able to spend more of your time concentrating on what you consider to be priorities. Facts that have been concealed can be brought to light through secret investigation. These might better be kept secret until the time is ripe for exposing whoever is at fault.

24. FRIDAY. Good. Carry on the good work. You should be feeling fairly pleased with the results that you have been able to achieve so far this week. Confidence will be riding high at the moment. Influential people will be impressed by all of your recent efforts. A slow beginning to this day was indicated. But as the hours roll by, it will become even more positive than yesterday for advancing your joint financial affairs. Today is starred for straight talking and for clearing the air in private. Other owners of funds are more than likely to agree with the Sagittarius native's plans for investments. Take advantage of this unexpected cooperation and act with due speed.

25. SATURDAY. Disturbing. Relatives are contrary and oversensitive. One of your main problems today is likely to be that of getting along with other people. You may feel that your style is being cramped. Changes might have to be made in your personal plans. If you go ahead and please yourself as to how you spend your leisure time, then the resulting upheavals that you have to face could turn out to be intolerable. More than normal self-control will be necessary to prevent anger and loss of temper. This will not be a particularly happy day for romance. Long-standing relationships could be broken off suddenly. Travel should be postponed. Distant affairs may contain unexpected problems. These should be attended to before they become unsurmountable.

26. SUNDAY. Good. You will be able to smooth over past differences with dear ones quite successfully. Compromise solutions to emotional problems would appear to be the best ones. Today is good for making long journeys, which can be assigned without too much warning. You usually enjoy sudden changes of plans. People you come into contact with will make excellent company. The impulsive nature of the Sagittarius-born person will most definitely work to their advantage now. Sudden moves will bring new opportunities for the future. It will be to your advantage to initiate informal chats with professional people. You will undoubtedly find they are as eager as you to exchange ideas.

27. MONDAY. Variable. Health difficulties, not necessarily personal ones, can interfere with your plans for this first day of the working week. If it is not your own physical condition that is giving you cause for concern, it will probably be that of a dear friend or relative. You may have to put yourself at the disposal of a family member who needs your assistance. It is not going to be easy to combine business with pleasurable activities. Study or travel plans will have to be altered at a moment's notice. Today is favorable for concentrating on mental pursuits later on and making important financial decisions. These may relate to income tax problems, now that you are nearing the deadline for filing returns.

28. TUESDAY. Quiet. This is just the sort of a day that your mind and your body will thrive on. You will be able to relax and unwind easily. This is just as well, as you seem to have been under a considerable amount of pressure of late from many sources. Go over work that requires attention to detail. This will be a pleasant and constructive period for those who are working from their home base. It is a better time than ever for consolidating gains. It is equally good for making preparations rather than for attempting to start up any new operations. Business and public activities will be about normal, but they will not be particularly interesting; don't allow boredom to cause mistakes.

29. WEDNESDAY. Successful. This is one of the best days of the year so far for getting your affairs in better order. You must pay more attention than usual to income tax and insurance matters. With more determined efforts, you can probably win over those people behind the scenes who may have been difficult in past years. Do your best to obtain interest from background figures for your original projects. These could make a lot of money for you if they are handled correctly. Today is favorable for persistent efforts to advance all of your affairs. Perseverance will win through in the end. Reunions are possible after long absences. These should give a great deal of pleasure to everyone included.

30. THURSDAY. Good. You certainly seem to be ending the first month of the year in fine form. Your relationship with business associates seems to be very good indeed. This is especially true of those who are higher up the ladder of success than you are. You can do quite a lot today to ensure that you get some sort of promotion or salary increase in the not-too-distant future. This is the sort of day that most Sagittarius natives will enjoy because there will be plenty of scope for activity. It looks as though you will be involved quite frequently with good friends and acquaintances. Social activities could provide business opportunities that will eventually evolve into lucrative contracts and a fairly high return on investment.

31. FRIDAY. Lucky. Sagittarius natives will have some good luck about now. This will be helpful to them in their mental endeavors. Professional advice will be most valuable. You should be able to discover new and more simplified ways to cope with problems of income tax and insurance. There will not be a great deal of pressure to contend with from loved ones. This will enable you to map out your day and stick to most of your plans. New information that is supplied to you is likely to bring you gains. Interesting people with unusual ideas may be met. Urges for freedom are likely to be stronger than ever this evening. Maybe you have itchy feet and want to flee winter's chill for warmer climes. Or perhaps you're just longing for the weekend ahead.

FEBRUARY

1. SATURDAY. Variable. People in the background should be watched. Someone who could have a disruptive influence on your life behind the scenes may be out to cause some trouble for you. Do not pay attention to rumors. More consideration for the feelings of others will be necessary. Show your mate or partner that you trust him or her. You will win unreserved gratitude. Try to word any necessary criticism with more tact. This is especially true for people born under your sign who have to have any sort of dealings with government officials. Today is favorable for contacts with emotionally sensitive people whom you might be able to help. They probably lack confidence and need a boost to their morale. This is an area where you excel.

2. SUNDAY. Disquieting. Sagittarius natives will become easily irritated. You must watch your temper with loved ones. Any emotional outbursts from you in the early part of the day could cause aggravation within the home. And that could be almost impossibly difficult to overcome. Count to ten before you utter words that you know you will have cause to regret later on. This is not the right time to make important decisions, especially about work. Your thinking may be faulty about career matters. All impulsive moves should be postponed. People will be difficult later on if you do not keep your promises to them today. After all, once they know they cannot take you at your word, they might lose respect for you.

3. MONDAY. Upsetting. Little things will irritate you. They could possibly even stop you from making progress in certain areas of your life. And this could be important to you from the financial standpoint alone. This will not be an easy period for getting things done. Loved ones may be making demands upon you that cut right across your working schedule. Conditions at your place of employment will also be difficult. There could be disruptions. It may well be that there are unexpected changes in schedule that do not meet with your approval. Even worse, there will be nothing you can do about it. People you usually get along so well with may be cold and unfriendly. There is no easy answer, but you are probably not to blame. They may be undergoing some home-front trauma.

4. TUESDAY. Fair. Strained relations can be improved quite a lot. You should be able to use your charm, as well as your drive and energy, to good effect. You do still have to keep a check on the impulsive side of your life. You must be prepared to meet other people halfway. Otherwise, it will be very difficult for you to promote anything that would require teamwork. Be sure that you do not take any action that would bring radical changes about for you or your job. They may not prove to be advantageous in the long run. Romance looks especially happy and exciting. You might have the chance to get together with someone you care quite a lot about, but have not been able to see much of recently. This will do you both a world of good.

5. WEDNESDAY. Deceptive. You may think that you have more time to complete certain duties than you really do. It is vital that you make an early start this midweek day. Complete routine affairs that must no longer be shoved to one side as you have been doing. Contacts with people behind the scenes may be useful for reaching financial agreements. You might find that a working lunch can produce some valuable results. Secret transactions will be favored if you are discussing wages with superiors. Conditions later on will be deceptive. These may warn against taking anyone or anything for granted. But you have been around long enough not to do so, and you are probably a good judge of character.

6. THURSDAY. Good. Romance is highlighted. Those of you who are thinking of getting engaged or being married should go ahead and put the finishing touches to your plans now. Sagittarius natives who do not have a steady date at the moment could find themselves getting involved with someone new and exciting. It may be someone who has just arrived upon the scene. Short trips can bring the Archer into the company of the kind of people they enjoy being with the most. Ties of affection can be strengthened through correspondence. Keeping in touch with dear ones over the telephone is an ideal way to maintain good relationships today. One way or another, remember to show that you care.

7. FRIDAY. Variable. Today should find you in a period when you have more energy at your disposal than usual. Be sure that you use it constructively. Come to grips with jobs that you do not find very rewarding and may have been putting off earlier in the week. Channel any upsurge in driving force along productive lines. Do not fritter it away. Do not allow yourself to be talked into involvement with friends who want to spend time seeking pleasure and entertainment when they should be working. Today is favorable for making short trips. These may be used to gather knowledge or information that you could not come by in the normal run of things. They may prove to be far more valuable than you could ever have imagined.

8. SATURDAY. Good. Today is probably the best day of the week for making contact with influential people you wish to have important discussions with about the future. You will find that superiors are understanding and show a great deal of sympathy for your hopes and wishes. Public officials will be available to discuss any plans that you wish to put into practice with regard to property matters. Today is quite good for discussions about leases and mortgages. Financial plans can be taken even farther than you may have hoped for. Do not be afraid to think about opportunities that come your way. But don't stop after thinking about them. Get out and make them come true.

9. SUNDAY. Rewarding. It seems that you have had a hard, although pretty rewarding week. Now that Sunday has come along, you should do your best to enjoy yourself. That will include bringing happiness to those who are closest to you. This is a fine time for getting away from the old Sunday routine and going in for a bit of adventure. Try new areas of experience. People may come up with some bright ideas that would not cost a great deal of money to carry out. Short trips can be a means of meeting with like-minded people. Favorable business opportunities could arise from casual contacts. Explore every angle and don't discount the possibility of developing a successful account.

10. MONDAY. Important. It looks as though you will be feeling full of vim and vigor after your weekend break. You will be keen to make new starts with projects that are very close to your heart. It would appear that your creative ideas will have a special appeal for influential people. And these same people just happen to be in the position to offer you some sort of backing. But this is another one of those days when Archers have to watch the impulsive sides of their nature. It is a good time for using unconventional methods. At the same time you do not want to upset people you may have to rely on at a later date by your actions. So tread softly and be wary of whomever you might inadvertently offend.

11. TUESDAY. Good. Keep on the track that you have set out on. It looks as though you are on the trail of something particularly lucrative. You will be able to use your charm to very good effect in areas that have not given you easy access to date. Romantic adventures will be happy and could contain some exciting incidents. This is especially true if a change of environment is involved. Today is excellent for becoming engaged or for making business proposals. Good luck can make concentration on mental pursuits most worthwhile. Sagittarius natives will most certainly be at their communicative best. You talk well on your feet and your presentations are filled with items of interest. You can also write reports others enjoy reading.

12. WEDNESDAY. Fortunate. Although pleasure-related activities may not come quite up to your expectations, there will be opportunities in other areas of your life that will more than make up for this. At your place of employment, for example, you will find that you will be very popular. This will lead you to attempting to take on exciting challenges. More money can be earned. It might also be possible to add to your income by making better use of your natural talents. Second-string jobs could bring you in some lucrative bonus payments: Sagittarius natives will be more serious and determined than ever. This can be helpful in the handling of the affairs of children. But it can also be a boon to them when making deals that require forceful negotiations.

13. THURSDAY. Productive. Speculation will offer you good opportunities for making more cash. A calculated risk might pay off well. Just be sure that you investigate thoroughly all information that friends present you with before you dip into your reserves to make a new investment. Perhaps the advice of professional people, such as your bank manager or your stockbroker, would be the wisest to follow if you are thinking about the purchase of shares. Today is good for using advanced ideas to make mental and creative efforts more appealing to the public at large. Family affairs will be fairly active this evening. Maybe there is a birthday at hand, or perhaps a celebration of a promotion.

14. FRIDAY. Good. Although this will be a quiet day at your place of employment, it could be a very valuable one. It would appear that you have quite a lot of correspondence to catch up on as well. You also have other desk work that should not be neglected a moment longer. All routine affairs would be most effectively handled in the early part of the day. At that time you are likely to have the greatest driving force at your disposal. Employers will find it easier to obtain the cooperation of their work force. Today is fortunate for real estate affairs. Offers that you make for property are quite likely to be accepted. Be sure you have investigated every angle of whatever deal you make before committing yourself. Once you have signed on the bottom line, it's a valid contract.

15. SATURDAY. Disquieting. This day could be something of a letdown for you. But perhaps this is only because you have been expecting so much from it. Efforts to obtain the cooperation of family members are not likely to be very successful. Any ideas that you had for making cutbacks in expenditures are unlikely to be very well received. You may be a little shocked on checking up on your bank statement. You may find you do not have quite as much cash at your disposal as you thought. You could have made an error in your accounts. In spite of some hard work on your part, not a great deal is likely to be accomplished. This is disappointing for you because you had pinned your hopes on making it a productive day.

16. SUNDAY. Strenuous. More care has to be taken not to overdo. The week that has just come to a close would appear to have left you feeling pretty drained of energy. Sagittarius natives would tax their strength too much if they spent a lot of their time rushing hither and thither. You may have to be firm with family members who expect you to be at their beck and call all the time. People may be taking unfair advantage of your easygoing and amicable nature. Mental restlessness can interfere with concentration on mental endeavors. Driving will require special care and attention this Sunday. The traffic is usually extra-heavy as evening approaches. And daylight fades fast in winter months.

17. MONDAY. Demanding. After a somewhat tricky weekend, you are not likely to be in any mood for work. Sagittarius natives are likely to awaken feeling moody. Do not take your feelings of bad temper out on dear ones. You must not do anything that would help to create an uneasy atmosphere within the home. This is an especially sensitive day for health problems. You may not be feeling your usual self physically. Be alive to the dangers of accidents through negligence. This is especially important if you are handling equipment that you are not entirely familiar with at the office or factory. Don't risk physical injury or damage to a machine because you let your attention wander.

18. TUESDAY. Variable. It will take quite a lot of willpower on your part to keep up with or better your schedules. You are not going to find it at all easy to concentrate on routine matters first thing. Readers who earn their living through buying and selling may not have the drive and ambition that is usually present. However, on the plus side, this is a time when you will be able to obtain more cooperation from members of your family. There are not likely to be any new domestic problems for you to cope with. This will be a happy day for romance and for bringing new companions home to meet the folks. Try to avoid contact with relatives other than immediate family. They are difficult to please and inclined to be fault-finding.

19. WEDNESDAY. Fair. This will be one of those days when superiors and fellow workers are likely to be suitably impressed by your output. They will also note your enthusiastic attitude toward your job. This is the right day for making attempts to promote anything that would require a team effort. Jobs that you have been finding rather dreary and commonplace will be much easier to keep under control if they are shared. Better-paying jobs may soon be offered because of the activities of today. Joint financial affairs will be sensitive, though. You need to be a little more careful with your money. You have shown a tendency of late to throw it around quite a lot. This practice may have grown slowly and you had not noticed.

20. THURSDAY. Good. What will please you most about today is the fact that family members will be cooperative. They will be in almost complete agreement with most of your plans for changes within the household. This is the perfect time to discuss new savings schemes that you are eager to launch. The Sagittarius homemaker should be pleased that he or she is able to make considerable savings when doing any early shopping for the weekend. Keep your eyes open for the bargains if you are purchasing in bulk. This will not be a particularly active day on the work front, but you will have plenty to keep you busy when dealing with domestic matters. Health, either your own or that of a dear one, may need professional attention.

21. FRIDAY. Quiet. This will be an easygoing and quiet sort of a day. It is good for puttering around the house and catching up on odd jobs. You certainly will not want to be stuck with menial tasks when you take a weekend break. Sagittarius will want to get ahead with their regular chores now so that they know they will have the chance to spend more time with dear ones. Get your accounts and your financial statements in better order. Time should be given to examining joint financial matters. But on the other hand, this is not the right time for making any important monetary decisions or large purchases. You must first review your budget and decide how to apportion spending and how much to save.

22. SATURDAY. Sensitive. Professional advice can be helpful to personal affairs. You may have been having marital or partnership problems. You have felt ill at ease in trying to discuss these difficulties with other members of the family or with friends. If so, it might be more beneficial for you to talk the matter over with someone whose profession it is to shed more light on such issues. It is important that you do not keep emotional feelings bottled up inside you. This will be a sensitive day for your relationship with your opposite number. Problems that you thought had long since been overcome may rise to the surface once again. You will find that it will pay to say exactly what is on your mind, and then listen carefully to what your partner has to say.

23. SUNDAY. Variable. You will find that today will be very similar to yesterday in many ways. You will still be looking for answers to emotional problems that you have been keeping to yourself. It may well be that you get some sympathy from an older relative. Since such advice has proved to be invaluable in the past, you would do well to consider it seriously. You may prefer to get away completely from the domestic environment at some point in the day. You will probably be able to relax more readily with friends than with close family. Today is good for sudden departures and for setting out on long journeys. Impulsive and erratic actions involving romance do have to be avoided, though. Otherwise, you may find that you will earn a reputation for reckless behavior.

24. MONDAY. Mixed. It will pay Sagittarius people to compromise more with others rather than to try to have their own way too frequently. Give way on minor issues if it will add strength to your hand at a later date. That could be a time when you are attempting to thrash out matters that are of great importance to the future security and well-being of you and yours. Independence should always be treasured. However, if you try to exert your free will too often, you could well be the one who winds up the loser. This will not be an easy time for carrying out your personal plans. Feelings of frustration could lead to loss of temper. Keep your cool because losing control is self-defeating. Plan your strategy carefully and be as tactful as possible. But be sure to have a back-up plan.

25. TUESDAY. Disquieting. Business associates will not be prepared to tolerate your unpredictable actions. You must not try to force through changes without first getting the okay of people in authority. A disturbing price will be exacted from you unless you are prepared to compromise. You could avoid disturbing scenes at the office or factory by showing a greater willingness to cooperate. Sagittarius people will probably be able to accomplish a good deal if they are involved in any buying and selling. This is quite a good time for getting rid of articles that are no longer useful to you. If you have items of value, it would pay you to have a professional set prices on your belongings. Otherwise, you may end up giving away some very valuable pieces, either of furniture or jewelry.

26. WEDNESDAY. Deceptive. Do not try to pull the wool over anybody's eyes. This matters especially with close family members. Play it straight with loved ones. You will most certainly discover that the maxim that honesty is the best policy is absolutely correct. Do not make up stories about having important business appointments when you are really attempting to carry on secret romantic meetings. Sooner or later, you will be in the soup. And that could lead to grief and pain, as well as disillusionment. The financial advice and propositions of friends should be shunned, because they could cause great loss. Deception, either intentional or otherwise, is likely where money is concerned. Keep your affairs aboveboard and consider friends' advice carefully.

27. THURSDAY. Good. You are probably going to consider this one of the best days of the week so far. You will probably find it easier to exert self-discipline. If you are thinking of starting any real exercise program or taking a course in nutrition, then now is undoubtedly as good a time as any to commence. Get yourself into better shape physically. You may find that you take a keen interest in yoga. Some other exercise program new to you could appeal even more, however. The ideas of friends will be of considerable help to business finances. Plans may be presented to you that will enable you to boost your reserves with entirely satisfactory result. Sagittarius people should attempt to introduce the progressive ideas they have been evolving into club or group activities.

28. FRIDAY. Fair. Today is a so-so ending to the month of February. Mixed trends are indicated for business. The early morning period can bring some fortunate developments connected with the mental endeavors of the Sagittarius person. Writers and those of you who live by your wits can have some good luck. You must not go in for lavish or extravagant spending, though. Friends can be instrumental in your realizing some secret wish or ambition. The day is favorable later on for handling financial plans that you need to go over under the cloak of secrecy. Consider them carefully and keep your own counsel. New acquaintances can be helpful in changing viewpoints that have become a little old-fashioned or outdated.

MARCH

1. SATURDAY. Good. This first day of the month gets off the something of a swinging start for you Sagittarius-born people. Although this is the last day of the week, there is quite a lot that you can achieve. Set up jobs that you will wish to carry out after you have taken a weekend break. Family members will be more than usually in accord with the hopes and ideals of the Archer. They will do what they can to assist you in any way that they can. You will also have a greater feeling of freedom. That is something for which you have been yearning for quite awhile. A great deal of internal pressure seems to have been exerted upon you. Today may allow you to ease up a bit.

2. SUNDAY. Disquieting. Perhaps you have not been finding it very easy to get to sleep of late. You will have to try to learn the art of relaxation. Do not rush about as much as you have been doing. The early part of the day is the best time for handling family matters. But if you are doing any home entertaining, you must be careful that you do not ask over any more people than you can reasonably expect to cope with. Subtle tactics are advisable if you have to deal with relatives who have been emotionally demanding and draining. Opposition may arise later, which could interfere with your pleasure plans. Try not to let this spoil what should be a pleasant weekend day.

3. MONDAY. Tricky. Concentration will be difficult to attain and maintain. You may be feeling rather drained of energy. Your weekend appears to have taken quite a lot out of you. It would be best to concentrate on jobs that you can handle with very little effort rather than attempting to make any new starts. This is also a period that calls for a good deal of tact and tolerance. You must keep trying to get loved ones to see things from your point of view. Individual freedom could be at stake here. Extravagance must not cause you to lash out wildly. It would be more effective to explain calmly, and in a rational way, why it must stop. Winning someone over to your side will never be done by anger.

4. TUESDAY. Variable. Family relationships will continue to be under some considerable strain. You will be feeling torn between your domestic responsibilities and your desire to get out and about. This is not the right moment for trying to make any changes in the running of household and domestic affairs. Later on, conditions will gradually ease up when your opposite number becomes more congenial. Bankers will be inclined to be more generous than ordinarily if you are trying to raise any loans. Real estate can be made more profitable. Try to keep a balance between outside affairs and family matters. One should neither interfere with the other nor take most of your time.

5. WEDNESDAY. Happy. Any property involvements should be carried out to conclusion. You will feel that you have a strong bargaining hand. If you are selling real estate, it will probably not be too difficult to get the price that you demand on the open market. Fortunate results will lead to additional cash being deposited in your bank account. The goodwill and assistance of influential people can be reasonably expected. Home affairs will be more stable than usual. Family members will be happy to accept your plans for going out, as long as they are included in your trips. Take them along. You might have a good time, and they will certainly appreciate your consideration.

6. THURSDAY. Rewarding. Strike while the iron is hot. Push hard now to clinch bargains with your mate or partner that will give you the sort of freedom you crave. Family members will be inclined to welcome romantic partners. You had been feeling a little apprehensive about introducing to them. For the single Archer, social activities can lead to new attractions being formed. You might be able to put your love life on a much more stable footing. Today is good for setting up new homes or for making present ones more attractive and comfortable. Propose your plans and ideas to all family members and ask for their feelings. You may well find that some of their ideas are even more progressive and practical than your own.

7. FRIDAY. Good. This will be the third in a cycle of days when you seem to have been making tremendous headway in sorting out your personal problems. Now that you have made some useful progress on the domestic front, you will have a better chance to turn your attention to business matters. Get started immediately with jobs that you do not want to have to leave to one side until after the weekend break is over. You will have a good deal more energy than usual. You might be able to dig your heels in at the office or factory and win. Superiors will show greater sympathy and understanding for your long-term aims and objectives. If you feel you have won their confidence and approval, you will be likely to do an excellent job.

8. SATURDAY. Encouraging. You have plenty of energy and desire to achieve good results today. This is one of those Saturdays when, in the early part of the day at least, you will be itching to get going. You should immerse yourself in jobs that will be helpful for completing useful agreements. Try to get superiors to sign on the dotted line. Attempt to get contracts that have been hanging fire for all too long signed, sealed, and delivered. All projects contain the possibility of some unexpected improvement. Get started with writing and correspondence. Answer letters to friends, which have been piling up. Make it your first priority to accomplish all the backed-up jobs you have neglected for some time.

9. SUNDAY. Fair. Mothers and housewives will have quite a lot to accomplish today. This will be even truer if there is any all-day family entertaining planned involving ten or more. It would appear that today's guests are all members of immediate family, and you will be eager and willing to go all-out in preparing a sumptuous meal. There will not be too much unnerving pressure placed upon you because family members will pitch in and give you all the help they can. You may be feeling a bit concerned about your health. Minor ailments should not be neglected. Perhaps you have not been getting quite as much sleep as you should. Take care of yourself. Romance will be happy with those concerned in affectionate and cooperative moods.

10. MONDAY. Variable. Don't allow the independent streak in your nature to gain the upper hand. You may feel like wanting to ride roughshod over people with whom you have had long-term relationships. The reason for this might be in order to obtain momentary happiness and excitement. This, of course, would be a big mistake. Do not alienate people with whom you have a lot in common. You have shared many experiences in past years, including trials and tribulations. Don't risk destroying friendships lightly. This will be quite a favorable day for work. It is good for launching cooperative projects with associates. Give-and-take is the order of the day. This allows for plenty of exchanges.

11. TUESDAY. Tricky. You may feel that you are getting away with telling little untruths. But the members of your family know you well enough to realize what you're up to. Do not make up false excuses if you are going to get home late from work. You only put yourself in a bad light, open to suspicion. You will most decidedly discover that honesty is the best policy. Pleasure and recreational activities will be most enjoyable. As long as you do not have an inflexible deadline over your head about when you should be home, you can take your time. Do not be extravagant or overindulgent. There is a strong chance of trickery if you attempt to make money through speculation. Play it safe today.

12. WEDNESDAY. Difficult. Family members will not be in accord with your personal plans. Arguments can develop at home. These are not likely to be out in the open. They may take the form of long silences and obvious moodiness. You will find this very difficult to endure. Differences of opinion connected with influential people will make it hard to launch creative projects. You were hoping they would lend support to get these underway. Property transactions are also not likely to be clinched at this time. Better control of your quick temper will be necessary. But you are definitely not entirely to blame. Conditions are poor which makes it seem as though everything is going wrong. Just be patient for now.

13. THURSDAY. Variable. It will probably be a mixed sort of a day. Any good news that comes through will only arrive rather late, if at all. This will be a particularly frustrating and nail-biting period for those of you who have recently taken examinations or been given auditions. But it would be silly to get yourself in too much of a state about matters you are powerless to alter. Sagittarius people must not be drawn into risky, speculative business propositions. Risks must not be taken with your physical welfare. Too much daring when you are driving could lead to accidents. Abide by speed limits and commonsense precautions. If you happen to be a passenger in a car being driven too fast, or in too reckless a manner, ask to be let out. High-speed accidents are usually fatal.

14. FRIDAY. Routine. You have not had the chance to take a break for most of this month. Now is a period when you will be able to slow down the tempo of your life somewhat. This will be a routine working day, but you will have the chance to settle any recent disputes with your nearest and dearest. It will be well worth your time to do so. At the office or factory, work to lay the groundwork for a salary improvement. You will be hoping to see that your efforts receive due recognition some time next week. Be sure, too, that your boss is well aware of any overtime you have been putting in. Otherwise, he or she may be unaware of your dedicated zeal.

15. SATURDAY. Good. You will be able to get a move on now. Try to turn the present situation at home to your advantage. You should be able to get family members to go along with any plans you have for tightening up on big expenditures for the household budget. Extravagant people for whom you have some financial responsibility must be told to economize immediately. Show that you yourself are prepared to make sacrifices if others are prepared to follow suit. The day is favorable for any activities pertaining to real estate transactions. Pleasing new arrangements can be made with your mate or partner. These may relate to personal schedules or to such matters as renovations to your home.

16. SUNDAY. Variable. Domestic harmony must be maintained at all costs. Do not do anything that could alienate the support you have recently been able to obtain from loved ones. You will probably have to work a bit harder at personal relationships than you would have liked to. But this will pay off in the long run and you will realize how worthwhile it was. It would not be a good idea to try to promote unpopular changes in the smooth running of your domestic life. It will be a good day for real estate affairs. It will be entirely feasible to build upon recent profits successfully. Social activities will go very well today. This will be especially true if you are entertaining within your home. You have most of the day free for preparing food and deciding on special entertainment activities.

17. MONDAY. Disturbing. You will certainly not be in the mood for hard work on this first day of the working week. But it would appear that you do not have any excuse for not showing up. So don't try to fudge on your obligations at the office or factory. If you do it, then why not everyone else? A more conciliatory attitude would be helpful when trying to overcome tensions that have recently been building up in your home. You must try harder to see present domestic problems from the point of view of other members of your family. This is certainly not a day when you should be pushing too hard. Physical risks must be avoided. Don't neglect your health. It is one of your most valuable assets in life.

18. TUESDAY. Worrisome. You will be feeling under considerable strain. You must try a little bit harder to relax. It is not going to do you any good to try to rush routine jobs that you do not really like carrying out. More haste will definitely mean less speed. Family members are not likely to agree with your traveling plans connected with entertainment. This is especially true if you had not intended to include them. Marital arguments will be more serious than you may have envisaged. Much more consideration will be required to prevent hurt feelings. You must not put your personal desires before those of others in the family. There should be a lot of give-and-take on everyone's part.

19. WEDNESDAY. Disquieting. This is a midweek day when you are likely to find yourself having to handle quite a few temperamental people. You must be careful that you do not put your Sagittarius foot in it. You might alienate business associates upon whom you may have to rely at some time in the future. It would be extremely unwise for you to take a live-for-the-moment attitude to life. Resources can be endangered through extravagant or unwarranted spending. Cut back on money that you have been splurging on pleasure and entertainment. Shared savings should not be used to support speculative propositions; at least, not unless the ones involved are fully agreeable to the idea.

20. THURSDAY. Variable. Today will be good for reaching solutions with older relatives. They have probably not been in agreement with you about the way you have been living your personal life. You might be able to explain successfully to parents and other relatives just why it has been necessary to act as you have been doing. New savings arrangements will help guarantee your keeping more money in your bank account. You will thus ensure that there will be no problems in meeting regular bills when they come in for payment. Of course, this refers to the regular, monthly bills. It does not apply to large expenditure, nor for emergencies.

21. FRIDAY. Fair. Working behind the scenes will be helpful to ensuring that you can obtain the support of influential people. They prefer to maintain a low profile, even anonymity. Boardroom meetings for the Archer who is discussing big business deals will have a greater than usual chance of success. Their chances will be even better if the meetings are carried out behind closed doors. Do not allow yourself to become involved in gossip or in spreading rumors. Real estate affairs can be successfully promoted as well. Property matters that have been hanging fire can be brought to a satisfactory conclusion. You should get great satisfaction from knowing you were able to get so much done by week's end, leaving your way clear for the weekend break.

22. SATURDAY. Good. This is an up-and-at-'em day. Do not hold back. All your old fire and drive will be very much in evidence.

Tell your boss just what, if anything, has been troubling you of late. You are likely to get a much more sympathetic hearing from superiors than you would have thought possible. Promotion or some great improvements in office or factory conditions would seem to be in the cards. Unexpected events will be helpful in furthering your personal affairs. Romantic involvements that have been worrying you look as though they are well on their way to improving. This will prove a great boost to your morale and renew your hope for the future of your romance. Don't ignore health problems.

23. SUNDAY. Special. This is one of those Sundays that you have been yearning for. You will be able to clear the air at last with loved ones. It is especially true of areas of your life in which tensions have been building up without anything having been mentioned. Speak your mind. It is sometimes difficult for Sagittarius people to talk about matters that may be open to arguments. But honesty will most definitely be the best policy to stick to, not only now but always. You will have more time to attend to serious mental pursuits. This will be especially true if you have a keen interest in writing or the arts. You may want to visit special art exhibits in museums, or browse in those that specialize in very old books and manuscripts.

24. MONDAY. Disappointing. You won't be in the mood for work. You must apply yourself diligently at your place of employment though. Put your nose to the grindstone. There could be a backlog of jobs that you would rather pass up, too. But unless you attend to these chores, you will get in your bosses' bad books. Don't try to take the initiative and be too independent. You won't have much opportunity, either, to earn any additional cash. Plans of other family members could cut into your working day, which is likely to cause even more problems for you. Short trips will turn out to be a complete waste of time. All in all, you can expect a frustrating day, and there is very little you can do about it.

25. TUESDAY. Worrisome. Emotions will be running high today. There will be an atmosphere at home that most signs of the Zodiac would be unable to cope with. Because you are a Sagittarius, however, it will be easier for you to ignore the tensions and demands that you feel are most unfair. These may be made on you by other members of your family. At your place of employment too much pushing and too many attempts to obtain premature results could only end in disaster. Later, friends may well be responsible for problems, too. You may feel that you have to make a trip to support a close associate who has come to your rescue in the past. You should be glad that you have the opportunity to do so.

26. WEDNESDAY. Deceptive. Things may appear to be a lot better on the domestic front. But this could be only on the surface and be misleading. People will still be extremely resentful about the way you have been carrying on your personal life, although they will be hiding their true feelings. It would be wise not to get drawn into discussions about opposing issues for the time being. Be pleasant, but go your own merry way and do your own thing. Possibilities for deception will be so strong that Sagittarius people will have to be on the alert. Speculation will contain the chance of a serious loss. Do not invest cash where there is the slightest possibility of risk. Influential people cannot be relied upon. This may only be a temporary state, so you can afford to be patient and wait.

27. THURSDAY. Good. After what appears to have been a tricky couple of days, you would appear to be back on top of the heap. You will be pleased about this now that the end of the week and the month are looming ahead of you. Money can be made in addition to your normal income. A boost to your resources will enable you to meet your quarterly bills. This will come about without as much hassle as you had envisaged. The organizational abilities of the Archer will be much to the fore and will impress influential people. Your boss will be pleased with the additional effort that you appear to be putting forth. Since you realize that you are in a favorable light, make the most of this chance to excel.

28. FRIDAY. Encouraging. This will be another first-class day for work. People behind the scenes will be helpful. They might supply valuable information for those people who make their living in the real estate business. Short trips could lead to outstanding affairs being concluded even more amicably than you could possibly have foreseen earlier in the week. Today is perfect for contacts with hospitals and similar institutions. Get in touch with older friends and relatives. They may have been feeling ill or emotionally upset recently. Thinking about the past is a likely occupation this evening. You will enjoy reminiscing about old times and perhaps going through photograph albums, remembering those good old days.

29. SATURDAY. Quiet. Take it easy today. You may be feeling uptight and nervous. But you must try to do your best to relieve all anxieties that have been brought about by emotional tensions and pressures. Some time spent alone will be valuable for assessing past mistakes and ensuring that you do not repeat them. Try to keep tensions in check. You may be feeling at loose ends later in the day. But do not allow yourself to be misled by friends who want to spend a lot of money in their quest for pleasure and entertainment.

Meditation and thinking about philosophical issues will help you to regain a state of calm before retiring for the night. Just put your mind at rest and get a good night's sleep.

30. SUNDAY. Variable. Sagittarius natives will be feeling fairly carefree early in the day. You will be looking forward to what this Sunday has in store for you in the way of social interaction. But you might find that family members are somewhat unreasonable about your inviting friends over to share the family scene. Your mate or partner will be particularly glum and uncommunicative. Hobbies can be a source of pleasure. They will help you take your mind off worries that are really of minor importance. A more serious and thoughtful mood will take over later. You may start to plan the coming week and reflect on how you can make the most progress. Or it may be that you will be thinking about family matters.

31. MONDAY. Sensitive. There may be too many little tasks to attend to for your liking. But if you want to clear the way, you will simply have to knuckle down to them. You will, of course, be more interested in seeking pleasure and recreation. But you have to leave these affairs until later on if you hope to earn your keep. Do not do anything that could upset your immediate boss. It will be a better day for those who can get out and about in connection with their work. This will give them a greater sense of freedom. Today is favorable for romantic ventures. But play it cool if you find that more than one person is showing interest in your feelings. This is a new development that you find both flattering and intriguing.

APRIL

1. TUESDAY. Mixed. Don't be an April fool. Look after your own interests by all means today. But by doing so do not put your long-term happiness and understanding with a loved one under any strain or in jeopardy. This will be quite a good time for making new beginnings on the work front. You may be able to influence a superior to back one of your creative ideas. New ways of making money may be discovered. This would, quite understandably, come in very handy to say the least. Family members will be all the more inclined to cooperate with any budgetary schemes that you wish to put into action. This could be a refreshing change in their point of view. Just be sure to let them know how much you appreciate their attitude.

2. WEDNESDAY. Disturbing. Emotions seem to be a little unstable today. A relationship that means a lot to you could be showing cracks. Some of these may be more serious than you had originally imagined. Any form of overindulgence would have a detrimental effect on your health. Just because you are down in the dumps does not mean you should go to extremes when eating and drinking. Sagittarius natives are well advised not to be too daring or to take risks. At your place of employment it is best to stick to tasks that you know and understand. Do not take on more power than has been vested in you. You will only draw attention to yourself and you may put yourself in an unfavorable light. At best, little good will come of it.

3. THURSDAY. Changeable. All activities must be kept well and truly aboveboard. Any double-dealing will not work out as you may have been led to believe. Although certain people will be well-meaning their ideas for making money will not work. Their get-rich-quick schemes will be way off the mark and will probably lose money. You are eager to get on in the world, but you must not do anything that would upset your boss. Impetuosity will be frowned upon. Today is good for making long-term agreements that will ease unavoidable responsibilities in the future. The health of others could interfere with your plans for tonight. The problems may be related to family members who had planned to be included.

4. FRIDAY. Good. This will be the best day of the week so far. Push hard to get agreements signed that you do not want left dangling in midair during the weekend. Sagittarius people will discover that there could be lots more opportunities available to them to further their plans. People met in casual circumstances can provide unexpectedly helpful information. Short trips, and getting out and about generally, will give you a welcome break from the rut that you have been living in. Give your opposite number a special treat. This evening you will be surprised at the delighted reaction you get. And you may also be surprised to find how much you can both enjoy a night on the town.

5. SATURDAY. Productive. Family members will cooperate with your plans for the home. It is a good day for arriving at a fair agreement with loved ones that will enable you to save more cash in the weekly budget. See what you can do through your own efforts and creative talent to make your surroundings more attractive and comfortable. It is the time of the year to have a good old spring cleaning. Get rid of rubbish and unwanted articles that may have been cluttering up your house during the winter months. Money spent on property will more than help you to maintain its value. It will also help you add to its worth and make it a more attractive offering when you decide to sell it. Real estate holdings usually grow, and you may find yourself the owner of a prize nest egg.

6. SUNDAY. Good. All in all, this will prove to be another happy and constructive day. If you take Friday and Saturday into account, you will realize how pleasurable they were. Now adding today, you feel that this has been one of the greatest weekends you have experienced for quite a long time. This is also a congenial period for domestic relationships. You and your family will not have too much difficulty in agreeing on how to gain the very best this day has to offer. Continue with your efforts to make your home more luxurious. New arrangements can be worked out that will give you a greater sense of freedom. This may relate to staying out one or two nights a week without arousing anger or resentment at home.

7. MONDAY. Disturbing. It could be that you are feeling somewhat tired and drained of energy. This is a period when you could easily make financial mistakes. You are not concentrating as you should. It would be best to stick to jobs of a routine nature. Be careful that you do not make any casual remarks to fellow workers that could be taken the wrong way. That would get their backs up and you won't get cooperation. Don't gamble. Employment affairs contain the possibility of secret enmity, which can make conditions most upsetting. People whose company you are in later on may be dreamy and selfish. This will serve to throw a pall over the evening's entertainment. You may even wonder why you bothered.

8. TUESDAY. Variable. Impulsive actions could cause hurt to others. Do think before you do anything that could upset your mate or partner. People may be keeping their emotions bottled up inside of them. Try to ensure that you do not do anything that could increase their pain or heartache. This will not be an easy day for the Archer to obtain cooperation from people. The exception will be those who usually operate from behind the scenes. Secret arrangements can be agreed upon which will be helpful to financial plans. Too much independence will prove counterproductive, though. In other words, do not try to carry out ambitious plans on your own without consulting with others who are involved.

9. WEDNESDAY. Fair. As long as secret affairs are avoided, you should not have to worry about too much today. Keep all of your business dealings strictly open and aboveboard. This applies in the personal area, too. Self-employed Archers will have excellent opportunities for adding to their earnings. Be prepared to work longer hours, not only today. It will be well worth your while to do so from the financial angle alone. Those of you who are in the buying and selling game will be able to use your forceful personalities to good effect. Commission payments and privileges can be increased. You should work very hard for both as they will add a lot to your regular income.

10. THURSDAY. Useful. This will be a day that will be very similar to yesterday in many ways. The accent seems to be very much on work. Continue to push hard for what you know you are capable of achieving. Sometimes you really do not make enough effort. Be alert for opportunities to impress superiors. You may be able to put yourself first in line for promotion by showing your true zeal and initiative. Jobs can be made more rewarding with some imagination on your part. Or new work could be found that offers higher pay and more prestige. Determination can work wonders; but secret deals are not advisable. You might be burning your bridges behind you and left without any job.

11. FRIDAY. Rewarding. This can be another eventful day for the employed Sagittarius persons. Through your efforts this week, you should have been able to build up your savings to a considerable degree. Certainly people in positions of authority at your place of business will be very pleased with the way you have conducted yourself. See what you can do to teach and encourage younger people at the office or factory. They will then be able to take over jobs that are less important to you, leaving you free to concentrate on priorities. Some good luck can reverse a difficult situation. This will be a load off your mind and open the door to a carefree weekend. That is, of course, provided no other difficulty arises to mar your good fortune.

12. SATURDAY. Good. The weekend would appear to be rounding off very nicely, cross fingers. It looks as though you have overreached some of your wildest dreams at work. Today will see you with more opportunities to mix business with pleasure. It might be a good idea to arrange cocktails or dinner with a person whose influence could be useful to you in the future. Business propositions that you discuss now are more likely to be worthwhile. People may change their minds. That will bring about favorable changes in the current state of affairs. Pleasure and recreation will be easier to arrange for and can be found at a reasonable cost. You should make every effort to take advantage. You work hard all week and deserve a break.

13. SUNDAY. Misleading. Perhaps you will not have slept very well last night. Or perhaps you ate something that disagreed with you. For whatever reason, you will not be feeling in tip-top shape. Promises should not be made or if they are, they should not be believed. Watch what you say. Sagittarius people may say things on the spur of the moment, then change their minds at a later date. This kind of uncertainty could earn you a reputation for being unreliable. Commitments made now could turn out to be a terrible nuisance tomorrow. Money can be lost on real estate ventures that were based on luck alone. It would seem like a heedless way to lose your hard-earned cash.

14. MONDAY. Variable. Marital partners will be unusually sensitive. You might not be able to devote quite so much time to work as you would like to. There will be many emotional demands made upon you that will, of necessity, use up your time. Older relatives, in particular, will be looking to the Archer for aid, sympathy and comfort. Sagittarius must be careful to avoid being overly blunt or direct. The tactful approach is the one that will work to your best advantage. Impulsive action would only create ill feeling. Today is favorable for speculative ventures only with close associates. Alone you will find yourself out of your depth and getting into real trouble. You need guidance and help from someone more knowledgeable than you.

15. TUESDAY. Tricky. Finances require more caution than ever. If you are dealing on the foreign currency markets, you might be well advised to wait for a more favorable time before you clinch any big deals. Be sure, too, of the credentials of the people with whom you are dealing. This will be especially true if they come from distant places. Caution is the watchword of the day. Joint resources must also be handled with extreme care. It would be all too easy to have nothing to show for money that you have paid out. It will be a useful day for conferring with people behind the scenes about secret matters. These may be connected with business or family affairs. But do not reveal the content of your discussions.

16. WEDNESDAY. Important. The day is more favorably inclined for efforts to improve working conditions or pay. Have a chat with your immediate boss if you feel that is is about time that your salary were reviewed. Perhaps you can work out a way that you can earn more cash. It might be through increased output or perhaps additional bonus overtime payments. Co-workers will be cooperative. You might be able to join forces with your colleagues to force the hand of superiors. Today is good for giving the office a touch of brightness with flowers or wall hangings. Throwing an impromptu party to bring people closer together will undoubtedly arouse a lot more interest and add to their feelings of camaraderie.

17. THURSDAY. Variable. Today will be good for in-depth investigations and searching inquiries. If you need to get hold of any information that has not been available to you to date, now should be a good time to do so. Get in touch with background figures who have helped you in the past. New facts may come to light that put a different slant on sensitive issues at your place of employment. You will be able to understand the erratic actions of your co-workers a little better now. The income of partners or spouses can be increased. But this is not a day for setting out on long journeys. If you had made reservations, try to get them postponed. If that will not work out, just cancel them and reapply later.

18. FRIDAY. Quiet. It is just the sort of day that your mind and body will require. You should take things at a slower pace. It seems that you have been pushing yourself fairly hard during the first part of the month of April. You need to take it a little easier now. Come to grips with jobs that you have been putting off. Desk work should play an important role in your affairs. Pay up on outstanding bills so that you have a clearer picture of your financial situation as a whole. Today is useful for preparing for new starts in the future, but not for jumping into action until after the weekend, at least. Once that gets underway, however, stop thinking in terms of work and future moves.

19. SATURDAY. Good. This will be a tip-top day. You will be feeling rested and happy to get back again to jobs that require a lot of physical strength and mental determination. Loved ones will show a greater willingness to join forces with you. This is especially true if there are tasks around the home and garden that require more than one pair of hands to complete successfully. Professional advice will be useful to health problems. If it is not your own well-being that has caused you concern, then it will be that of a dear friend or relative. Today is good for associating with in-laws. Contact with professors and universities can be important. You could research a writing project or investigate teaching techniques.

20. SUNDAY. Variable. Sagittarius people must avoid any activities that could endanger their health. Watch your diet. Make sure that you eat the right kind of foodstuffs. Do not go to extremes with drink. People may be pushing you to get involved in entertainment plans that do not really appeal to you. Stand firm. This is your day of rest, and you must spend it as you feel inclined to. Any business that is carried out today will probably be profitable. But it is also likely to create resentment among family members. That is because they will feel neglected. They think that Sunday is a day for sharing recreation of some kind with you. Or if not that, they want your undivided attention.

21. MONDAY. Mixed. Don't be in too much of a rush to get your new plans going. Although there seem to be many projects that you wish to get launched, this may not be the right time to push influential people too hard. There will be better chances of earning higher pay in the period after midday than during the first portion of this Monday. Some time may have to be devoted to older relatives, like parents. They might be relying on you rather more than usual. Compromises should be made with friends about pleasure plans in order to stop serious differences from breaking out. Office romances could be starting up for some of you about now. Reputations can be enhanced or damaged, depending on who is talking. Guard against making harmful remarks. You may harm someone.

22. TUESDAY. Deceptive. You may feel that you have more time to cope with work than is actually the case. Get down to important desk jobs first thing. If you don't, you will never complete them. Do not allow people to talk you out of dealing with business affairs. Friends who have more time on their hands than is good for them may be trying to influence you in a negative and counterproductive way. Sagittarius can be imposed upon because of your kindness and your generosity. Today is favorable for making new acquaintances through clubs and societies. You may find that they are very serious and are eager to become active in your area of work. This could possibly prove to be a great boon to you.

23. WEDNESDAY. Good. This midweek day puts you in fine fettle. You seem to be in the good books of a special person. He or she is certainly in a position to be of great assistance to you in your work. Aim high. Meetings with superiors under social conditions could lead to valuable agreements being reached. These will ensure that future security will be much more of a reality. The use of novel and original ideas can help Sagittarius win popularity and increase spheres of influence. Today is favorable for surprise activities with friends later on in the afternoon. It will be a lively period in which people will be refreshingly unconventional. Enjoy the experience as it offers you a novel change of pace.

24. THURSDAY. Disquieting. Health problems, not necessarily personal, are likely to require more time and attention. You may have to neglect some of your duties. If you are going to be late for important appointments today, you had better let the other people who are involved know about it in plenty of time. This, of course, is so that you do not get a reputation for being unpunctual or unreliable. This will be a disappointing day for getting things done. Frustration will mount up inside of you, which could cause you to lose your temper. You are undoubtedly feeling unappreciated and unrewarded. Your best course is to overlook any slight, intentional or not, and carry on with whatever you wish.

25. FRIDAY. Quiet. There is too much to do today, but you are not likely to have many complaints about this. As the week is drawing to a close, you will be better able to concentrate on the small jobs. You have had, of necessity, to put these to one side over the past few days. This will be a slow period. If you are attempting to get any exciting creative projects off the ground, it looks as though you are going to have to wait until after the weekend. Influential people, with whom you might like to meet, will probably not be available. Conditions are too slow generally to sustain progress. Today is useful for giving more time to health problems and for visiting hospitals where others are confined. Don't forget how lonely they can get and how totally out of touch with events.

26. SATURDAY. Difficult. Perhaps you have been expecting too much from today. For whatever reasons, you are likely to be having feelings of doubts and frustration. Perhaps loved ones will not be quite so prepared to fall in with your plans for pleasure and entertainment. You will, however, have some good insights. These will help you to plan ahead for business moves that you will be wanting to get underway during the early part of the month of May. Today is favorable for short trips to discuss personal matters with people you have not had the chance to meet face-to-face for some time. These discussions should go well, and will help to clear the air of any lingering misunderstandings.

27. SUNDAY. Disturbing. People born under Sagittarius have to guard against being erratic. Do not let friends down. You may not feel like keeping appointments that you made last week. But people will see through your excuses if you try to weasel out of engagements. You will only be creating problems for yourself if you do not deal with others as straightforwardly as possible. Unconventional ideas or conduct will be hotly resented. Speculation would not be a good idea, as it is likely to be more hazardous than usual. More care should be taken not to leave money lying around in obvious places. No matter who it belongs to, it should not be put at risk. If you are directly responsible, you will feel badly if it is lost.

28. MONDAY. Deceptive. There will be more opportunities for you on the job to attract the attention of superiors. Just be sure that you do not take on more responsibility than has been vested in you. Your progress will be watched with keen interest. All of your business and financial dealings should be strictly open and above-board. Superiors and other influential people are unlikely to be in the mood to discuss pay raises for the time being, so the subject would be best not brought up. Evening is definitely a period for being with close family members. You know, and they know this is true, but also that it does not always work out. There are outside interests or even overtime than can interfere.

29. TUESDAY. Uneventful. Tidy up your affairs. Get the record straight. Go over your business and other personal savings accounts. Try to get a clearer picture of your financial standing, as a whole. Loved ones will be helpful. It will be a day for cooperative efforts at your place of employment. Boring tasks would best be shared so that you can get through them much more quickly. The risk of deception that has been hanging in the air is more than likely to be reduced. But remember that the whole year warns against taking any financial propositions at face value. Try to find some investment firm in which you can rely completely. Then get some of their ideas of what kind of ventures you could invest in with safety. Don't try to act on your own. You could lose everything very quickly.

30. WEDNESDAY. Variable. Co-workers will be uncooperative. You will be very much on your own today. If you want a job done, you are undoubtedly going to have to do it yourself. This is not new. Do not delegate duties to underlings. Check and double-check all financial figures. Superiors will not be easy to win around. Perhaps your charm will not be working quite well enough for you. Influential people may want more time to think things over before they sign important documents. But cooperative ventures with mates or spouses can have most fortunate results. Today is better than usual for romance and for social affairs than it is for work. The former will entail spending money, the latter will earn it. As you know, spending money is all too easy while earning it takes hard work.

MAY

1. THURSDAY. Encouraging. The merry month of May starts off with your feeling somewhat more optimistic about a proposed venture. You had been harboring considerable doubt about this over the past few weeks. It now seems that you have a better chance of receiving backing from influential people. This will do a lot to alleviate your worries. Pleasure and doing what you please will offer you great temptation. You are likely to have more than a usual amount of spare time on your hands. You will have no doubts as to what use you will make of it. Today is especially good for making short trips and renewing contacts. These will stand you in good stead during the remainder of the year.

2. FRIDAY. Enjoyable. Relatives and neighbors will spring pleasant surprises on you. Other people can be relied upon to organize enjoyable entertainment that will have a particular appeal to the Archer. Your company will be very much in demand. You will enjoy mixing with large groups of people and attending parties. New ideas can be helpful to creative enterprises. Be a little more inventive. Do not put any limits on your fresh and original thinking. Many interesting people who can be helpful to you in your job can be met through social affairs. Today is good for those readers who are moving or attempting to improve their present homes. Make the most of this period.

3. SATURDAY. Happy. This will be the third in a cycle of good days. You people born under the sign of Sagittarius certainly appear to have gotten off to a flying start this month. More goodies seem to be on the way. This is a most pleasant day. You will have the golden opportunity of devoting a lot more time to home and family affairs. You will also have many matters of importance to discuss with your nearest and dearest. One of the most important and crucial of these will be the budget. Optimistic feelings about the future will assuredly be fully warranted. These vibes will apply equally at business and in your home. What's more, your family will feel the same.

4. SUNDAY. Quiet. Take it easy. It looks as though you have been putting quite a lot of effort and energy into your plans recently. It would be a good idea to relax and to slow the tempo of your life down. It would be in your best interests not to take on any heavy manual work. If you wish to keep yourself pleasantly occupied, stick to your many desk jobs. Answer letters and pay bills that have been overdue since the first third of the year. Get to bed earlier than usual. Your recent late hours appear to have been taking their toll. Contacts with romantic companions will be pleasant but not particularly exciting. Relationships often reach a certain plateau, and then become routine.

5. MONDAY. Exciting. With a bright start to the working week indicated, your confidence will be riding sky-high. You should be able to push even farther ahead with your original ideas. Arrange meetings with professional people. You know they are in a position to offer you good advice if and when you are thinking about making any new investments. Do all in your power to ensure that any cash you have in a savings account is earning the best possible interest rate. This can be an interesting and important day for creative projects, too. Sagittarius people will be more than usually methodical and painstaking. This means that details will have to be handled with more thoroughness. Romance is starred.

6. TUESDAY. Lucky. Speculative ventures will contain more opportunity for gain. A calculated risk has a better-than-even chance for paying off. It would be wise to listen to older and more experienced friends who have given you good tips in the past. They are more reliable than people who you know to be younger than yourself. They may have more enthusiasm than common sense. This will be a day to play hunches, although not expressly so with money. The more daring approach is likely to work in establishing new romantic relationships. New ideas that have been rejected in the past as too unconventional can be used to improve creative projects. You may be surprised at how successful they will be.

7. WEDNESDAY. Fair. Employment affairs include the possibility of higher pay. If you are offered a salary increase, you would be wise to accept it even if you were hoping for more. Influential people may withdraw earlier offers if you start to haggle at this point. More glamorous positions may be obtained. Sagittarius who have been working as secretaries may be promoted to personal assistants. Use your imagination to attract more attention from those people in authority. Archer shoppers should keep their eyes open for bargains. This will be important especially if there are any sales going on in your area at the moment. Be alert for ways to save.

8. THURSDAY. Excellent. Today is probably the best day of the whole year so far. A letter or telephone call that you receive will make you feel very happy. It will also make you a lot more confident about the future well-being and security of you and yours. Prevailing conditions offer exceptional opportunities. You must be sure that you do not miss out on any of them. All new projects that you start out on today are more than likely to be successful. This is a good time for impressing influential people who are in a position to offer you a salary increase. Income and security can be greatly improved through good luck. But don't depend solely on luck, of course. You must exert the most influence and impetus.

9. FRIDAY. Quiet. This will be an easygoing sort of a day. It would be advisable for you to keep impulsive tendencies in check. Take life slowly. More time ought to be devoted to home and family affairs. This will also be a reasonable working day. But you must nevertheless knuckle down to jobs that you might have been avoiding for one reason or another. Perhaps it is routine matters that you have been shying away from. Affairs left from yesterday can be advanced, but at a considerably slower pace. It's a day in which personal relationships should be reviewed and some screening done. People in general will be inclined to be friendly and cooperative. For those who are not, just avoid them.

10. SATURDAY. Worrisome. It will be a difficult day for coping with emergency situations. Partnership affairs will be especially sensitive. You will find it impossible to fathom the thinking of a loved one. Perhaps you are simply not on the same wavelength as to the best way for solving an emotional issue. Do not do anything impulsive that could jeopardize future happiness. This is especially important if offspring are involved. Home entertaining can end in hurt feelings and perhaps even worse. You want to be on your guard against people who may be interfering in personal matters that really do not concern them. If they happen to be relatives, you will have to choose your words carefully.

11. SUNDAY. Confusing. It looks as though you will still be making attempts to solve personal problems that arose yesterday. This is likely to take up a good deal of your time. Discussions with dear ones will undoubtedly go on for long spells without any definite conclusions being reached. It will be difficult for the Archer not to interfere in relationships with others. He or she feels confident of settling disputes. Perhaps it would be wise to let relatives and friends do most of the talking. The less frequently you express your opinions, the better it will be for all concerned. It is the kind of day when impatience and impulsiveness will only start arguments.

12. MONDAY. Tricky. Secret activities can be somewhat helpful to financial affairs. It would be a good idea to get in touch with people better informed than yourself. They will supply some background knowledge on matters in which you are not, perhaps, very experienced. This is a sensitive day for financial affairs. It is most definitely not a period for spur-of-the-moment investment. People and circumstances can be very deceptive indeed. Do not allow yourself to be lured by the prospect of quick profits. Risky ventures could affect your resources rather shatteringly. You are not in a secure enough financial state to risk any but the most minor of losses.

13. TUESDAY. Variable. Some good luck can help the Archer to improve the possibility of making a profit from joint financial affairs. This is a period when two heads will definitely be better than one. Get together with like-minded people if you are attempting to promote a creative venture. Personal spending can be immoderate and will require some curbing. Do not dip into funds reserved to pay regular bills just to supplement living beyond your means. Money can be squandered without your having too much to show for it at the end of the day. You must learn to live within a budget. It will make your financial position more stable.

14. WEDNESDAY. Worrisome. You may have to contend with the demands of discontented loved ones. It looks as though you will not be able to spend as much time on business affairs as you would have liked. But if you wish to keep the peace at home, you will have to compromise. Your mate or partner may have a valid point, as it would appear that you have been spending rather more time away from home than usual of late. Partnership pressures could be building up to such a point that there will be an emotional outburst if you do not try harder to calm things down. Close relationships can be broken off without much warning.

15. THURSDAY. Good. After surviving a somewhat difficult stretch, you seem to be back on the right track now. The situation at home will be eased considerably. A touchy problem looks as though it has been worked out, at least for the time being. Those born under the sign of Sagittarius will be in a stronger position today, able to get others to accept their plans. Today is good for making long-distance journeys. These are necessary for drumming up support in other towns or cities. Trips that you make will have a considerable bearing on the future. Today is good for dealing with professors in an attempt to gain expert knowledge. This may be job-related information, or connected with side studies.

16. FRIDAY. Mixed. This is not a day for making any radical changes. No alterations should be made in places or types of work.

You may be feeling bored with the present setup, but you would be silly to throw away security. You are not in a strong enough position to follow up on all of your dreams and your ambitions at the moment. Existing employment affairs offer good opportunities for improving your earnings. But you must be willing to put in a bit of overtime. Outstanding affairs can be brought to a satisfactory conclusion. The day is favorable for all types of travel. Make the most of any opportunity you get to enjoy a change of scene. If your trip is business-related, there could be time for sightseeing.

17. SATURDAY. Variable. Perhaps the plans that you had made for the weekend cannot be fulfilled. There will probably be changes that could leave you at somewhat of a loose end. It is also possible that you will have to devote more time to business affairs. There are outstanding matters which have to be completed before you can get more involved in home and family life. Sagittarius must not give in to pessimistic feelings. Setback are likely to be only temporary. Problems may be exaggerated. Dubious people or organizations should be avoided. Any work that is done will carry with it personal satisfaction, as well as bringing in more money. This is an ideal combination that many strive for, but never quite achieve.

18. SUNDAY. Sensitive. Family members will be even more resentful than yesterday if you spend a lot of your time on outside affairs. Be sure that you do not ignore the emotional needs of your mate or partner. Try to arrange a trip out that would include your close family only. Although you are eager to get on with certain business matters, such dealings should wait until the working week gets underway. Promises should not be made unless you are absolutely sure that you can keep them. Evening is a time for answering letters and for doing what you can to map out your plans for Monday and possibly the remainder of the week. Don't overdo, however. You will probably want to start the work week well rested.

19. MONDAY. Tricky. Many minor problems are likely to beset you. It may be difficult to trace cash that is owed to you. People will be elusive and evasive. You may have to make an unexpected journey to meet a person face-to-face. He or she is reluctant to discuss certain affairs with you over the telephone. You could well have to go to the expense of seeking professional advice in order to obtain what is rightfully yours. The good hearts and generosity of Sagittarius people can be exploited. Be alert for those who would have no qualms about taking advantage of you. They are aware that you can be a soft touch and will exploit your generosity.

20. TUESDAY. Disturbing. Depressed feelings will overtake you first thing. People upon whom you can normally rely for some sort of support will not be of too much assistance to you, either. You will have to summon up reserves of courage and determination if you are going to be able to cope. Money pressures are likely to mount. It will not be easy to get hold of ready cash. Bank managers are not likely to be very obliging if you are attempting to obtain any sort of loan, even if it is to be small. Hunches should not be played, as they will more than likely be wrong. Put your mind to work and figure out an alternate way of obtaining a loan.

21. WEDNESDAY. Fair. On the whole, this will be a fairly promising day. You reach the midweek period with one or two rather tricky hurdles still to overcome. But social affairs will be more congenial than usual. This is a happy day for making amends to friends and neighbors. Your relationships with them have been somewhat strained of late. Activities with people who are close to your mate or partner will help to end the rupture of peace within the home. Harmony will be easier to maintain in all relationships. Early today is good for making new romantic attachments. It will also be important for strengthening present ties of affection. Don't ignore these opportunities, thinking there will be a better time.

22. THURSDAY. Good. It will be an especially happy day for the Sagittarius person in love. You will find it much easier to get good vibrations from a person who means a lot to you. Existing relationships can be put on a stronger and more permanent footing. The support of influential people will be easier to obtain. This augurs well for harmony at the office or factory. Just be sure that you do not take the goodwill of your boss for granted. All salary increases will have to be worked for. Try to be of some assistance to people less well off than yourself. Some charitable work would not go amiss. This is not news to you. You have done your share in past days and enjoyed knowing you can help out.

23. FRIDAY. Disconcerting. Guard against feeling sorry for yourself. An up-and-at-'em attitude will be necessary today. After all, who is going to help you to become successful unless you are going all-out to achieve that success yourself? No one and nothing should be taken for granted. Teamwork is not likely to bring about the sort of results that you had been hoping for. Personal affairs seem to be heading for some sort of crisis. Somehow, you do not seem to be able to cope with this emotionally at this time. Difficult decisions cannot be ignored for very much longer. Some uncertainty and possible suspicions are likely. Trust in your usual good judgment and try to keep from being suspicious of others.

24. SATURDAY. Disturbing. Family affairs continue to be most sensitive. Loved ones will be obstructive. You are probably going to get the feeling that personal freedom is going to be restricted in some way or another. People born under the sign of Sagittarius dislike intensely having any sort of restrictions placed upon them. It would appear, however, that you may have to bow to the will of others unless you are willing to face some very serious consequences indeed. Personal plans may conflict with those of people who are being depended upon, so that upsets are likely. Risks of any sort must not be taken with your physical welfare. Good health is a very valuable asset and one you should not jeopardize.

25. SUNDAY. Demanding. Conditions at home may appear to have improved considerably, but this is likely to be only on the surface. You still have to be very cautious about taking other members of your family for granted. And this applies especially to your mate or partner. Thinking will be unrealistic. This will increase the possibility of mistakes being made in your financial affairs. Do not listen to the speculative suggestions of your friends. They are quite likely to be way off the mark. Important decisions about cash should be postponed, and no long-term commitments made. Secret attractions may develop, which are happy if time can be spent with the person of your desire. Otherwise, you will find it difficult to maintain much of a relationship.

26. MONDAY. Variable. It looks as though you won't be in the mood for work today. You will be suffering from the blues. You will also have a great deal of difficulty in concentrating and getting into top gear. The urge to spend recklessly will continue to be strong, but you must resist it. Do not take a live-for-the-moment attitude to your life. This Monday can be lucky for Sagittarius in some ways, however. Business transactions involving real estate could turn out to be lucrative. Family affairs will contain some fortunate developments that will make the situation at home considerably less pressured. This will be a tremendous relief to you. Your otherwise unfortunate events earlier will now seem less drastic.

27. TUESDAY. Disappointing. You may have been hoping to conclude some useful business agreements with people behind the scenes. They are probably going to turn out to be rather difficult, however. You would be well advised not to be too pushy. This applies especially to those of you who are involved in the buying and selling of merchandise. Trips are not likely to work out as satisfactorily as you had hoped for. In fact, you may be put to a lot of unnecessary expense. Secret enmity will be present that will be hard to detect at first. Tact will be needed to prevent broken relationships. This is the kind of day in which you must be on guard all the time, whether dealing with business partners or family members.

28. WEDNESDAY. Fortunate. A complete reversal of yesterday's somewhat dismal trend would seem to be in the cards. Your luck will be on the rise. A person who is in a position to pull a few strings on your behalf will probably be prepared to do just that. This will not be a particularly busy day, but it can be used positively to strengthen relationships that have been under quite a lot of strain. The cooperation of partners or spouses will be helpful, probably because of the knowledge that they can provide. Today is good for making arrangements with relatives or neighbors. You have plans to be away for several days and want to safeguard your home. Someone may agree to watch it, or a relative may live there.

29. THURSDAY. Uneventful. Peace and calm will reign all day. You will be happy to take a break from the recent pressures that have been a burden to you. Furthermore, these have not all been of your own making. This is a period when you should turn to home and family affairs. Your loved ones will be more responsive than usual. Fix up a special outing that would appeal to all members of your family. As long as you are not trying to make any important decisions about domestic issues all will probably be well. Today is not the right time to make any moves with regard to the buying and selling of property. Time given to improving private collections of books, stamps, antiques, etc., is likely to give great satisfaction.

30. FRIDAY. Mixed. Marital differences are likely to develop over family issues. The domestic scene will be tense. Differences will be breaking out, probably over money. You may feel that loved ones have spent rather extravagantly on themselves. If you are honest about it, however, you have perhaps been a bit of a culprit in this area yourself. You will have to be more considerate if you wish to avoid injured feelings. Later on, property investment may be a means to make a little bit of money on the side. Have a closer look at the real estate situation. At the same time, don't act on impulse. Be sure to get all facts and figures before you make a move.

31. SATURDAY. Sensitive. Property affairs may demand that you do quite a bit of running around. This is important especially if you want to catch professional people whose advice you require before they take off for the weekend. Results will be worthwhile if you are prepared to exert yourself more as far as real estate matters are concerned. You should certainly be aiming to increase profits in this area. Today is good for working on your home and making it more attractive. Be more of the handyman and carry out odd jobs yourself. This is cheaper than going to the expense of calling in a professional person. But too much independence or failure to consult others will result in ill feeling.

JUNE

1. SUNDAY. Productive. It would be so easy for you to put off all of those little jobs around the house and garden. But you know that you ought to be getting ahead with them without delay. Come to grips with them first thing, then you will be able to enjoy your leisure time with a clear conscience later on. This will turn out to be a fairly good day for relaxation and entertainment so long as you do not spend too much cash in the pursuance of pleasure. Creative projects should be concentrated upon. Pay special attention to those that give you an outlet for your natural talents. Try to include some sort of entertainment with family or friends. Get out and see a show or have a gala dinner as a change of scene and pace.

2. MONDAY. Variable. New ideas will be helpful to creative ventures. Plug away at hobbies that you have not had the time nor the inclination to turn your attention to in recent days. The imagination of the Archer will be much more active and productive at this time. Do no neglect your day-to-day job though. Influential people must not be rubbed the wrong way. They might get the feeling that you are not pulling your weight at the office or in the factory. Changes of plans on the social scene could lead to some exciting developments. But unecessary spending and wasteful impulses should be avoided. You set an example for the rest of your family.

3. TUESDAY. Mixed. Contacts with people who operate from behind the scenes are not likely to be very successful. It would not be a good idea to try to get the support of influential people who like to keep a low profile. It seems that they will not want to put themselves in the firing line and take any risks on your behalf at this point. Slow down a bit. Impulsive tendencies, such a well-known trait in the Archer's makeup, must be kept in check. Secret enmity may be revealed at the office. It is going to be tricky to promote teamwork with colleagues whom you can usually rely upon. Maybe there are some rumors around about your personal life.

4. WEDNESDAY. Variable. This first week of the month of June does not appear to have really gotten off the ground for you.

Perhaps you have been expecting too much. This could be the reason you are feeling down in the dumps without any really good cause. People born under the sign of Sagittarius can gain from legal settlements, however. Any court actions that are settled this Wednesday will most probably favor you. Rediscover old talents and give them more time. Family affairs can take an unexpected turn for the worse. Arguments will erupt within the home. These should be settled before words are spoken which cannot be retracted. You act as arbitrator and keep the peace.

5. THURSDAY. Good. It looks as though the dark clouds that have been hanging over your head will be rolling away. You will feel free of certain restrictions that have been placed upon you at your place of employment. Your boss will be easier to approach. If you want to talk over the possibility of a salary increase in the not-too-distant future, this is probably the right moment to do so. It will be a day in which money matters can be sorted out with some straight talking. Health can be improved by spending money on keep-fit programs. But equally important are diet and exercise outdoors. Watch your weight and keep away from fats and sugar.

6. FRIDAY. Disturbing. One bright spot in this otherwise difficult day is that Sagittarius people are out and about. They may be in the big department stores hunting for bargains they are quite likely to find. Do not go in for buy-now-and-pay-later arrangements, though. You should not take on any more responsibility in the financial area of your life. This is all the more important if you have not consulted with your loved ones first. Today is better for solo activities than cooperative actions. People will not be very helpful or amenable to your suggestions. They will be more inclined to be overcautious and even suspicious. This development will both surprise and disappoint you. It is not often that people mistrust you.

7. SATURDAY. Mixed. Exceptional opportunities will be available to you today. But whether you will be sharp enough to grab them first thing is the question. You must not be slow-thinking. Be quick off the mark, or your competitors will beat you to the punch. Partnership projects are highlighted. Associates may see things that you would miss were you to attempt to go it alone. The chances of people born under Sagittarius being too independently minded would only lead to aggravation that you could well do without. Gains can come through loved ones and their ideas for improving savings. This should show you how important it is to discuss mutual affairs within the family. Watch out for your health.

8. SUNDAY. Deceptive. Your hopes and schemes for having a good time of it this Sunday are likely to be thwarted. Members of your family and close friends may have entirely different ideas about what constitutes a good time. They appear to be too inclined to be lethargic to want to do anything out of the ordinary. You might well find yourself at loose ends, which could be extremely boring for you. It looks as though you have plenty of energy to burn up. Perhaps it would help if you were to get involved in some form of physical exercise. Arguments could easily develop over financial decisions that would have some long-lasting effects.

9. MONDAY. Disquieting. The Monday morning blues will hit you rather badly. Chances are the day will get off to a somewhat unsettled start within the home. Loved ones will continue to be critical of your financial planning, and some readjustment would seem to be unavoidable. Arguments will develop that may take rather longer to resolve than you would have believed. Tempers will become very easily frayed. It will stick in your throat that what you are trying to achieve for the good of all is simply not being appreciated. Firmer control of partnership spending will have to be exercised even if it leads to head-on-collisions. Attempt to make it clear that your partner must obtain your approval for any cash outlays.

10. TUESDAY. Difficult. This will be still another day when the feelings of those close to you will be sensitive. People you share a good deal of your life with will be easily hurt. Old wounds that you had thought were healed will be opened up anew. It is not going to be easy for you to concentrate on employment affairs. Associates will not be very sympathetic to or understanding of your plight. People born under Sagittarius will have to battle all the way to get their financial ideas accepted. The refusal of others to cooperate will only add to your expense. But you are used to handling rough periods and to overcoming obstacles. You can go it alone.

11. WEDNESDAY. Variable. Slow down. The Archer seems to be in too much of a rush to complete deals that by necessity will really be painstaking. It will take many more days yet to bring them to a successful conclusion. Partnership affairs continue to be under a lot of strain. It might be a good idea to bring in a professional adviser to give you an outsider's point of view on the present difficult situation. More willingness to cooperate on your part will avoid the possibility of flare-ups and blowouts. Unpleasantness could sour the relationship that you have built up and treasured over all these years. It would be better to work out a compromise solution.

12. THURSDAY. Mixed. Today will be quite similar to yesterday because you will be aiming for reconciliation. People born under Sagittarius will find it easier to speak openly and frankly with youngsters, though. This will help clear the air for parents who may feel that they have been growing away from offspring. Influential people will be more inclined to give you a fair hearing. This will hold especially for your schemes for streamlining present working schedules. Household expenses will be a bone of contention. You will have to trim your family budget to suit your pocket. Since this is a family affair, why not get everybody involved? Suggest ways to cut spending and make savings, however small.

13. FRIDAY. Uncertain. The superstitious among Sagittarius people may be expecting ill luck to overtake them. Such an event is unlikely to happen, though. It would not seem that this will be a particularly inspired day. You will still be haggling over problems that seem to have been troubling you for some time. This is particularly true where household expenses are concerned. Business transactions do contain better possibilities of larger profits. These, however, may not come through as quickly as you might have hoped. Suspicion or a noticeable lack of warmth in others can be worrying. You may be imagining this because of their coolness.

14. SATURDAY. Good. This will probably be the best day of the week. You will be able to talk over your monetary worries at last. You can talk frankly with people with whom you have been having differences of opinion for almost all of the week. Important decisions can be made. It might be possible and more productive for you to discuss business matters over the telephone or write letters. This will save you the time and trouble of having to make journeys to see people. Financial affairs willl be looking brighter. New agreements will be easier to negotiate, which will ensure greater security. But do not devote all of your time to business matters. Keep in touch with your friends.

15. SUNDAY. Variable. Partnership cooperation will be difficult to obtain. It is unlikely that it will be possible to arrange pleasure outings with loved ones. They will have ideas very different from your own. Their wishes as to how to spend their leisure time this Sunday won't hurt you one bit. Marital differences will develop. It might be best for you to get away from the domestic environment for awhile. You will only become gloomy if you do mope around the house. Get in touch with friends you have not seen for a long time. Not only will they cheer you up, but you will get caught up on news of their doings. Try to find some form of entertainment you all enjoy and have a good time.

16. MONDAY. Quiet. This is not one of the most exciting starts to the working week. Still and all, there is quite a lot that you can achieve by plugging steadily away in the background. Your boss will be most impressed if you show that you can stick to tasks that require a lot of attention to detail. This easy day contains opportunities for pleasant contacts with friends you have not seen for some time. Your company will be in demand socially. You will prefer getting involved with smaller groups, though, rather than going to places where there will be large gatherings in attendance. Entertainment may consist of a small card party or an art show.

17. TUESDAY. Sensitive. If you have not been feeling too well, perhaps you should consult your family doctor. You should be able to get some good advice on the best way to relax and unwind. You probably need to get rest and far more exercise than you normally do. Diet may also be an important factor. If you eat improperly or don't take time out to let your meal digest, you are asking for trouble. Friends may be turning to you for financial assistance. But you must not put out cash for people who have not paid you back in the past. Be a little bit firmer and more logical. Do not fall for the old pal's act. All financial affairs will be sensitive and contain the possibility of arguments.

18. WEDNESDAY. Routine. All the little jobs that have been piling up can now be dealt with. You will certainly be pleased to pay all your outstanding bills and get a clearer picture of the overall financial situation. Now is the time to arrange meetings with your bank manager and other professional people. See if there is the possibility of a loan in the not-too-distant future. If you are still anticipating expanding your present business interests you are going to need money and know it will be available. As the day wears on it might be boring for people who like to keep on the go. It is likely that thoughts of the past will be persistent.

19. THURSDAY. Good. This will be one of those days when it is quite possible that you will have several opportunities to get on in your career. You should grasp the chances that come your way with great speed. If you delay, you are not likely to get a second bite of the apple. Financial transactions can be advanced through employing secrecy. Do not let too many people know how you are redeploying your reserves. Listen to professional people and not to friends who might be unable to assess the situation accurately. Windfalls can also come through home and family connections. Joint financial affairs are all the more likely to bring gains.

20. FRIDAY. Lucky. This will be still another good day. You seem to be gaining in confidence all the time now after a somewhat uncertain start to the month. People who are in positions of respect and authority will encourage you to go farther. Compatible people, who could turn out to be long-time friends, may be met while making trips. You will find strangers most interesting, especially those who come from walks of life different from your own. You Sagittarius people may find that you are split in your loyalties. Decisions on which way to turn will not be easy to make. But if you take time to reflect in peace and quiet, you will make the right choice.

21. SATURDAY. Variable. Although you will have lots of petty little jobs to cope with, you should not moan and groan about it. Get on with chores that have been piling up at home. Homemakers should try to get the weekend shopping in early. If you delay, you could get caught up in long lines, which will cause frustration and irritation. Be on the lookout for bargains, too. Try to cut down on what you pay out for the weekend budget. Unsettling decisions may have to be made today, possibly connected with the home. Influential people should not be asked to grant favors, as they will not be very cooperative. It will be a good day for house hunting and property transactions of almost any kind.

22. SUNDAY. Ordinary. This will be a most welcome day of rest. You should not take on any more than you have to. Do what suits you best. What is likely to suit you best is more attention to hobbies and to anything else that takes your mind off the hassles of the work-a-day week. Talks with loved ones could bear fruit especially if it is the financial situation that you are mulling over. Parents born under the sign of the Archer should play with offspring and draw closer to them. Time can be taken to get your accounts in better order. But you should also try to do something you don't have time for during the week. Get together with friends and go on a picnic or have a barbeque supper outdoors.

23. MONDAY. Mixed. This will not be an easy day for keeping track of where the money goes. You may have to pay cash for a lot of items. Be sure that you keep all of the receipts for your purchases. You will then be able to do a thorough check later on. Accounts must not be allowed to get sloppy and out of hand. Additional expenses are likely to arise. Loves ones may feel that you are not contributing enough for the home maintenance. Property deals could work out well and will offer chances of gains. Those Sagittarius who are involved in the real estate business won't have too much to complain about. There is more than enough action to go around.

24. TUESDAY. Disquieting. You always seem to be in such a hurry. Take it easy. The Archer who is a traveling salesperson should spend more time getting to know clients better. In this way you will win their confidence and their friendship. This will ensure that you take bigger orders, which will bring you in a higher commission. Flirtatious actions could be misunderstood. Don't get romantically involved with people at work, as this could start fights with your steady partner. Money should not be wasted on long-distance phone calls. Attempts at writing for publication may fail. This is not a profession you can break into readily.

25. WEDNESDAY. Good. Don't beat about the bush. Although your outspokenness can get you into trouble at times, this is no day for mincing your words. Influential people will appreciate your no-nonsense attitude. This could lead to promotion. You will win the respect of your associates, too. Your original ideas look as though they will be adopted by those around you. This day offers you better opportunities for carrying out your plans. Your hunches should be given a try, as they are likely to succeed. It will be a good day for music lovers. Artistic matters will rank high in your list of priorities. Put your talent to work. It will bring great satisfaction.

26. THURSDAY. Variable. A little worry is likely today over home and family matters. Perhaps there is some problem with your mate or partner that is emotional. It might be of great help to talk this situation over with an older relative. Their experience could enable you to see things in an entirely new light. You must avoid being impulsive and erratic at all costs. Do not let infatuations with ships that pass in the night make you lose the confidence of someone with whom you have built up a very special relationship over the years. Today is good for joint financial ventures. People who suddenly emerge from the past can be important. It may be that they have expertise in the area that you require.

27. FRIDAY. Mixed. You will be in an open and generous mood. This must not cause you to be silly about the moves that you make with money. People may be trying to touch you for a loan. Before you give them cash, try to obtain built-in guarantees that the money will be paid back by a definite date. You will be very popular with your friends. You will have plenty of varied invitations to choose from if you are contemplating hitting the town tonight. People born under the sign of the Archer do have to avoid being impulsive and erratic, though. These traits could lead to misunderstandings and complications. And if they were at all serious, you might find that you will lose a friend or two.

28. SATURDAY. Difficult. You need to work out a schedule for this last day of the week. The less that you rely on the other people in your life, the better. Plans that are made by friends are not likely to work out as you may have been led to believe. The urge to gamble, although strong, should be resisted. All speculative desires could cause losses that will lead to arguments with loved ones. Today is favorable for pleasure that does not cost you a lot of money. Trust can easily be misplaced where cash is concerned. Don't be too late getting to bed. You could be overtired after your exertions of the week that is about to come to a close. You don't want to sleep tomorrow away and lose the benefit of a free day.

29. SUNDAY. Variable. There may well be a lot of desk work to deal with on this usual day of rest. You had been unable to complete it in the office during the week. Maybe you do not relish the thought, but once you have settled down to it, you are not likely to find it very much of a dreary job. This will be an enjoyable day for Sagittarius later on. Something may be taking place in the entertainment field that will add spice and variety to your life. It will not be difficult for you to find congenial companions. New friendships can be formed with unusual and interesting people you would not normally come into contact with. Make the most of your chance.

30. MONDAY. Disquieting. You might be asking yourself certain serious questions about the purpose of life today. But you really must be careful that you do not let your work suffer because you are in a daydreaming mood. Some discontent with your employment conditions would appear to be inevitable. Try to keep quiet and not to voice your differences too loudly in the presence of your boss. The Archer must beware of making unfavorable moves. Driving requires caution. Do not speed or take any undue risks while on the highway. Study and education programs can be disappointing or perhaps interrupted by circumstances beyond your control.

JULY

1. TUESDAY. Excellent. The second half of the year kicks off to an excellent start. You may receive some good news, dropped onto your doormat this morning. It looks as though some money that has been outstanding for a long time will come through to you at last. It will be an interesting working day for the employed Archer. Opportunities at work will mean that you can stretch yourself and show off your natural talents to their fullest degree. Partners' incomes can also be boosted, which will further swell the family coffers. Emotional ties can be strengthened through travel. Sharing adventures and new experiences can forge bonds that you will treasure for a long time.

2. WEDNESDAY. Sensitive. Don't make promises that you may not be able to keep. It might be best not to make weekend arrangements too far ahead. You might not feel like keeping them when the time comes. Also, today is not a time when you should change your kind of employment. Those of you who are in a secure job should hang onto it. Don't do anything that would antagonize people in authority. Differences may arise with loved ones. Health problems could interrupt working schedules. Secret activities in some areas of your life would best be avoided. However, everyone has personal matters that are only shared wth those involved.

3. THURSDAY. Uncertain. Short trips can be especially helpful to partnership affairs. The Archer who has been contemplating setting up business in some area that is not in the immediate vicinity would be well advised to go full steam ahead. Get in touch right now with associates and let them know of your decision. Don't beat about the bush. Give it to your colleagues straight from the shoulder. Some depression is likely over health or other personal circumstances. Perhaps all is not as you would like it to be at home. It is a day in which you must try to keep smiling. Everyone has a low period from time to time; it is not unusual. Things will pick up.

4. FRIDAY. Demanding. Impulsive words and actions could lead to broken relationships. Do not upset those close to you. That impulsive streak that seems to run through the Archer must constantly be checked. Do not allow your emotions to have too great a sway over your actions. It's a case of allowing your head to rule your heart. Avoid reacting quickly to people at the office or factory. Do not alienate associates to whom you might have to look for support later on. Mental or physical restlessness is likely. More consideration will be necessary before making any moves. You don't want to put yourself out on a limb with no way to retreat. Try to get another point of view and gain new perspective.

5. SATURDAY. Quiet. You might well be seeking the action today, but you aren't going to find a great deal of it. If you were looking for friends to organize pleasure plans, you will be disappointed. Opportunities should be watched out for to improve mutual resources. The best way for you to keep more cash in your bank account is to make cuts in expenditure. Look out for the bargains when doing your regular weekend shopping. Compare prices before you buy at the big supermarkets and department stores. All affairs should be handled in a responsible way that leaves nothing to chance. Don't forget to include some fun and entertainment.

6. SUNDAY. Good. It should be a happy day. All in all, you won't have any complaints. Opportunities to become more closely involved in the affairs of youngsters will be available to the Sagittarius parent. Although conditions on the surface may be quiet and uneventful, this is a very important day for the Archer who is involved in joint financial arrangements. Moves made today have every chance of ending up successfully. People will be more inclined to cooperate with your moneymaking propositions. Influential people may offer backing. But don't spend the whole day on business affairs. You need a change of pace and some fresh conversation and exchange of ideas. It will recharge you for the week ahead.

7. MONDAY. Variable. Don't put off till tomorrow what you could just as easily handle today. You might be in one of those moods when you would prefer to postpone the writing of business letters and the handling of tax affairs. This would be most unwise. Joint activities continue to contain the chance of some good luck, but you must not rush too hastily into making any monetary moves. Much caution is necessary when handling your reserves. You Archers must keep more control of your own resources. Today is favorable for having joint discussions with loved ones about family assets. The health of a family member may be worrisome.

8. TUESDAY. Fair. Thinking can sometimes be entirely too optimistic. Don't get carried away on a wave of enthusiasm. It would be unwise to listen to friends who live by their wits. Don't get involved in speculative ventures for which you would be putting up most of the backing. Mistakes of the past can be repeated. This is true if you do not learn a little more from recent experiences where you have got your fingers burned. Distant affairs can be helpful to long-term security. Today is good for starting more advanced studies to deal with higher education problems. Professional advice will be helpful. Consider all options before making a final decision.

9. WEDNESDAY. Encouraging. An upsurge of energy is indicated. You will be able to do quite a lot of catching up. Some of you readers can get ahead with chores you would have preferred to have gotten rid of as long ago as last weekend. At work, it is one of those times when the impulsive action of the Sagittarius native could turn out to be just the right thing to do. People in authority will admire your spirit. Favorable circumstances can present themselves without your having to engineer them. Today is good for sudden departures to faraway places. Be alert for your options with regard to mode of travel. Much will depend on whether your trip will be for business or pleasure. You may have time for sightseeing.

10. THURSDAY. Variable. Romance can blossom through travel or through contact with people at or from a distance. You will find it most invigorating to keep on the move and to visit distant places that you are not entirely familiar with. The early part of the day is best for dealing with all sorts of desk jobs and similar types of routine work. Superiors will be impressed by your enthusiasm if you show you are capable of handling more and harder work than some of your colleagues. But nothing should be done in the personal area of your life that could possibly endanger your reputation. This, of course, includes office romances, no matter how brief.

11. FRIDAY. Rewarding. It doesn't look as though much can possibly go wrong for you today. People who have the power to influence your career will be only too pleased to assist you in any way they can. Artistic jobs will have a lot of appeal. Those of you who have a hobby that takes you into the realms of show business might be able to turn this talent into something more reliable and enduring. Later in the day things will heat up considerably. More determined efforts can make the possibility of increasing your income a reality. Today is good for collecting outstanding debts and for helping people fulfill their ambitions. Whether or not you can manage the latter is open to question.

12. SATURDAY. Disquieting. It will be easy to fall out with family members. Loved ones will be obstructive, especially where your plans for savings come into the picture. Don't be too forceful or dogmatic with your mate or partner. Perhaps a compromise would be the best solution to your present worries. You yourself have to watch out that you do not get the reputation for being too extravagant. Transactions that involve property or the home should be postponed. Too much optimism could lead to business mistakes. Consider all your options realistically and keep an open mind. Also, plan for some recreation later in the day.

13. SUNDAY. Good. Any entertainment that is offered will be most stimulating. If you did not have anything special planned for today, why not check through the entertainment pages of your Sunday paper? You might find that there is a film or show on that you and your mate or partner would love to see. Also, you will be able to further business opportunities by dealing with people you were not able to track down during the last working week. Home entertaining will be fun as well as giving you the chance of advancing your career prospects. You should invite important business heads who have influence with their firms. They may be able to introduce you to an association which will benefit you.

14. MONDAY. Variable. Your phone will start ringing early in the day. Or someone might be waiting to see you and talk to you at your place of employment almost as soon as you arrive. Don't get in a flap. Any friends who are attempting to get in touch with you now could be the bearers of good news. Just be a little wary of being drawn into any speculative ventures, however. This would not be the right day to try to make a quick buck through get-rich-quick schemes. Loved ones must be given more attention, as they will feel extremely discontented if they are neglected. This is understandable and you are not trying to ignore them deliberately.

15. TUESDAY. Sensitive. Deep insights into people of the past are possible. But you do find these a little unsettling. You may have doubts about the true feelings of a person you had previously thought you could count on. Something is likely to take place now that will cause you to reexamine a relationship that has been longstanding. You may have to summon the strength of character to make an important and life-changing decision. This is not the time to set out on any long trips unless they are absolutely necessary. Charm and tact will help to win new friends and influence people. These traits are invaluable, whether in business or social affairs.

16. WEDNESDAY. Fair. Today is good for working behind the scenes. Operating away from the public can enhance your reputation. This applies to those people who it is not always easy to meet with. Don't have any qualms about airing your views and your opinions. Your boss would much rather have it straight from the shoulder from you even though it may be criticism. Real estate affairs could be another source of income. Problems of the past that have been nagging away at the back of your mind will be easier to handle. Some lucky developments are possible. Distant affairs will be sensitive. If these entail business, you may be sworn to secrecy.

17. THURSDAY. Useful. In many respects this will be a day quite similar to yesterday. You will be carrying on with what you started with then. You will be in a more serious frame of mind. This will help you to look a little deeper into problems that you have only been skimming over on the surface for the sake of convenience. Personal affairs can be sorted out and put into better order. You and your opposite number should have a much clearer idea where you are going and exactly when. But differences can develop with people important to career or public activities. Be alert to these and do all you can to avoid any direct confrontation. These might otherwise affect your progress and cause you great distress.

18. FRIDAY. Variable. Impulsive action on the part of Sagittarius people could endanger their physical welfare. Do be careful if you are handling any tools or equipment that are new to you. Don't tamper with electricity or appliances unless you are certain you know what you are up to. It would be better to call in a professional repair person, even if it does cost you quite a lot of cash. Don't show too much daring or take on challenges just as a lark. Unless you have a hundred percent chance of succeeding with a dare, it is not worth the risk. Personal spending could be immoderate. Don't splurge on luxuries. You probably don't need them.

19. SATURDAY. Tricky. People behind the scenes may be able to assist you. You are trying to sort out a trickly problem connected with your financial affairs. You may be a little unsure about an income tax or insurance matter. It would be in your best interests to discuss your options with a person who is more of an expert than you in that particular field. You must not make any promises about investing in speculative projects in the future until you have had the chance to examine them more closely. Caution is necessary to avoid the possibility of deception or trickery. If you lack sufficient information, it is up to you to get it somewhere.

20. SUNDAY. Variable. The direct approach will most definitely be the best one when handling financial matters. If you have any criticism of the way loved ones have been spending money, speak your piece now. It might cause some hurt to your mate or partner, but at least he or she will know what is on your mind. And everyone will agree it will be for the best in the long run. Today is good for property transactions. Home buying and selling might be nearing the completion stages now. Sunday activities offer business opportunities that you do not usually associate with the weekend. However, keep these matters to a minimum. Concentrate on relaxing and having a good time with family members.

21. MONDAY. Sensitive. Contacts or agreements involving professional people are more than usually difficult to negotiate. The small print of documents could delay the signing of contracts that you had been hoping to complete today. Distant affairs need very tactful handling. Be wary of what you put in letters. This is no time for acting on impulse. Today will be good, though, for making far-reaching decisions about the personal area of your life. Loved ones will show greater understanding for what you want the future to hold. This will include the plans you have made for the good of all of your family. Be sure that you keep them informed and also that you ask for their opinions and ideas.

22. TUESDAY. Good. This can be a very handy day for making short trips. You should get out and about more. People born under your sign, who make their living through buying and selling, must make more effort. They should try to make contact with those people who have not placed orders with you, to date. Your charm may well win over superiors who have proved to be difficult to bargain with in the past. Relatives will be congenial and can be especially helpful with their ideas. Any changes forced on you Sagittarius people can probably be turned to advantage. The evening will be a happy time for romantic meetings. All in all, this will be a pleasant day, and one you will enjoy remembering.

23. WEDNESDAY. Mixed. The charm and charisma that you people born under Sagittarius have in abundance can be put to excellent use today. Those who are connected with show business or the arts will be able to get along famously if you are attending auditions. People who are interviewing you will like your outlook and your outgoing ways. You will win many new admirers and supporters. Financial decisions will be easier to make. You should be able to get your monetary affairs into better shape. Bankers will be understanding and forthcoming with professional advice. You may want to make arrangements for a fairly large loan now.

24. THURSDAY. Variable. Don't act on the spur of the moment. Hasty or impulsive action will be regretted, if not now, then later. You must not try to force the pace at your place of employment. Jobs that would require some sort of team effort will not be at all easy to launch. This is also a time to give a very wide berth to dubious company and their propositions. Loved ones may be demanding and selfish. Your spare time is not going to be as easy to spend as you would wish. But real estate affairs can be made more lucrative. Some interesting bargains may be involved. You may want a piece of property as a hedge against future inflation.

25. FRIDAY. Good. It looks as though this will be one of the best days of the month for you people who are born where Sagittarius rules. Others will be easy to influence. You ought to be able to get your way in many areas where the door has been slammed in your face on previous occasions. Influential people may at last be willing to listen to some of your original ideas. Make people in authority more aware of your natural talents. Don't hide your light under a bushel. But great care is necessary in signing documents. Romance looks much more exciting than has been the case for many a long day. Be sure to take advantage and not pass up the opportunity to make new friends. Also take care of your health.

26. SATURDAY. Changeable. The week comes to an end with your experiencing mixed feelings. You seem to have made gains in certain areas, but perhaps there are still difficulties in your personal life. You have not been able to resolve these in a way totally satisfactory to yourself. Speculative ventures should be avoided. They are not likly to bring you the gains that are promised. Financial affairs should be kept as free from risk as possible. The search for pleasure could turn out to be more expensive than you had anticipated. But health difficulties can be handled with greater ease. This will be a relief and take a load off your mind.

27. SUNDAY. Disturbing. No financial commitments should be made this Sunday. You might be sorely tempted to get involved in some sort of deals. In fact you had convinced yourself that a particular one would make you some easy money. But this is not the way things would probably turn out. Once again, you must be warned that your impulsiveness could get you into deep waters. Joint financial resources should not be dipped into for gambling purposes. Attempts on your part to obtain the goodwill of influential people have not much chance of being a success. Health problems of others, possibly people living at a distance can interfere.

28. MONDAY. Disquieting. Yesterday's many problems will be much on your mind. But it will be a pointless exercise to dwell on the past, especially since the past cannot be altered. You must take more of an optimistic and positive outlook particularly regarding your job. The reputation of the Archer also needs a good deal more protection. Do not do or say anything that could upset your boss. Get on with your job and do not upset everyone else by complaining. Secret romantic affairs are definitely a no-no area. Do not get involved in any new emotional entanglements. If you cannot settle down and be content with someone, wait for the right person.

29. TUESDAY. Rewarding. An upsurge of energy will enable you to get on with jobs that need physical as well as mental application. Push hard to get through chores around the home. Handymen should try to do repair work and redecorating where necessary. Try to increase the value of your property by the improvements that you are able to make. Jobs can be changed for the better. These will offer you better opportunities for fulfilling your ambitions. It might be a good time to make a move you have been contemplating for some time. Good luck can bring outstanding affairs to a happy conclusion. This comes as a wholly unexpected development and makes you extremely happy. You are eager to share the news.

30. WEDNESDAY. Disappointing. It's a case of up one moment and down the next. You had not expected it as the month of July draws to a conclusion. Partnership affairs, especially, contain the possibility of worry. The health of mates or spouses will require more time. Furthermore, it could also force you to alter your personal plans. You will have to make certain sacrifices if you are going to fulfill your obligations. This is not an easy day for getting the boss to understand your problems. Physical welfare must not be endangered. Activities this evening might also be marred by the unexpected. It will be one of those dreary days you will want to forget.

31. THURSDAY. Worrisome. Home affairs interfere with your plans, both business and private. Loved ones will be demanding time that you feel would be better spent elsewhere. Difficulties with business associates are also in the cards. Colleagues may feel that you are not pulling your weight. Team effort could turn out to be a complete waste of time. Favorable agreements that you had hoped to wrap up before the month of August are not likely to be consummated. People born under Sagittarius must beware of difficulties involving women. The possibility of scandal exists if tact is not used. Don't flaunt a relationship that could be detrimental to your progress.

AUGUST

1. FRIDAY. Difficult. The month of August starts with your feeling in very much the same mood as you did when July came to an end. It seems that the problems within the home continue to cause havoc with personal plans that do not include other members of your brood. Conditions also continue to warn against taking risks with your good name. Women may be the cause of some of problems for the male Archer. It is not going to be at all easy for you to make up your mind about an emotional matter. Since this will have an important bearing on your future happiness, you can understand the gravity of your dilemma. Arguments can lead to broken relationships. And those will breed unhappiness and resentment.

2. SATURDAY. Deceptive. Continue to tread very carefully in your love life. Romance appears fraught with problems for you. Promises must not be made if you are not one hundred percent sure that you will be able to keep them. You Sagittarius people should not allow others to have control over your money. Deception or fraud is possible. A firmer hand will be necessary with marital funds. Loved ones may be in the mood to squander your hard-earned cash. Savings must not be dipped into to boost extravagant impulses. This is not an easy day for getting to the bottom of problems, although secret methods may produce good results.

3. SUNDAY. Good. Today will be a better day than the last two. A little honesty and frankness on your part would not go amiss. Talk out your problems with dear ones. Now is the time to speak your mind. You will find that open discussion goes a long way to enabling you to release many of your pent-up emotional feelings. This will be a pleasant period for all home and family affairs. You will be content to spend more time with people close to you. The day also offers chances of new financial partnerships, especially relating to property. It will also be happy for romantic trips with your partner. These may be of short duration like an all-day sail.

4. MONDAY. Fair. This will be a fortunate day for the Archer who is on the go. Short trips are more than likely to have a successful outcome. Your services will probably be in great demand, and you will be able to boost your income. Make this a day for getting on in your job. Show superiors that you are not one to shun hard work. You could even put in a bit of overtime if it is necessary. People may be willing to offer you loans, but be careful. Strings are likely to be attached to such offers. Be on the lookout for some bargains if you are visiting the big department stores. Late hours warn against becoming involved in secret affairs. Furthermore, you should be careful of your reputation.

5. TUESDAY. Encouraging. Progress can be made with the launching of new projects. This is a first-class period for promotional ventures. Those who earn a living through buying and selling ought to be able to make a handy bonus in addition to their usual take. Publishers and advertisers among you are likely to hit on some original ideas. These could make it easier for you to push new products. Influential people will be impressed by the imaginative streak in your nature. Long journeys that are started now will very probably have a successful outcome. Distant affairs can be more satisfactorily handled by using unorthodox approaches.

6. WEDNESDAY. Rewarding. This is one of those easygoing midweek periods. It will give you the opportunity to cope with a number of small tasks. You should really have dealt with these before the end of last month, but postponed the tasks. Write letters and pay outstanding bills. Do not keep people like small shopkeepers waiting to be paid. You Sagittarius folk should also give as much time as possible to study and educational programs today. Concentration will be easier. You will not have much difficulty in retaining knowledge either. There are not likely to be any demanding people or circumstances for you to wrangle with. This will be a big relief to you and give you a sense of satisfaction.

7. THURSDAY. Lucky. You should be feeling in an optimistic and positive frame of mind. After what appears to have been a reasonably easy day yesterday, you should now use plenty of determination and initiative. You must attempt to get influential people to accept some of your original and inventive ideas. Routine work that has become something of a drag can be streamlined. Business transactions contain the possibility of important financial gains. Expenses may be a little higher than usual. People born under Sagittarius, however, are likely to have a good time enjoying the things that their cash can buy them. These could include entertainment, meals, trips or video tapes, whatever is their preference.

8. FRIDAY. Demanding. People with whom you thought you had reached some sort of business agreement are more than likely to go back on their word. This will be particularly annoying for you. It seems that you were close to clinching a deal that would have been most lucrative for you. This took place before you left for the weekend break. Sagittarius will have to curb anger and impatience.

Little will be gained by a show of temper. Perhaps it would be better for you to use take-it-or-leave-it tactics. More care will be needed to avoid accidents due to haste or lack of concentration. If you are driving, you must exercise extreme caution.

9. SATURDAY. Tricky. Tread warily. Although this will be a happy day for associating with friends, you should be very cautious about accepting invitations. You don't want to go to places of entertainment unless you are sure that you can afford them beforehand. Social affairs can lead to new romantic attractions. But once again, this is another area where you should not move too swiftly. Existing ties of affection can be deepened for those who have been going steady for some time. Caution is required with finances. New propositions must be examined with great care, as they may be deceptive. Take your time in reading prospectuses.

10. SUNDAY. Satisfactory. It will be another day that will be most enjoyable for get-togethers with friends. You may even be doing some home entertaining. If that is the case you will certainly realize that there is plenty of fun to be had without having to spend a great deal of cash. In any case, you should be trying to put some sort of limit on your extravagant tendencies. Don't forget that you will have some hefty bills coming in soon, and you must adjust your expenses accordingly. Someone who has really only been a friend could become a lover. Or a person close to you could invite you to a social gathering that could lead to a romantic linkup.

11. MONDAY. Disquieting. It could be that you are feeling a little tired and unprepared to work this Monday. You will certainly have to shake yourself up a bit. Otherwise you are surely to incur the wrath of superiors. This is one of those days when all financial matters will require special caution. The danger of deception will be stronger than ever. The propositions of friends should be looked at more closely before you commit to any investment. People who come to you with speculative schemes are likely to have their information all mixed up. This alone should be a clear warning for you to keep hands off. You certainly don't want to risk any money in an unsound venture whose promoters are not even sure about.

12. TUESDAY. Variable. So long as you keep your feet firmly on the ground, you should be able to cope reasonably well. Once again, you have to be on the lookout for dubious propositions. Friends will continue to try to influence the way that you handle your investments. Time can be meaningfully spent attempting to get in touch with people in the background. They are in possession of information that you would not normally be able to obtain. Some good luck can come through people or events from the past. But health problems or the circumstances of distant people could interfere with your plans. You will have to find out.

13. WEDNESDAY. Demanding. It will be difficult for you to settle down. Those born under Sagittarius do not appear to have got into the swing of things at work at all this week. You will have to roll up your sleeves and concentrate much harder if you are going to succeed. All activities that you have to handle today will be more tedious than you would have anticipated. You will find it difficult to be your usual cheery and optimistic self. But phone calls or letters involving distant places may contain some heartening news. This could relate to an unexpected windfall such as an inheritance. Or perhaps a friend who has been away for years is resurfacing.

14. THURSDAY. Changeable. Impulsiveness is something of a problem for you. It looks as though you will have to keep a very tight rein on the sudden urges that you get. A good deal more self-discipline will be required from you. Moves that could have a serious effect on your future welfare and security, and that of your nearest and dearest, should be examined under a microscope. It will be a very favorable day for those who have the chance to travel about a bit. It will be dreary and dull for those of you who have to sit in offices. Either way, there will not be much that you can do about things today. Just hope for a radical change at your office.

15. FRIDAY. Confusing. Feelings and emotions could cast a cloud over your judgment. This is not the right day to try to make definite decisions about what future you may or may not have with a member of the opposite sex. Important financial decisions should also be postponed. Go over your accounts. Be sure that you are putting in enough cash to one side every week to meet the regular bills that will be coming up shortly for payment. Reputations can be damaged or business prospects adversely affected. More care with your driving is also imperative. It is another summer weekend eve and traffic will be leaving the city in droves. Speeding will only earn you an expensive traffic ticket.

16. SATURDAY. Disturbing. Arguments over money are likely. The amount of a recent debt will possibly be a bone of contention. Someone who you thought you could trust may have acted in a way that shocks and surprises you. Older family members might also be needing your assistance. This would be still an additional drain upon your reserves. All business propositions that are put to you require closer examination. Get-rich-quick schemes could well turn out to be disastrous. Loved ones will be in an extravagant mood. Money may be spent with very little to show for it at the end of the day. Of course, if you had to buy groceries for a family to last for the weekend, that could take a lot of cash.

17. SUNDAY. Quiet. Give yourself a break. You surely should deserve one. Chances are, the week that has just come to a close has been an exasperating one. In many ways it has also been a nervously upsetting one. Take life at a slower pace. Try to spend more time in the company of dear relatives and loved ones with whom you find it easier to relax. No important financial activities should be started. But you can formulate one or two business plans that you will want to put into practice, once the working week gets underway. Get to bed reasonably early. But allow time for some fun somewhere in your busy schedule. Otherwise, you will become a workaholic, all business, no play. You show signs of this now.

18. MONDAY. Variable. Pleasure and entertainment could turn out to be too expensive for your pocketbook. You will have to watch the pennies. Don't make loans unless you are sure you can really afford to. Friends who have been known to waste money with extravagant ways and gambling may be looking to you as a soft touch. Differences may arise with close associates over cash. You would be wise to refuse to assist people. These are the ones who have not paid you back when they said they would in the past. Social affairs will be favorable and can lead to happy romantic experiences. Follow up on these or it will seem that you don't care.

19. TUESDAY. Worrisome. Sagittarius people are likely to be faced with some difficult decisions today. You are not going to be able to postpone talking out important issues with other interested parties any longer. You may find that you feel cornered in some way. It is not going to be too easy to get along with superiors. Some recent checks on your work may have revealed some serious mistakes. Jobs may have to be done all over again by you. This will allow very little chance of adding much to your income. Loved ones may be hurt at some of the decisions that you make today. But honesty will definitely turn out to be the best policy in the end.

20. WEDNESDAY. Good. This will be one of the best days that you have experienced for some considerable time. After a lengthy period during which you have been plagued with doubt and confusion, you should at last be able to see your way ahead. Your job prospects will be brighter than ever. This can only add to your self-confidence. Make an effort to economize in the home. Make cuts in any area where there has been unnecessary expenditure of late. Today is favorable for dealing with delays that you have been experiencing in real estate affairs. These can now be made more profitable. It is time to consummate any pending agreement.

21. THURSDAY. Successful. Make hay while the sun shines. This is a follow-up day to yesterday in the same upbeat pattern. You should work hard to consolidate any gains that you made then. You will find that professional people will be helpful to your aims if you require their assistance in any special areas. This can be a lucky day as well as a pleasant one. Windfalls can come through other members of your family. Today is favorable for home entertaining and for meeting people from different walks of life. Business propositions involving the land or its products should be given more careful consideration. They are far more likely to bring you in increased profit now than has been true recently.

22. FRIDAY. Tricky. Speculation may be very tempting today. But at the same time, it would appear to be extremely hazardous. A person who entered your life only quite recently may come to you with a proposition for making money. The idea appears to be a very simple method on the surface. But remember that nothing comes free and clear. You would be foolish to dip into your savings without built-in guarantees that you will get some definite return for your investment. Much care is needed to avoid hasty actions. Children's affairs could involve you in unexpected additional expense. Weigh all these factors very carefully before you do anything you will later come to regret.

23. SATURDAY. Happy. In all probability, you may have some work to wind up first thing before you take a weekend break. But the accent should definitely be on pleasure and entertainment this Saturday. You are in need of some fun. Let your hair down and enjoy yourself in the company of people who always have an uplifting effect on your spirits. Today is good for journeys, which will be helpful toward satisfying your personal desires. It will be favorable too for meeting unusual types of people. Their ideas could start a change in the long-standing views of the Sagittarius native. You must consider all the angles, of course, and weigh your views against whatever their propositions are.

24. SUNDAY. Variable. This is likely to be a routine sort of a Sunday. Nothing very out of the ordinary is apt to take place. You Archers will probably be more interested than usual in staying near to your homes. You will not feel like rushing hither and thither in search of pleasure and entertainment. In fact, energy may be at a low ebb. It would be best not to accept any invitations that would entail a great deal of travel. You may have difficulty in getting home at the hour you would prefer. If you have to leave transportation arrangements in the hands of others, that likelihood is almost certain. Why not relax, seek pleasure in the company of good friends, and forget the frenzy of travel?

25. MONDAY. Fortunate. You will be anxious to make a good impression on influential people. Today you should have the opportunity to do just that. Put your original ideas up for consideration. They should get more than a fair hearing from someone who is in a position to offer you financial backing and the benefit of their expertise. Pay-raises or some sort of promotion will more than likely be on the way fairly soon. Romance will be happier and more stable than it has been in recent months. Your love life seems to be entering a very exciting period after a rather quiet stretch. This is good news and should give your spirits a real boost.

26. TUESDAY. Sensitive. Difficult people, probably elders, can cause delays that you will find upsetting and irritating. Parents will be making more demands on your spare time, which will mean that you have to change around your own plans in order to fit in with them. Chances to exploit good opportunities that you made for yourself might well be lost. You will find it hard to keep control of your temper and your emotions. This is not a period when you should mix with friends or associates who could have a depressing or pessimistic effect upon you. Make things easy for yourself if you can. Your health is good, so your future looks promising.

27. WEDNESDAY. Quiet. This should be quite a restful sort of day. Peace and tranquility will be present both in domestic surroundings and at the office or factory. Some time can be given to going over the books. Get your accounts for August into better order. Those Archers who are contemplating taking a late summer vacation may find this is the right time to make inquiries as to where to go. There may be some emphasis on partnership affairs later on in the day. But no new partnerships, either the business or romantic kind, should be started. People will be friendly but not especially energetic. They will probably not defy you openly, but neither will they be inclined to follow your advice.

28. THURSDAY. Mixed. Differences with spouses or partners could easily develop. These could be over issues that should really only be of minor significance. You and your opposite number may get on each other's nerves. There may not even appear to be any one reason for this mutual antagonism. It might be a good idea to give yourself a break and spend more time away from the domestic scene. See what friends are up to. There may be something going on socially that will stimulate you. Just be sure not to overdo, though, as it looks as though you will have to have your wits about you tomorrow. There are plenty of ways to have a good time.

29. FRIDAY. Sensitive. Financial affairs will be extremely sensitive. Watch out for people who may be trying to pull the wool over your eyes. This is not the right time for signing contracts. For that matter, it's not good for any other legal document that would tie you down too far into the future. Do not allow fast-talking people to pressure you into taking any action. It might turn out to be against the best long-term interest of you and yours. You need time to study the proposition carefully. Today will be good for operating from behind the scenes. This will be particularly true of conducting secret investigations to gather information that will be useful to you in the future. Try to wind up outstanding projects today.

30. SATURDAY. Disturbing. Firmness will be needed today with loved ones. You will have to make sure that members of your family do not give in to their extravagant impulses. The best way that you can get others to make cuts is to show them by example, how you yourself do it. Your opposite number may be taking a somewhat selfish attitude, though, and might not wish to cooperate with you. The evening is a period for get-togethers with small groups of close friends. This should be preferable to seeking pleasure in expensive places of entertainment that may not be worth it. Even if they are fun, you do not get much chance to exchange viewpoints and reminisce. And, too, they may cost you a lot of money.

31. SUNDAY. Upsetting. Thoughts are likely to turn to matters connected with your work today. Matters directly related to your career will probably be uppermost in your mind. It would be best not to get too carried away with the ideas of business friends, though. Although close associates are well meaning, their advice is not apt to be applicable to you. Loved ones will be a continued source of worry where spending is concerned. You will get the feeling that unless you draw up a new budget soon you could have trouble in meeting all of your obligations. Short trips will be pleasant and could offer you some welcome light relief. This will be especially true if the trip is for recreation rather than for business.

SEPTEMBER

1. MONDAY. Variable. This is a very favorable day for all efforts aimed at furthering your career prospects. Take a long-term view of your employment affairs. Try to arrange meetings with people who can be of assistance to you. You will have to be willing to work slowly. Get-rich-quick schemes are not likely to work out satisfactorily for you. This is not a propitious period for trying to conduct business that is tied up with foreign affairs. People at or from distances can be difficult. They may also perhaps be a bit deceptive, intentionally or otherwise. Your best move would be to concentrate on those closer to you. Distant people will come to you.

2. TUESDAY. Good. Get out and about today. You should try to open up lines of communication with people at a distance. You have not been able to talk things over with them, person-to-person, for quite awhile. In fact, the more that you are able to keep on the move, the better it will suit you. And the more territory you cover, the more you will be able to enhance your chances of improving your business prospects. Professional advice will be important to those who are trying to get anything new launched. Today will be favorable, later on, for parties and other social activities. You may, in fact, find yourself acting as host or hostess at a dinner party you arranged for at a club. Whatever the setup, you should enjoy it.

3. WEDNESDAY. Mixed. Perhaps you will not be able to make quite as much progress as you were hoping for at your place of employment. But this is no reason for you to become disheartened in any way, or be down in the dumps. An influential person who you were looking forward to meeting with may have to cancel the arrangement at the last moment. If you do suddenly find that you have time to spare, then for goodness sake, use it constructively. Subtle and less direct tactics are more likely to succeed in your efforts to advance your financial plans. Personal health may be below par. Care should be taken to guard against infections. Good eating habits and regular exercise are essential.

4. THURSDAY. Variable. Get to the point. Sagittarius should not beat about the bush. A straight-talking and no-nonsense approach will serve you best. This will be true especially if you are trying to collect money that has been outstanding to you for some time. People will respect you more if you let them know exactly what is on your mind. At times you tend to take the line of least resistance. This would be quite improper today. Activities are likely to be more strenuous than usual, but you will be able to accomplish much that is good. Career changes should not be made. Family affairs will probably involve some additional expense. This could be a matter of health problems, or additional school expenses.

5. FRIDAY. Confusing. Impulsiveness could be your worst enemy today. Slow down a bit. You seem to have made certain limited gains so far this month. You do not want to throw them away by being hasty. Financial thinking could well be faulty. Optimism that is rising in you could be misplaced. Don't go on the advice of friends. People born under Sagittarius could deceive themselves as well as being deceived. Hard-luck stories that are brought to you could well be bogus. But long-lasting new friendships can be established. You may meet people on the job during working hours, or later at some sort of social gathering.

6. SATURDAY. Disconcerting. Problems that cropped up yesterday are likely to spill over into today. You may have to put yourself at the service of someone who requires your immediate assistance. Or you will perhaps have to keep an appointment that you do not really relish. Don't allow yourself to run into debt in your attempts to keep up with the free-spending habits of your close associates. Expensive night-spots should be avoided. But you must not attempt to make economies for which other members of the family would have to make most of the sacrifices. Domestic opposition can erupt at any time if you are not careful. Keep the peace at home.

7. SUNDAY. Good. This is an idyllic sort of a day. It will be just the sort of Sunday that will suit you best. You will have the opportunity to see friends and loved ones who have been out of sight, though not out of mind, for all too long. You won't have to take on more responsibilities than you wish to, however. This will ensure that you can put some time aside for rest. It will also allow for attendance to some of your favorite hobbies. Today is especially good for secret associations. Romantic relationships can be deepened and made more special. Loved ones can be financially helpful. Or they will cooperate in attempts to reduce expenses. Whatever way, their help will be deeply appreciated by you.

8. MONDAY. Mixed. Excessive independence is likely to work against your best long-term interests. Be careful that you do not cross someone from whom you might well have to ask for some sort of assistance in the future. It would be easy for you to surrender long-term happiness for momentary pleasure and satisfaction. Sagittarius people must become more aware of what effect their actions may be having upon others. More willingness to compromise at your place of employment will certainly help. Family members may raise objections over the amount of time that you are spending away from home. Try to make them understand why you do it.

9. TUESDAY. Important. This will be a day for pushing ahead, regardless of the obstructions that other people try to put in your way. Go with your intuition. It is not likely to play you false. There will be much varied activity, which will certainly suit the Archer. Exchanges that you have with people from walks of life different from your own will build up your knowledge of matters that have always been of considerable interest to you. Contacts with public officials may be of some value too. This will hold especially for those of you who are after planning permission or some other concessions connected with property. You may need a variance.

10. WEDNESDAY. Changeable. This is a day for people born under Sagittarius to attempt to obtain obscure information. Go out of your way to collect knowledge that will be of use to you at a later date. Because there will be a slightly slower pace today, you will be able to take your time making important decisions. Moneymaking schemes that you have been holding back on can be successfully launched. Working behind the scenes can be an advantage to you. People may confide important information. Today is favorable for secret affairs, especially of the romantic kind. The health of a loved one may be worrying you. You might have to take time off from work to make arrangements for home or even hospital care.

11. THURSDAY. Disquieting. Don't act in an erratic way. Unpredictable actions on your part will backfire. You will have to pay the consequences for any wrong moves that you make on impulse. It is not going to be an easy day for you to get along with superiors. You won't be in the mood to toe the line laid down by people in authority. If you are not aware of what you are doing at all times, you can easily damage your business or career reputation. Don't place too much dependence on getting the support of influential people as it may not be forthcoming. You don't want to be left with no alternate plan for getting help. It might come too late.

12. FRIDAY. Good. Determination will help you in all areas of your life. The only way that you are going to get what you want today is to grit your teeth and to go out and grab it with both hands. Moneymaking efforts, in particular, will be more successful. This is quite an important day for Archers who are in the buying and selling game. Travel will bring you good results. You should find that you can influence the thinking of people in faraway places in such a way as to earn you additional profits. Secret activities can lead to contacts with powerful people who control others from behind the scenes. Be sure that you do not inadvertently reveal any names. You might lose future support.

13. SATURDAY. Pleasant. This will probably be the best day that you have experienced this week, if not this month. You will discover that many of the personal problems that have been worrying you will now be sorting themselves out. Loved ones will be easier to get along with and will not be so demanding. Contacts with influential people should be made as early in the day as possible if they are going to be of any advantage to you over the weekend. Today is good for making important decisions or moves affecting business or career activities. It is also pleasant for social interaction. Since you do not have to get up early tomorrow, stay out late.

14. SUNDAY. Variable. No secret approaches should be made today. If you attempt to have any business dealings at all, you must make certain that they are kept over the counter. Play it straight with influential people whom you meet socially. Do not make promises on the spur of the moment that you may not be able to keep. People to whom you feel inclined to confide secrets may betray confidences. Deception has to be guarded against. Today is favorable for having serious conversations with older relatives, which may help you to make decisions about the future. It is far more satisfactory to discuss matters of such importance together so that everyone is aware of any decisions made.

15. MONDAY. Buoyant. The working week gets off to a flying start. You are in a sprightly mood, and your optimistic attitude is likely to rub off on others. Relatives may be inspirational for you. Older family members may be able to provide you with knowledge that will make you all the more enthusiastic about certain aspects of your career. All mental endeavors that are undertaken today are likely to be successful. New ideas and methods can be tried out with more probability of success. The independent nature of the Archer will act like a magnet attracting others to them. Use this to your advantage, but do not abuse it. Nobody wants to be taken for a patsy.

16. TUESDAY. Sensitive. Arguments are likely to crop up with friends. There are probably just silly disputes with close associates that come out of nothing at all, really. If you want to avoid antagonizing others, you will have to be more aware of the way you can put your foot in it. You do that by saying the wrong thing at the wrong time. Social activities are likely to be more expensive than you had bargained for. If you are taking people out for a meal today, then you had better check up on the various prices that restaurants will be charging. This is so that you can get a good idea of what you will be required to fork out. Otherwise, you could be caught without the necessary cash.

17. WEDNESDAY. Fair. Sagittarius will fare well today so long as they watch out for excessive spending. You must not give in to a sudden and impulsive mood that is likely to sweep over you. In all likelihood, it could cause you to splurge. Money can come through business transactions that you have been negotiating for some time. You may now begin to see the fruits of some of your recent endeavors. Today is good for teaming up with family members to add to the value of your home or property. Some good luck is likely to bring you a financial windfall. But care is necessary with the use of all electrical equipment.

18. THURSDAY. Demanding. Speculation and other risky ventures must be avoided. You must be very careful about the way you handle your money. People may not be entirely honest with you when explaining ventures that they would like you to invest in. The Archer must not be so inclined to take chances as usual. Activities with friends may be more expensive than you had bargained for. They are likely to be looking to you for some sort of cash support or loan. But today is favorable for persevering with creative enterprises in the face of setbacks. Put your worries out of your mind and determine to concentrate on your own endeavors. Otherwise, you will end up doing a lot, but nothing well.

19. FRIDAY. Exciting. Because you are an optimistic person, you like to take life very much as it comes. And this is the sort of day that is likely to suit you down to the ground. Lines of communication that have not been open to you will now be available. You may be able to save yourself one or two short trips by making telephone calls. Unexpected events are likely to develop as the day goes on that will help the person born in Sagittarius to move a step nearer to some cherished goal. Hunches can be played, which will lead to some exciting meetings or experiences. Today is good for using new ideas to further your creative projects. Take every opportunity you get to work on these.

20. SATURDAY. Uneventful. Take life at a slower pace today. Loved ones should be given more attention. This is an easygoing sort of a day. You will have the opportunity to make it up to people to whom you have not been able to devote as much attention as you should. On the entertainment scene, not much is likely to take place that will be either exciting or stimulating. Social activities are not going to be as pleasant for you to attend as the picture that friends had painted of them or may have led you to believe. Today will be useful, however, for concentrating on creative enterprises, including hobbies. These are among your favorite pastimes.

21. SUNDAY. Tricky. Keep impulsive tendencies under control. Pay more attention than usual to your domestic responsibilities. You seem to be headed for a showdown with your mate or partner. You simply must make more of an effort to prove that you have his or her best interests at heart. Employment affairs will contain certain difficulties for those of you who have to attend to them. There could be arguments with co-workers about bonus and weekend payments. These will not be easy to resolve. Health problems could interfere with romantic meetings. Secret affairs can lead to regrets or remorse. Don't act in haste as you will regret it.

22. MONDAY. Rewarding. Health problems must not be neglected. This is a period when you should be making more of an attempt to get yourself into better shape physically. Those of you who have not been to the dentist recently for a checkup should make an appointment without further delay. Physical fitness courses are recommended for any one of you who has been putting on weight. Additional attention to your diet would not go amiss either. Today is good for making job changes that have been thoroughly investigated. Sagittarius will find that people are more inclined to follow their lead. This is good news because their ideas are innovative and they follow through on projects once started.

23. TUESDAY. Upsetting. You may have to face up to some home truths that you find somewhat unpalatable. Those Archers with children in their teens may have some difficult decisions to make about offspring. Arguments that take place within the home will be emotionally upsetting for you. You might find that you are being pulled in different directions. Personal plans that would take you away from your nearest and dearest will raise objections from your mate or partner. The health of close associates may require that time be taken away from other activities. This, of course, causes delays. Personal health should not be risked for whatever reason. It is a valuable asset that few recognize until it is lost.

24. WEDNESDAY. Variable. Close associates may refuse to accept the advice that you offer in good faith. People will not be quite so trusting of your motives as you may have hoped. This will make teamwork very difficult to promote. Arguments will be confusing to resolve. It might be best to steer clear of contentious subjects. Any threats to freedom or independence will be strongly felt by you. Impulsive moves should be avoided, as they would bring drastic changes. You may not really be ready to make these yet. But friends and their activities can provide you with some pleasure and distractions later on. These will be a welcome relief no matter what the entertainment is.

25. THURSDAY. Quiet. This is a pleasant if somewhat lackluster day. You will not be called upon to take any out-of-the-ordinary action. People will be agreeable enough, but not very enthusiastic about making any new business starts that would require a great deal of teamwork. Differences that took place yesterday between you and people you have to work alongside will be easier to resolve, however. Today is useful for sounding out others about making cooperative moves in the future. But it will not be good for starting any joint ventures immediately, as the day is too slow to maintain momentum. When you do launch such ventures, you need to have every possible bit of momentum going for you.

26. FRIDAY. Mixed. Your company is likely to be very much in demand today. But it could also cause you to dig deep into your pocket. Close associates may be hard up and will be looking to you to provide the wherewithal to meet pleasure and entertainment expenses. This is not a day for backing the speculative propositions of others. Group activities may include chances of confusion due to impractical and dreamy people. But today is good for joint financial ventures that are aimed at improving savings. Try to concentrate solely on the good features of the day. Building up savings is a worthy endeavor. And your company will enliven any social gathering you attend. Not only they but you will have fun.

27. SATURDAY. Demanding. Pressure will be on you to dip into joint funds to buy luxury articles for the home. This is not the time to listen to dear ones who advocate a policy of live for the moment. You must be careful with cash that will be needed to pay regular bills, like income tax and insurance, at a later date. Don't go in for extravagant entertainment, either. Invitations to visit clubs and similar places should be investigated further before you commit yourself. Friends will not be entirely reliable where money is concerned. Not that they mean to be dishonest, but some people don't keep track of money, or account for it. If the funds belong partly to you, it would be wise for you to offer to handle it.

28. SUNDAY. Good. Communicating with people at or from a distance will be pleasant. Perhaps someone who you have not been in touch with for quite a while will be dropping in to see you. This is a good period for reviving close relationships that once meant a great deal to you. Helpful information may be supplied that will be of value when it comes to drawing up personal plans. These you wish to put into action in the not-too-distant future. Social activities can provide meetings with influential people who can be helpful to business and financial planning. But secret activities are not advisable. Even if they are innocent of guile, people tend to be suspicious.

29. MONDAY. Sensitive. Misunderstandings could easily develop with loved ones over stupid and insignificant details. You will have to be very careful of arguments that blow up out of nothing. Some of them tend to get too heated. There could even be walkouts that lead to separations. Keep that impetuous side of your nature under control. Try a little harder to see sensitive situations from the other person's point of view. The health of close associates could lead to visits to hospitals. Long journeys can be helpful to personal affairs, but they may involve some sadness. Attempts to help others may be misunderstood. Some people tend to misconstrue the intentions of well-meaning people. Pay no heed.

30. TUESDAY. Rewarding. This will not be a very busy day. However, progress can be made when it comes to tying up the loose ends of business. You do not want to have any of them hanging over your head when the month of October gets underway. There will be some refreshing progress with financial matters that have been causing you some headaches. Any meetings that you have with accountants or other professional people will be entirely helpful to you. The day is favorable for attempts to make good names even better in club and society circles. Great publicity can be obtained. This will generate a great deal of interest in other areas, and could lead to more generous contributions. These would probably support some worthy charity.

OCTOBER

1. WEDNESDAY. Variable. Domestic activities may press for attention. Women Archers, in particular, are probably going to find that they have a lot of catching up to do with personal chores around the home. People may drop in unexpectedly and interrupt you. It may not be possible to give over as much time as you would like to regular employment affairs. New starts on creative projects might best be left for a more propitious day. Today is not favorable, either, for initiating any important moves with regard to real estate activities. Later hours can be good for spending more time quietly with loved ones. Everyone needs a quiet time, occasionally, just to catch one's breath, so to speak.

2. THURSDAY. Fortunate. With an upsurge of energy indicated, you will be in the mood to take on more than one of the exciting new challenges that are offered to you. Influential people may have been doubting your ability to accept additional responsibility. But you should be able to prove them wrong on that score. Any attempts by you to boost your reputation or get ahead in public affairs are likely to bring you in additional financial returns. Today is good for giving yourself a treat. Spending sprees could enable you to pick up some bargain buys. But be careful of those so-called bargains. If you don't need something, but buy it anyway, you waste money.

3. FRIDAY. Good. You will be delighted at the sudden turn of events that takes place. A problem that has been nagging away at the back of your mind for quite awhile might sort itself out. This will relieve you of having to do too much about it yourself and that suits you. An influential person will be able to give you some valuable advice about your career. This is important because it will enable you to make a decision about future planning. Sagittarius business people among you are more likely to turn their attention to financial matters. Plans can be made for increasing future profits. Friends can be helpful in enabling you to realize a secret wish.

4. SATURDAY. Worrisome. Readers who are interested in making the world a better place to live in can do a lot to help people who are not as well off as themselves. This is an important period for joining charitable organizations. You start to gain by putting yourself out a bit to assist people who are not quite as lucky as you. Your standing in the community will improve as well as your self-esteem. It would be best not to try to discuss your own emotional problems with loved ones, however. Misunderstandings could result in accusations of selfishness being leveled against you. But do not allow yourself to be pressured into excessive spending.

5. SUNDAY. Disquieting. You had probably made plans much earlier in the week as to how you were going to spend your leisure time. But now you might not be too happy about keeping your word. Perhaps you will be involved in making trips or even long journeys to see friends. Probably you would prefer to spend your time quietly at home with close family members. This can be a rather disturbing day for Sagittarius. You might find that you are simply not on the same wavelength as a person you have known as a close associate for many years. Although you might try not to show it, you are likely to go around as if nothing were wrong.

6. MONDAY. Good. Pleasure will come from employment affairs. Perhaps you have been taking an introverted look at yourself over the weekend. It will certainly do you good to throw yourself, body and soul, into your job. You will find that people with whom you have to work will be cheery and constructive. Now is the time for team effort in order to reach objectives that will be of a benefit to all concerned. This can be an important day for those born under Sagittarius with regard to romance. Nothing outward may happen, but love affairs are likely to be on your mind for much of the day. Is it the result of an unexpected romance over the weekend?

7. TUESDAY. Disappointing. The positive flow of yesterday's upward trend looks as though it is going to be halted. Those born under Sagittarius are likely to begin this day with a strong determination to succeed. But it appears that forces will be conspiring against you to thwart every move that you attempt to make. It might be a good idea to stick to routine jobs where you would not risk your savings. This is better than chancing everything with new investments when there could be an element of risk involved. People or events will force you to slow down your pace and bide your time. In some ways, this will be of great benefit to you.

8. WEDNESDAY. Strenuous. It looks like a topsy-turvy sort of a period for the Archer. Perhaps you will have no choice but to do things the wrong way around this Wednesday. It will certainly be very difficult for you to stick to a set agenda. Perhaps your boss will keep changing his mind. You may be halfway through one job only to find that you are transferred to something entirely different. It would be best for you to take life very much as it comes. Those who are self-employed and have some definite aim in mind may be able to achieve some sort of breakthrough. This could be just what you have been waiting for, so be sure to take the opportunity.

9. THURSDAY. Tricky. Sagittarius people will become painfully aware that they have not been as successful as they thought in balancing their books. Perhaps there will be larger bills to pay than had been anticipated. In any case, the Archer will probably have to dip into funds that he or she would have preferred not to touch. It might be necessary to look at various other budgetary methods anew in order to get the financial house in better order. The thinking certainly seems to have become confused where cash is concerned. But contact with people behind the scenes who have assisted you in the past can be helpful. This will free your mind.

10. FRIDAY. Variable. Government officials will be putting pressure on you to toe the line where money is concerned. It seems quite likely that you will be having some lengthy discussions with people who hold public office about taxation or insurance matters. Influential people will be pulling their weight. It would be best to listen to what those in authority have to say. If you argue about everything, they will, in all probability, pull rank on you, and you will lose out anyway. Loved ones will not only be able to support you in a quiet and unassuming way, but may also offer possible financial assistance. Sagittarius may not even have been aware of such help being available, so the surprise will be total.

11. SATURDAY. Changeable. You will be in the mood to put across your point of view with vim and vigor. This is all very well as long as you do not alienate people. They might otherwise be willing to assist you if you were just a little more yielding. Be willing to make compromise solutions. If these will enable you to get contracts and other legal documents signed it will be worth it. They have been long delayed and you want to take a break for the weekend. Do not do or say anything that could result in gossip or resentment by neighbors. If Sagittarius people are serious and totally honest, others will automatically recognize their sound motives.

12. SUNDAY. Sensitive. Travel plans are likely to cause some dissension among loved ones. It is not going to be easy to get other family members to go along with your agenda for pleasure and entertainment. Your mate, or partner, is likely to be in more of a mood for staying at home. Perhaps you should give way a little and make an effort to ensure that everyone close to you gets something positive out of today. Short trips will be best. Social gatherings in your area could lead to contacts with people who may turn out to play an important role in your life. But even if this does not turn out to be true, you would be better off getting to know your neighbors. Some day, one could have an important place in your life.

13. MONDAY. Variable. Hunches should be played, but only to a limited extent. So long as the risks that you take with your reserves are calculated ones, they will have a better-than-even-money chance of paying off. It might be a good idea to discuss with your bank manager or your accountant the investments that you are considering making. Their advice could be invaluable and even prevent you from making silly mistakes. Later in the day you will have the opportunity to deal with any health problems, whether they are personal ones or ones connected with other members of the family. Either way, it is important that these be dealt with immediately.

14. TUESDAY. Productive. With a little bit of luck you may be able to increase your regular salary. Perhaps you will have the opportunity to do some overtime work. Or it may be that you are asked to take on a part-time job in your leisure hours that brings you in some very handy spare money. Family members will be particularly helpful and understanding. They will fully comprehend that what you are attempting to achieve is for the benefit of all your brood. Secret business arrangements with older relatives could also prove to be particularly lucrative. These benefits may not show up right now but be security for later years. Your overall financial picture is in good shape now so you do not need to worry over that.

15. WEDNESDAY. Disappointing. You will be in a more than usually creative mood. The major problem for the Archer today is the fact that you are going to be expected to deal with many run-of-the-mill, routine jobs. Since you would understandably prefer to be giving free rein to your natural talents, this will be tough. You won't get much sympathy at home or at work, however. People will be indifferent to what you are feeling emotionally. You will have to rely upon yourself more than ever at this particular time. More hours spent with children could help you to fill a gap in your life. They will not be critical in anyway, they will give you lots of pleasure and fun, and they might even broaden your perspective.

16. THURSDAY. Quiet. Recharge your batteries today. Take stock of the situation that you are now in. Prepare moves that you will wish to make when certain constraints and limitations are removed. The Archer should find that they are comparatively free from pressing obligations and duties. This is a better period for catching up with writing letters and doing accounts. Don't try gambling as a means of supplementing your income. Speculation is not likely to bring you the returns you were anticipating. Sporting engagements can be made. Sagittarius people should consider spending more time than usual with their loved ones.

17. FRIDAY. Disturbing. Self-doubt could well grip you this Friday. You may be asking yourself a lot of fundamental questions. Perhaps you are feeling the effect of recent stresses and strain. You definitely would seem to be in need of more rest. Check your diet. Make sure that you have been getting all the vitamins and other essentials that your mind and body require. You may be forced, through the routine of social events and obligations, to spend more time dealing with club and society affairs. Opportunities that are now open to you will offer you less chance of obtaining pleasure than you would have thought possible. So it's up to you now to find some form of recreation before the weekend starts.

18. SATURDAY. Variable. More time should be spent dealing with your regular job. This applies to all of you, even workers who do not usually put in an appearance at their place of employment on a Saturday. Many of you may find that there are matters that you can tidy up from your home base. You certainly want to do all that you can to clear the decks so that you are free to enjoy your weekend in relative peace and tranquillity. Service and self-sacrifice will be rewarded financially. Health problems can arise, possibly through contact with people with infectious illnesses. Precautions should be taken. It would be best to keep a great distance from them. Try to find some form of entertainment for the evening.

19. SUNDAY. Mixed. A spouse or romantic partner will be doing all in his or her power to persuade you to do some traveling around. Those born under Sagittarius do not usually need a push to get out and about. This is one of those Sundays, however, when you wouldn't object to spending more time within the confines of your own four walls. A little solitude may appeal to you. Perhaps there are matters that you want to think over quietly on your own. Your health may not be as good as usual. Take care of your well-being, both mentally and physically. But don't neglect to have some fun and to meet with some long-time friends you haven't seen lately.

20. MONDAY. Disconcerting. Arguments may erupt at home. Differences of opinion are likely to become obvious between you and certain members of your family early on. Try to refrain from being critical. Leave other people to make decisions that you really have no right to interfere in. Think it over and see if you are being honest about it. Personal projects that you were hoping to launch are not likely to have very much success. Influential people may not give you the backing that had been promised to you verbally last week. More care than usual is required when driving. You should never drive on busy highways or streets unless you are fully alert and concentrating on road conditions. There is too much at stake.

21. TUESDAY. Variable. Additional problems will be caused by the demands that are made upon you by a spouse or other loved ones. Work schedules may be interrupted. You will become very frustrated if you are not allowed to get on with your regular employment affairs first thing. In-laws could be acting in an irresponsible way and cause difficulties in the life of your opposite number. You will have to try to give people who look to you for guidance and advice a helping hand. In all personal affairs your opinion is likely to carry considerable weight. This is a nice tribute, but it does carry a lot of responsibility. You must be fair-minded.

22. WEDNESDAY. Encouraging. This will probably be one of the best days that you have experienced for quite a while. You will be in a better position to please yourself as to how you go about your day-to-day affairs. Members of your family will be better able to stand on their own two feet. Loved ones and romantic partners may be able to make some valuable contacts with influential people with whom you had not been able to get an appointment yourself. At last it looks as though you will get the green light to go ahead with a new and exciting business matter. This is exciting news and will give your morale a huge boost. You have had a long, tedious wait, sometimes without light at the end of the tunnel.

23. THURSDAY. Deceptive. Tread very carefully today. This is not going to be an easy one for getting to the root cause of problems. Perhaps someone you thought you could rely on has not been entirely honest with you. Today is not the best of times to attempt to get any sort of team effort launched. News relating to taxation, insurance, alimony payments, or pensions can confuse those born under Sagittarius and probably cause them to panic. But calm down. There will be people available who can help you out with their experience and their advice. It may be necessary to use roundabout tactics and behind-the-scenes maneuvering to find them.

24. FRIDAY. Lucky. Influential people, especially those who hold high rank in government departments, will be more willing to assist you. This is a fine day for attempts to thrash out problems that have been requiring you to spend an awful lot of time on desk work and accounts. A weight is likely to be lifted from your shoulders. Spouses or loved ones may find some money is owing to them, which they may possibly have forgotten all about. Small inheritances or legacies may be forthcoming. This is a useful day for swelling mutual resources. Your partner may contribute as much or even more than you. Either one might win a lottery or other cash prize.

25. SATURDAY. Disturbing. Some people today will literally amaze you. People with whom you had definite and important appointments will let you down with very feeble excuses. You will feel most annoyed that you have been stood up on short notice and treated in such a shabby and offhand manner. This will be a frustrating period. And there does not appear to be a great deal that you can do about the problems that are currently besetting you. Information regarding distant affairs may be held back. Associates may not be prepared to share secrets with you. Superiors are unlikely to favor the plans of the Sagittarius worker. Your best bet is to forget the whole scene and go home.

26. SUNDAY. Disconcerting. This will not, perhaps, be the most pleasant of weekends. You seem to be lacking in confidence. Something is likely to take place today to cause you to feel emotionally insecure. Communication with distant places can be frustratingly hard. Long-distance phone calls could turn out to be a complete waste of time and expense. Relatives will be unsympathetic to self-improvement schemes that you were hoping to launch with their assistance. You will simply have to learn to be more self-reliant. Loved ones may have secret reasons for disapproving of the activities that you had arranged for today, but they won't say why.

27. MONDAY. Variable. Professional advice will not be very helpful. People like real estate agents, or independent sellers, who should be able to offer you sound guidance, will be uncommunicative. People born under Sagittarius will have to wait awhile before they take property matters any further. This is not a day for being too pushy or demanding. No definite arrangements or agreements should be made in connection with future business aims or goals. Charm and indirect methods will be the best way for you to contact influential people to help in financial affairs. And this might prove difficult to do. There would seem to be a great deal of resistance to loans in financial circles just now.

28. TUESDAY. Sensitive. Business people among you are undoubtedly out to improve your reputation and your public image. But they would be well advised to try a more roundabout approach when having to deal with people in authority. It might be best to meet under social conditions. This is especially true if you have anything important that you wish to discuss about the future with someone who is in a position to give you a helping hand. Domestic affairs may interfere with routine activities, and there could be delays in this area of your life. It is important that you do not appear cold or unfriendly when putting people off. You must use charm and tact and never let them think you are not interested.

29. WEDNESDAY. Tricky. In attempts to further their efforts in their chosen field of endeavor, people born under Sagittarius can easily become too drastic in their actions. Their unconventional ideas will also cause great concern. If you wish to make progress in your career, you will be advised to bridle your erratic and sometimes overly independent nature. The decisions that you make in a hurry could be ones that you will live to regret for quite a long time. Listen to what older relatives have to say. They will be advising you with your best interests at heart. Just remember that they are trying to help you, not to interfere. Experience makes them experts.

30. THURSDAY. Deceptive. In areas where money matters are concerned, people born under Sagittarius are advised to keep a watchful and not too trusting eye on so-called friends. It is also advisable that you do not leave valuables lying around. Take more precautions against the possibility of theft or deceit. Even at the best of times, you can be extremely gullible without even realizing it. It will not be easy to fathom what superiors may have in mind for you as far as future career interests are concerned. The evening will be a period when you will be happy to put your feet up and relax. You can't eat and sleep and live with your problems.

31. FRIDAY. Rewarding. It certainly would appear that the month of October has had more than its fair share of ups and downs for the Archer. Still and all, you should be quite pleased that you are able to bring the month to a close on a fairly positive note. This can be an especially important day for anything and everything related to club and group activities. You may be asked to become a member of a society that you have long been trying to get into. Important people may be able to use their influence on your behalf. Some unexpected progress can be made in affairs that are very close to your heart. Inventive ideas will help you to boost profits. Don't waste your potential for dreaming up innovative ways for doing things.

NOVEMBER

1. SATURDAY. Fair. You will be striving hard in the background to further some new developments. You may stumble on some strange, but practical ideas for improving these. However, you want to be a little patient about putting them into practice. Among other considerations, you must investigate fully just how much it is going to cost you. There are not likely to be many difficulties in getting along with members of your family today. In fact, loved ones will understand if you have to do some of the work at home that you usually do at your place of employment. Your vivid imagination is likely to produce some lucrative schemes.

2. SUNDAY. Changeable. Perhaps you may be feeling a little tired and spent. This is one of those Sundays when you will wish to give plenty of time and attention to personal matters. Anything connected with career prospects can wait another day. Romance will be much on your mind. Secret love relationships could be important. It might be possible to arrange to see a person who means a great deal to you. You have not been able to get in touch for quite awhile due to difficult conditions. This is a time for keeping anything and everything to do with personal liaisons strictly within the circle of those directly concerned. Care is needed on the highway. Other road users, including motorcyclists, may be careless.

3. MONDAY. Variable. Today will be good for anything that has to be carried out under the cloak of secrecy. If you have any meetings that have to be attended to behind closed doors, these are very likely to go off better than you would have anticipated. People in other towns and cities whom you have appointments to see have not been as obliging as you would have hoped. Now, however, they will be easier to win over. You should have some success from short trips or journeys, the purpose of which you wish to keep to yourself. Later on, though, Archers are likely to be faced with difficulties and opposition to personal plans. This, no doubt, originates with family members. You must make a decision.

4. TUESDAY. Mixed. Family members will behave badly. You might be surprised at the low level of cooperation you are able to obtain from your nearest and dearest. Those of you who are trying to launch money-saving schemes will be disappointed. It might be best to rely on yourself as much as possible if you are going to avoid head-on confrontations. You must also avoid becoming overly self-righteous. In personal and business activities you will present a strong and convincing image. You should be able to have things your own way if you are attempting to clinch any important deals. You worked hard on all the preliminary steps to ensure that.

5. WEDNESDAY. Deceptive. There could be some wheeling and dealing going on behind the scenes at your place of employment. Up till now, you have not been aware of it. It might come as something of a surprise to you that someone with whom you have been angling to clinch a contract has also been seeing people who are your rivals. This could be the time when you have to go in for a no-punches-pulled attitude in order to get some answers from them. You Sagittarius people will also have to do some quick thinking where money is concerned. You must not take a casual attitude to financial matters. You have been altogether too easygoing.

6. THURSDAY. Excellent. There is little doubt that you will have great success in your business as well as in your personal life today if you are prepared to cut the frills and concentrate on essentials. Get off to an early start. Those of you who are trying to win important new orders should have an excellent chance of being successful. This is especially likely if you are dealing with people in other towns or cities. The more you travel, the better it is apt to suit you. You will have more energy at your disposal, which will make it that much easier for you to keep going. The generosity of family members, or those you Archers live with, can be helpful.

7. FRIDAY. Good. This will be a good follow-up day. Any verbal agreements that were reached yesterday should be pushed through. Get in touch with professional people in order to get contracts drawn up. Present business associates will agree with your plans for making progress and profit. It is important that you deal with career matters first before you contemplate seeking pleasure. However, it would be possible to combine the two if you are having a working lunch. See what you can do to add to the security of your home and family. Make sure that all insurance policies are up to date. Journeys to visit hospitals, institutions, and other similar places of care can have unforeseen benefits.

8. SATURDAY. Disturbing. The need to do some extra traveling in the morning could create problems between you and loved ones. Your mate or partner will not take very kindly to your having to give a lot of time over to work. It will be especially true if you had made certain, if vague, promises to spend more of your time dealing with family issues. You will have problems in resolving points of conflict. Your nearest and dearest may complain that they are coming off second-best in your life and are being neglected. Your health may not be one hundred percent just now. This will make it even more difficult for you to cope without losing your temper.

9. SUNDAY. Variable. You do hate to be pinned down with family obligations. But this is one of those days when you would be well advised to give more time to the desires of your nearest and dearest. You do want to smooth over past differences and avoid conflict in the future. Your mate or partner will be in a better mood, and you want to work on this. Propose some unusual ideas for going out. Trips would probably bring you some enjoyment and would certainly make people who depend on you feel wanted. You should also be able to get some useful odd jobs done in and around the home. Do what you can to pretty up your surroundings.

10. MONDAY. Mixed. Perhaps you won't be in the mood to push yourself too hard today. One of the main problems is likely to be the fact that you have a number of routine jobs to deal with that you would much prefer to leave until another day. Still, remember the old adage that if you've got a job to do, do it now. Influential people will be watching how you cope with tedious paperwork. If you want to improve your prospects for promotion in the not-too-distant future, you are going to have to knuckle down to it. Offers made from family members in connection with your love life are likely to be tempting. You may be feted at a family gathering.

11. TUESDAY. Encouraging. After an up-and-down period you seem to be in a better position for dealing with anything that has to be carried out in secrecy. This will be an excellent day for meeting with professional people. They might be able to explain the small print of contracts and similar legal documents to you. You will certainly be seeing matters connected with your career in an entirely different light. Transactions that have been hanging fire can be brought to a successful conclusion. This should mean a handy profit for you. The thoughts of you Sagittarius-born are likely to center very much on events from the past. These could be related to family events, such as marriages or deaths.

12. WEDNESDAY. Variable. Those born under Sagittarius are likely to be feeling a little tired and spent on this midweek day. You will perhaps think it is only fair that you should be given a break or a treat. But rather than fritter your time or your money away on useless pastimes, you will try to derive some pleasure from more serious kinds of activities. It may be that you will be able to give more attention to a hobby. That could possibly earn you money as a second-string job in the end. Travel should be kept down to a minimum, though. You will find it tiring and probably a waste of time. Unless you had made plans well in advance, you would not be able to take full advantage of side trips and evening entertainment.

13. THURSDAY. Fair. This will be quite a pleasant day. But if you were hoping to make progress in your career by leaps and bounds, you had better forget about it; because you will surely be barking up the wrong tree. Influential people will be pleasant enough and will be willing to listen to any minor complaints that you have. But they will not be willing to discuss the possibility of important promotions with you. This will be a straightforward kind of day. You Archers will be your usual uncomplicated selves. You should be able to use your spare time to get the best out of life. It should not be necessary to spend a great deal of money in order to do so. But romance requires some subtlety and caution.

14. FRIDAY. Changeable. This is a good day for Archers to bury their noses in their work and try to think of nothing else. If you really put your mind to it, you should be able to complete jobs that you should have worked out earlier in the week. You certainly do not want routine affairs hanging over your head when the time comes to take a weekend break. Even if your work is purely humdrum and routine, you should not have much difficulty in concentrating. Your intuition and your imagination will serve you well and possibly serve to bring you in some extra money. In the evening you should concentrate on satisfying the needs and the desires of your loved ones. This could even mean dining out.

15. SATURDAY. Sensitive. You have not perhaps been making quite the progress that you had been hoping for in your career. But at least your relationship with superiors would seem to be quite promising. You do not appear to have suffered any major setbacks. You may be able to get quite a lot of work done from your home base. This may save unnecessary journeys to places of regular employment. Later in the day, sports enthusiasts among you might be able to get involved in your favorite pastimes. It is important that Archers watch what they say to influential people during the course of social gatherings. Be careful that you do not put your foot in it.

16. SUNDAY. Disturbing. Many of you will have been looking forward to the peace and calm of a day of rest. Unfortunately, you might not be able to have the easygoing day that you were hoping for. Demands made on your spare time will be greater than you had anticipated. People who tend to pull strings in the lives of the

Sagittarius-born may require you to attend to the health of others in a way that can endanger your own physical or emotional well-being. Some difficult decisions may be required. These you would prefer not to have to make. You are also likely to be constantly aware that influential people are watching you.

17. MONDAY. Demanding. The problems that you encountered yesterday were not resolved. They are likely to spill over into this first day of the working week. You may find that you have to attend to the personal and emotional problems of loved ones. Work that you had hoped to make an early start with may have to be postponed. It might even be necessary to work through the lunch hour. Despite that, it may even be necessary to put in some overtime if you are going to keep your schedule up to date. Marital problems may require you to take on some extra responsibilities. It will be difficult to avert quarrels and bickering with spouses.

18. TUESDAY. Sensitive. As long as you avoid erratic behavior you should not fare too badly. If you do give way to impulsive actions, this will have an extremely disturbing effect on marital as well as business partners. Try to win associates over to your side by the gentle approach. You might be able to snare some especially favorable contracts if only you are patient. Spouses will be willing to speak up on your behalf if you will agree to confide in them without holding anything back. If you try to be too clever, you will only outsmart yourself. The evening would be a good time to try to patch up any differences. These may have only recently arisen between you and older relatives, but they could have serious consequences.

19. WEDNESDAY. Tricky. This will be a period when you could find all sorts of good reasons why you should not knuckle down to your work. You may tell yourself that you have been pushing too hard and you need a break. But you will have problems with superiors if you do not give them a fair day's work for a fair day's pay. You must be honest with yourself as well as with others. Do not permit friends who seem to have a lot of time on their hands to bring too much influence to bear upon your actions. You must not allow yourself to be led no matter who it is. Misunderstandings over the handling of joint finances may require you to make some sacrifices by digging into your own private funds.

20. THURSDAY. Good. This seems to have been an up-and-down sort of a week. But today would appear to see you back on the track of something pretty lucrative. You appear to be thinking more straightforwardly about money. You ought to be able to discover ways to put more of your earnings to one side to meet those winter bills. They will all too soon be coming through your mailbox. Some thought should also be given to putting more cash aside to meet the additional expenses of Christmas. The festive season is not really very far away. The Sagittarius-born who handle money on behalf of others may be able to conclude some especially lucrative deals. But always be extremely cautious.

21. FRIDAY. Successful. This will be a pleasant day. You should find that you have an opportunity to deal with financial matters in a most agreeable way. Those of you who are expecting legacies or perhaps an inheritance should attempt to get in touch with influential people or government officials. These people who operate from behind the scenes could determine whether your legacy is in the pipeline. They may be able to give you information about such matters that you would not normally be able to find out. The more that you can make contact with such people socially, the better it will be. Official backing can probably be obtained for business dealings with large corporations or institutions.

22. SATURDAY. Variable. The Sagittarius-born will probably be more intent than usual on thinking seriously about the future. This will deal with the long-term security of you and your family. It would certainly be a good idea at this time to try to find ways to put more of your earnings to one side. You will certainly need to get your hands on more cash in the near future. If you are considering doing something out of the ordinary this Christmas, you had better start making plans now. If you wish to go away for the festive season and stay in a hotel you should get your bookings arranged without further delay. Otherwise, you may be too late.

23. SUNDAY. Fortunate. You will be delighted with the free-and-easy atmosphere today. It will afford you the opportunity to catch up with many jobs around the home. You have been itching to come to grips with these. It will also be favorable for all forms of self-improvement endeavors. Your true love of originality and your willingness to break new ground can make you an explorer in uncharted territory. People at or from distances are likely to offer you encouragement for personal schemes. This will give your self-confidence a tremendous boost. The evening will be a time for seeking pleasure and entertainment with close friends and family.

24. MONDAY. Variable. The pressure of business conventions and public taste may require Sagittarius people to lower their sights on their personal endeavors. This will be true even if they obtain the offical go-ahead for their schemes. You will find that some restrictions you could not possibly have anticipated will be placed upon you. This is not a good day to act. You must not be impulsive. The exercise of some extra subtlety and diplomacy can make routine business transactions more lucrative. Any spare time that you have should be used for bringing accounts up to date. It will be good for writing business letters to people in faraway places.

25. TUESDAY. Sensitive. With only a few more days left in the month of November, domestic affairs are likely to require a good deal more attention. There may be some slackening off at your place of employment. In fact, you may be able to knock off from work earlier than usual. Any spare time that you have should be given over to home and family matters. Sagittarius parents should give more time and pay more attention to the needs of children. Youngsters could have problems they would like to discuss with you. Try to be extra friendly and understanding in order to give them the confidence they need to broach certain sensitive subjects.

26. WEDNESDAY. Confusing. After an evening spent out on the town with friends, the Sagittarius-born may feel more confused than ever about money matters. The ideas of other people should not be followed blindly, especially if speculation is involved. Do not part with savings that you have painstakingly built up to invest in anything where the risk of loss is great. You must not allow yourself to be easily led. Keep all impulsive tendencies in check. This is a time to keep on the lookout for so-called friends who are simply preying on the generosity of their long-time pals. Take a firm stand when anyone asks for a loan or expects you to pay the whole tab.

27. THURSDAY. Good. Friends and acquaintances will tend to take the ideas of the Archer more seriously than usual. This is a splendid time to take the lead. If you have any pet projects that you have been waiting patiently to launch, this would be the right moment to get them off the ground. Your powers of leadership will be very much to the fore. It will be a great relief to all of you to realize that you are being treated with more respect at your place of employment. Later on, friends will be only too eager to supply you with particularly valuable information and tips. You know well how to turn these to your best advantage. And because of the timeliness of the information, you stand to make good gains.

28. FRIDAY. Happy. It would seem that you are on the track of something good at the moment. This is a first-class day for attending to the details of business and financial matters. Use it to your best possible advantage. But this is not the right time to put your ideas for change up to influential people. The more conservative-minded superiors will resist if you attempt to force them to follow your schemes. Do not attempt to overstep the authority that has been vested in you. So long as you only try to make relatively minor gains, all will be well. Friends will continue to be helpful and will also be good fun to be with during leisure time. You could probably plan something extra-special for this weekend.

29. SATURDAY. Fair. The Sagittarius-born are likely to be drawn into furthering some important developments in the background. Try not to get caught up in too much complexity or secrecy, though. It is vital that you keep your dealings with influential people as straightforward and aboveboard as possible. As it is nearing the end of the month of November, it would be a good idea to get your books into some semblance of order. Try to pay all your bills. You will then have a better idea of how much cash you actually have been able to save. Go along with the moderate-sounding schemes of people who act behind the scenes. These are the ones who have advised you well in the past. As before, they are not likely to mislead you or to advocate any risky ventures. They think too much of you to put your financial status in jeopardy.

30. SUNDAY. Quiet. It will be an ideal day on which to end the month of November. This is likely to be a typical family Sunday when you will not be called upon to take any important action. Give more of your time to home and family affairs than you usually do on weekends. You appear to have been neglecting them quite a bit lately. This is a period for the Archer to relax and take it easy, both mentally and physically. Perhaps you will be feeling a little below par, so you do not want to do anything that would endanger your physical well-being. You may prefer to spend some time in your own company. Daydreams may be a pleasant way for you to forget about problems connected with work and your career. Today will be appropriate for putting in an appearance at the Sunday markets. There may be some real bargains for sale. But remember, nothing is a bargain if you don't need it.

DECEMBER

1. MONDAY. Disquieting. The working week and the month get off to a somewhat unsettled start for you Sagittarius-born people. Young or old, single or married, you will have problems settling down to your work today. Also, when attempting to implement personal plans, it is advisable to focus on long-term interests and not allow yourself to be carried away by the whims of the moment. Otherwise, you will find yourself burdened with extra responsibilities that you are not in a position to take on. Family members should not be relied upon for support. There may be more broken promises than ones fulfilled, though these are not intended.

2. TUESDAY. Variable. The Archer should try not to be too headstrong or impulsive. Make sure that you let other people know exactly what your plans are at your place of employment. Do not say one thing and then go right ahead and act in a totally different way. You must work harder at getting a reputation for being reliable. Otherwise, influential people will not be willing to assist you to get on and gain promotion. They must be convinced that you can be trusted with additional responsibilities. Personal affairs have to be handled with sensitivity, especially if you are looking after the interests of others. Push tasks ahead with determination.

3. WEDNESDAY. Lucky. This is a day when you are likely to feel an upsurge of energy. It will certainly be easier for you to deal with many of the problems that have been crowding in on you over the past few days. Home life will be much more settled, and this will enable you to deal with outside interests, especially your job. People at your place of employment will be easier to influence. This will mean that greater teamwork will be possible. Some profound changes will be going on behind the scenes. Sagittarius people are advised to keep their ears to the ground, as they may be able to latch on to some lucrative financial deals. Don't miss out on them.

4. THURSDAY. Mixed. Perhaps you might have been hoping to make more gains than you will be allowed to this Thursday. It looks as though you were able to make some promising new starts yesterday. Now it appears that you will have to mark time with such projects. Today is good for looking into new contracts. You can also carry out negotiations that you will be planning to clinch at a later date. Influential people will be helpful. But financial support is not likely to be forthcoming in quite the amounts that you may have been expecting. Be sure that you keep your demands reasonable so that you do not alienate people in authority.

5. FRIDAY. Variable. Today is good for negotiating new contracts and agreements. See what you can do to get other interested parties to sign on the dotted line. People will be more amenable, and your powers of persuasion should be that much greater. You can put that Sagittarius charm of yours to particularly good use. But the odd word casually dropped into conversations can get back to loved ones and cause upsets. People may misconstrue your words, and this could get you into all sorts of trouble. Try to steer clear of people who gossip and who you know from past experience cannot keep secrets. The ability of Archers to express themselves fluently will help them to overcome barriers. These could have blocked fulfillment of their personal plans.

6. SATURDAY. Disquieting. This may not have been the exciting start that you had anticipated getting off to in this last month of the year. Perhaps you have been in too much of a rush. Don't try to launch any new projects at work of a business nature. This is not a period when you should be attempting to get financial backing from influential people. The Archer should be giving a good deal more time to home and family affairs if they wish to avoid differences with loved ones. Your mate or partner may feel that you have been ignoring the desires of those closest to you. You will have to give more time to others if you want to avoid arguments. This is not a period for making property moves either.

7. SUNDAY. Mixed. Any spare time that you have on your hands this Sunday should be used meaningfully. Come to grips with odd jobs around the house and garden. Remember that there is not very much time to go till Christmas. You might not have enough time to deal with matters such as presents if you leave them until the last minute. Loved ones will be helpful, and it will not be too difficult for you to promote anything that requires team effort. You should make attempts to get all major repair work completed and not left over until another day. It is important to bear in mind the desires of spouses and loved ones. They should certainly come before friends, no matter what the circumstances.

8. MONDAY. Sensitive. The impulsive and erratic actions of the Archer could get them in hot water. Do not put the success of projects in jeopardy because of impatience. Listen to the advice that older people are willing to give you. If you do not listen to superiors at your place of employment they may be unwilling to give you financial support. You desperately need it in order to launch your original ideas. On the other hand, swift action in connection with events behind the scenes can produce satisfactory and lucrative results. Evening is not a time to go gadding about town. Take it easy within the confines of your own four walls. Read a good book.

9. TUESDAY. Deceptive. This is one of those extremely sensitive days when you have to be very careful that you do not put your foot in it. One word out of place at the office or factory could do a lot of damage to a special relationship. You have enjoyed associating with an influential person who has been of help. Any strange ideas that you have about making a bit of money on the side can land you in trouble. This will be especially true if you take time off from regular employment affairs in order to attend to such matters. Self-deception or outright deception on the part of others is likely to mar any speculative endeavors that you undertake.

10. WEDNESDAY. Fair. Some improvement is indicated this Wednesday. So long as you do not try to rush things, you should be fairly pleased with the progress that you are able to make. The Sagittarius-born are likely to be feeling in good form. With an upsurge of energy indicated, you will be able to get through with more jobs than usual. This will impress people in authority with whom you may not have been getting on well of late. Creative endeavors will be particularly inspiring. You will be able to use your natural talents to good effect. You might even be able to get backing for ventures that involve an element of risk.

11. THURSDAY. Good. This is probably one of the best days that you have experienced so far this month. It is an excellent period for getting the bulk of your festive shopping done before the Christmas rush goes into full swing. Those of you who have a lot to do at their place of regular employment should knuckle down to their tasks early on. That way, you will have the opportunity to attend to more personal issues later. You should be able to catch up with any backlog of chores without putting yourself out too much. Hunches and intuitions should be acted upon as they are likely to be more reliable than usual. They should pay off if Archer workers are in a position to act on their own initiative.

12. FRIDAY. Variable. Your health may be below par. Minor ailments should not be left unattended. You should visit your doctor at the first sign of a cough or the sniffles. They may develop into something more serious if you choose to ignore the warnings. You may be feeling the strain of recent efforts. Loved ones might also be making extra demands upon you that you find are an increasing burden. It might be necessary to have a heart-to-heart talk with your mate or partner. Only then will you be able to clear the air about some prickly domestic issues. A genuine willingness to serve will be helpful in your relationships with older relatives. They will recognize your cooperation and realize how much you help them.

13. SATURDAY. Quiet. It will be one of those easygoing days when there is not likely to be much cooking at home or at work. You will be left to your own devices for a good deal of the time. You should use this opportunity to get your cards written and to buy and mail presents to people in faraway places. Remember there are not many shopping days to go now before Christmas. Department stores will soon be closing their doors for the festive season. Loved ones will not be making quite so many demands upon you. This development will come as something of a surprise and a relief. If you Archers are feeling a bit below par, you should take this opportunity to get some more rest and relaxation.

14. SUNDAY. Disquieting. Sagittarius people may find it impossible to get themselves understood by their mates or partners. This will be a trying Sunday for dealing with sensitive domestic conditions. No amount of talking or persuasion is likely to do any good when it comes to attempts to get your nearest and dearest to see thing from your point of view. It might be best to steer clear of contentious issues as much as you possibly can. If you are attempting to win over people in authority, it is important not to reflect an impression of being too independent or overly willful. Don't give in to extravagant impulses either. Just be yourself and impress others.

15. MONDAY. Upsetting. The demands made on all Archers are likely to be totally unacceptable. It looks as though you are programmed for a head-on collision with loved ones if they continue to push you too hard. Family members may be taking liberties where partnership affairs are concerned. You may have to take your mate or partner to task for spending more cash than you can really afford on Christmas shopping. It will not be an easy matter to balance the books today. Domestic issues can start brewing early in the day and come to a full boil before very long. Younger folks may rebel against authority and challenge the greater experience of the Sagittarius parent. Young people always think they know it all.

16. TUESDAY. Uneventful. You will be grateful that the pressure is lessened to a certain extent this Tuesday. This will be an easygoing day when you will have the opportunity to go over accounts and work out just how much cash you can afford to lay out over the coming two or three weeks. The atmosphere within the home will be very much improved. Loved ones will be more amenable to your ideas for making additional savings. This will be a more straightforward day all around. The Archer will have better opportunities for attending satisfactorily to cooperative partnership affairs. Take a closer look at your relationship with business partners too.

17. WEDNESDAY. Good. This will be a better day for getting things done. You will be pleased to discover that people are not making quite so many demands on you. You should be able to work out your own schedule for this midweek day, and by and large stick to it. This is quite a good day for getting rid of routine jobs and clearing the decks for making exciting new starts at a later date. Investments and mutual savings may have grown without your realizing it. The amount of interest that your deposits will have earned will be higher than you would have believed. Extra cash will be particularly useful for you at this expensive time of the year.

18. THURSDAY. Difficult. Don't be in too much of a hurry today. Those who are buying Christmas presents for dear ones should give more thought to planning. Try to imagine what people would like to receive or need. Sometimes one tends to think in terms of what you would like to buy for yourself. This will be an uneventful day. But you have to guard against upsetting other people by your unconventional behavior. Spend more time going over joint accounts. You should try to take more note of where the money has been going recently. You may have been acting more extravagantly than you realize. Ensure that you pay regular bills.

19. FRIDAY. Satisfactory. Problems of yesterday are likely to be encountered once again today. You must slow down a bit. You appear to be working too hard. You will not achieve more by pushing yourself to the limits. It will only be a case of more haste, less speed. You should try to find more time for doing your own thing. Women Archers will enjoy themselves more if they can get on with prefestive cooking. Get the Christmas decorations up at home. Then see what you can do to bring some fun and excitement into the lives of underprivileged children. School holidays will be starting about now so you can count on lots of help. Self-improvement endeavors are likely to appeal to you.

20. SATURDAY. Uncertain. You may encounter some secret opposition within the home today. Loved ones may not agree with all of your plans. But they may not wish to come right out with it and say so openly for fear of hurting your feelings. Your desire to gain extra qualifications may be thwarted for lack of time. It looks as though you will have to devote more of your spare time to household chores. It might also be necessary to drop in and visit relatives who you will not be able to visit during the Christmas holidays. It will be quite a good period for those of you who are involved in sporting activities, whether spectator or participant.

21. SUNDAY. Sensitive. It may be possible today to make some useful contact with influential people during social affairs. You may be attending a Christmas party where people who can have an influence on your career will also be guests. If so, you may well have an opportunity to have some fruitful conversations. You should make arrangements to meet them during the working week. This is a day when the Sagittarius personality can be put to particularly good use. People will enjoy your company. Superiors will take a favorable view of your ambitions and make some meaningful financial proposals. But arguments can erupt with family members.

22. MONDAY. Difficult. Perhaps you will feel that you have too much on your plate this first work day. There are sure to be many things to wind up at your place of employment. With Christmas only just around the corner, you are likely to find that the demands made on you are fairly substantial. Loved ones will show little understanding for what you are trying to achieve. You may find that the selfish manner of your mate or partner is difficult to fathom. The more that you can rely on yourself, the better off you will be. Some important progress can be made in career matters if you leave time to contact people behind the scenes.

23. TUESDAY. Upsetting. The Christmas rush seems to be getting you down. It looks as though you have your work cut out for you. You hope to be able to attend successfully to all of the chores that you wish to get out of the way. While advancing your efforts in your chosen field, you Archers must be aware of how easy it is to wreck your public reputation by any unconventional and erratic behavior. This is not a good day for proposing drastic changes or making innovations. Your career is likely to suffer if you do. Invitations should not be accepted for going out tonight if it means costing you a lot of money. A quiet evening at home will help you prepare for the holiday by giving you time to get organized.

24. WEDNESDAY. Deceptive. Festive celebrations may deprive you of your basic good sense about money. This is a time of the year when you could easily be tempted to throw caution to the wind and spend savings that you can ill afford to lose. Do not listen to friends who tempt you to take a live-for-the-moment attitude to life. People who are trying to pass themselves off as good buddies may, in fact, just be after your money. Any financial dealings with close associates are likely to lead to misunderstandings and should be avoided if at all possible. Don't stray too far from home tonight. Don't consume any alcohol if you are driving. Be on the lookout for carelessness on the part of other road users, too.

25. THURSDAY. Merry Christmas! It looks as though there will be many good things in store for the Sagittarius-born this Christmas day. Social gatherings, in particular, are likely to have a special appeal. This is especially true if you have the chance to visit people whom you have not been able to see for some considerable time. You will find an ideal outlet in the house of others for your verve and sparkle. You will feel free, for once, to do and say just what you want. Let your hair down and enjoy yourself in the company of like-minded people. There will be no real reason to feel reserved or inhibited. Nobody is watching to see how anybody else behaves on this holiday.

26. FRIDAY. Fair. Those of you who have overdone it should try to ease off today. If you have had a lot to eat or a great deal to drink, you should take self-disciplinary measures to cut down. Loved ones will be pleasant. If you have been gadding about, hither and thither, you will probably be pleased to spend more time with members of your family at home. Informal contact with people who play a rather large part in the lives of Sagittarius may produce some favorable results. Money problems should be brought up, as they will be more easily solved. Diplomacy can be useful. But it is important not to go overboard on secrecy, as results could be embarrassing. This will probably be a rather quiet day so you could catch up with personal chores.

27. SATURDAY. Harmonious. After all of the recent comings and goings of Christmas, you will be pleased to have an opportunity to spend some time alone with loved ones. What will probably appeal to you most is to stay within the confines of your own four walls. It could be that you are feeling a little drained of energy. If you have plans to go out tonight, you will want to rest up. You won't have enough energy left if you burn yourself out early on. You may wish to devote some time to tidying up generally and getting caught up with your letter writing. A highly enjoyable and stimulating time can be had in the company of older relatives.

28. SUNDAY. Quiet. This will be just the sort of a Sunday that you had been hoping for. The pressure will be off you. You should be able to please yourself as to how you spend your spare time today. You should be feeling fairly self-confident and satisfied with yourselves. You will be able to solve quite a few of your financial problems by going over such matters with dear ones and looking for new ways to cut down on unnecessary expenditures. Some time should be given to reviewing progress of the past year and for drawing up plans for the future. Ways should be examined for using personal initiative and talents to the best advantage.

29. MONDAY. Worrisome. This will be a most unsettling day for those who have to go to the office or factory to earn your living. You most certainly will not be in the mood to put your shoulder to the wheel. Concentration will be difficult to attain and maintain. This is not a day when the Sagittarius-born are likely to feel in a mood for playing around. They can be almost deadly serious in their application to personal affairs. Too much concern should be avoided, as it can give rise to friction among other members of the household. Today is good for getting down to the stores early and stocking up on provisions that you may have run short on. You may also find there are good sales of items that had been overstocked.

30. TUESDAY. Confusing. This is a sensitive day for romance. Do not take anyone or anything for granted where your love life is concerned. This is also quite likely to be an important day from the financial standpoint. But all dealings of a financial nature must be kept strictly open and aboveboard. Watch out for deception and misunderstandings when attempting to clinch important deals. Important documents should not be left lying around where eyes that they are not meant for can check them over. Conditions behind the scenes will be healthy for dealing with money matters. You will probably be happy to curl up with a good book or look at TV.

31. WEDNESDAY. Good. You should be able to look back over the past year, especially the last quarter, with some degree of satisfaction. Perhaps you have not been able to achieve all that you had set out to, but it looks as though you have gone a good way forward to realizing most of your ambitions. Today should be used for winding up unfinished business that you don't want hanging over your head. Family members may have some very important propositions to make. Those born under Sagittarius may be able to benefit financially. Today is favorable for paying out for home improvements that will add value to your property. It is also a lucky day for setting up home with loved ones.

October–December 1985

OCTOBER

1. TUESDAY. Fair. Although you are likely to have certain problems in getting along with your co-workers, you must not allow this to distress you. You will probably fare better if you operate under your own steam as much as office and shop conditions allow. Employed Sagittarians should be able to make a good impression on their boss and perhaps put themselves in line for a salary increase. You want to be careful that you are not too pushy though. The best way to catch the eye of those who matter is to plod along in your own way and not ask for any favors. Personal effort will be helpful for increasing profits for the self-employed. Activities with friends will provide pleasure.

2. WEDNESDAY. Slow. You may be feeling a little discontented today. It is not going to be easy for you to channel your energies in a positive manner. It might be advisable to stick to routine work that does not require a great deal of imagination. The day appears to be too slow moving to make it worthwhile to start up creative ventures. Do not overextend yourself. Good for resting and for doing what you can to improve your general health and well being. If you have been seriously thinking about starting an exercise course then you will have ample time today to do so. Employment affairs that you have to deal with at the office or shop are unlikely to pose any special problems.

3. THURSDAY. Disquieting. Sagittarians have to watch the side of their nature that leads them into erratic behavior. Do not be impulsive, especially when dealing with household matters. Watch that temper of yours. Do not be overly critical of loved ones who do not go along with your ideas for change. Reasoned discussions are best. Remember that everyone is entitled to their own opinions. Business associates may try to be dominating and this could cause you to have an emotional outburst. If you have been aiming to get promoted, then you will have to show people at the top that you have the right temperament that goes with additional responsibility, as well as the expertise required.

4. FRIDAY. Mixed. Office or work romances can be exciting but dangerous. Be very careful about getting too heavily involved with a person who you have to have a strictly professional relationship with. Sagittarians must also guard against letting their emotions run away with them and causing pain for people with whom they have longstanding ties. Do not throw away lasting happiness for fleeting gratification. Happy day for partnership activities with mutual friends of your spouse or partner. Evening will be a time to accept any invitations that come along that would get you out of your rut. Major changes within the home should once again be postponed until your finances are more stable.

5. SATURDAY. Lazy. This slow and easy day is favorable for making up to loved ones who you may have been treating a little harshly. On reflection you might realize that you have not really been giving loved ones a fair shake. Excellent day for long-term planning. Although it is still quite a way away, it might be a good idea to discuss Christmas plans if you are going to do something different this festive season. Remember how booked up hotels get in resorts at that time of the year. People with whom you have been at odds with will be willing to let bygones be bygones. A pleasant enough day but physical energy may be lacking.

6. SUNDAY. Disquieting. Although this Sunday is likely to begin calmly enough, as it matures you are likely to become increasingly irritated. One of the reasons for your emotional feelings will be the fact that friends turn out to be somewhat unreliable. Plans that you had made for going out could be cancelled at the last moment leaving you at loose ends. Do not spend too much money on outside entertainment that is unlikely to live up to your expectations in any case. Influential people may refuse to cooperate and it might be best not to discuss your career prospects outside of regular office or shop hours. Decisions to change investments must be made with more care than ever.

7. MONDAY. Good. This first day of the work week looks as if it is going to be the best day that you have had so far during the month of October. Conditions within your own four walls are likely to be much more settled. Your mate or partner is now likely to come around to your way of thinking with regard to certain changes that you have been itching to make in your home. At work, too, conditions will be greatly improved. People with whom you have not been able to cooperate will now be prepared to toe the line. This is also an especially favorable period for more energetic efforts to increase mutual resources or old-age security funds. Romance offers chances of new attractions.

8. TUESDAY. Varied. Distant affairs will be somewhat unsettled. It would be advisable to cancel any journeys until tomorrow or the next day if this is at all possible. If you are hoping to drum up business through making new contacts with leaders in commerce and industry then you are in for a bit of a letdown. People will be difficult to please and your Sagittarian charm will not be quite so useful for breaking down hostile barriers. Better day for personal interests; you will enjoy yourself if you can get out and around with friends who always lift your spirits. All information with regard to club or group activities does need checking however.

9. WEDNESDAY. Promising. The goodwill of influential people will be easier to obtain. You will find that this is an important day for job seeking. Sagittarians who are fed up with their present lifestyle and would like to make some changes may be able to find the very niche that would suit them. Scan the ad columns in the local papers; there may be an exciting challenge waiting for you there. Long journeys that you set out on in connection with your career are likely to terminate successfully. Needful changes can be made without upsetting the people affected. Friends can be helpful to business profits, probably through the knowledge and experience they can provide.

10. THURSDAY. Important. Another pleasant and productive day. You seem to be getting into high gear now. Your enthusiasm and confidence should be on an upward swing. People at or from distances will be particularly cooperative. Superiors will be doing all that they can to help you increase your knowledge in such a way that you will be able to up your earnings and thus secure a better standard of living. Family members will not stand in your way. Loved ones will show greater understanding if you have to spend more time away from home than usual. Good for Sagittarians who are involved in the importing and exporting business to make more cash. Secret contacts with professional people are favored.

11. FRIDAY. Doubtful. Activities that you wish to pursue are not likely to meet with the approval of co-workers. There could be walk-outs. You may feel that you are being tied to a course of action that you do not wish to follow. It would be best to operate on your own as much as possible. You might not be in the mood for it but you should get down to routine matters that you have been putting to one side during the earlier part of the week. Sagittarians must guard against being erratic in their actions. You will find that you have to exercise a good deal of discipline today if you have recently embarked upon a diet.

12. SATURDAY. Deceptive. The early portion of this day would appear to be the most favorable for advancing your plans. You should be able to make a certain amount of progress with work that you want to get finished before you take a weekend break. As the day goes on, however, you are going to find it increasingly difficult to get your own way. Be very wary about investing capital in friends' speculative ideas. Health difficulties will not be such a worry. Elders will be easier to cope with and are not likely to be making quite so many demands on your spare time. Club activities might be too expensive and not as much fun as you had been led to believe.

13. SUNDAY. Cooperation. A happy Sunday would appear to be in store for you and yours. Now is the time to try to improve your relationship with loved ones. There is a member of your family who you have not been getting along at all well with of late. Be big hearted. Bury the hatchet and show that you do not bear grudges. This is a starred day for social affairs and for getting together with friends who can supply you with valuable knowledge that you can put to good use in your career. Existing romantic relationships can be strengthened, new attractions formed. Dealing with people away from the public can be an advantage, but nothing should be put in writing until your facts are confirmed.

14. MONDAY. Fair. Sagittarians should try to avoid giving into feelings of restlessness. You may not be in the mood to get back into the work groove. It is not going to be an easy matter for the Archer to concentrate on the sort of tasks that are set for them by superiors. Thoughtless actions could create upheavals at home. Be sure that you do not act in a selfish manner when dealing with your spouse or partner. People will be emotional and should be handled with sensitivity. Secret affairs can be helpful to financial schemes but need very careful handling. Although you wish to assist those less well off than yourself, too much zealous crusading can actually delay or upset plans aimed at helping the less privileged.

15. TUESDAY. Disquieting. Promises that were made to you by people who you thought you could rely upon may be broken. This is a day when you could feel badly let down. Verbal agreements that promised to give you a break in your career are likely to be reneged upon when the crunch comes. Bankers will be less accommodating. It would be wise not to put in for a loan today. Your dealings with professional people may not be as amicable or reap the benefits that you were looking forward to. People, or conditions, behind the scenes can cause problems. Betrayal of confidences is possible. The health of relatives can involve you in quite a lot of time and effort. Trips in connection with making secret agreements should be deferred.

16. WEDNESDAY. Acceptable. Dark clouds may be hanging over your head. Shake yourself out of the doldrums. It is no use crying over spilt milk and mistakes that you are powerless to change.

Worry over health problems and other private matters could be the cause of your feeling down during the early part of the day. However, by midafternoon you should be feeling in a much better frame of mind; this could be because of a chance meeting with a friend who will have an uplifting effect on your spirits. Social affairs will become enjoyable. It will not be necessary to spend a lot of money to gain pleasure. Love affairs that have only recently started up should be exciting.

17. THURSDAY. Hectic. Attend to bills that need to be paid; you may have been leaving them aside for too long. Procrastination could become expensive now; go over your accounts. There may be people that you have been owing cash to since the end of September. You do not want to get a reputation for unreliability. Sagittarians can force unwelcome changes on themselves by acting impulsively or erratically. Ideas that you want to put into practice at your place of employment may be too progressive for others to accept. Feelings of loved ones will be sensitive. You may be accused of not caring enough about the happiness of a close family member.

18. FRIDAY. Improving. The cooperation of friends can be especially valuable to the more personal affairs of Sagittarian people. Singles who do not have a steady mate at the moment may be introduced to someone they take an immediate shine to. You are likely to feel much happier about your romantic prospects now. Influential people will be more inclined to grant favors. Good day for joining clubs and organizations where you can meet people who have the same career interests as you do. Conditions will be a little confusing for financial activity though. This would not appear to be the right time to tamper with investments. Romance will be rather expensive and unrewarding. Don't push your affections onto a member of the opposite sex who is playing it very cool.

19. SATURDAY. Smooth. The week comes to an end on a happy note. This is a fortunate day for financial affairs that you have been having some hassle with. You should be able to get to grips with knotty problems connected with your budget. Associates will be more helpful and cooperative. It will be easier to get hold of information that has been withheld from you. Old difficulties and those of yesterday can be rectified. People behind the scenes will now be willing to sign contracts that they have been sitting on the fence about. Financial pressures may also be eased because outstanding debts are paid.

20. SUNDAY. Mixed. Steer clear of influential people you want favors from. If you are attending social affairs where you will be mingling with superiors from your place of employment, then do not talk shop. Your boss will not want to be bothered with your requests for favors on their day of relaxation. Money should not be lent to or borrowed from friends. You must cut back on unnecessary spending in order to make ends meet. Friendship generally will be sensitive and will require more tactful handling if misunderstandings are going to be avoided. In contrast to the activity in the earlier part of the day, evening should be a relatively quiet period. You can settle down to desk jobs without fear of interruption. Remember to spend some time with loved ones.

21. MONDAY. Happy. Sagittarians should give as much time as possible to jobs that require the use of their imagination. This is a terrific day for those who are connected with the world of art and entertainment. You will find that you are very much in demand and you should be able to charge more for your services and therefore increase your take home pay. You will find influential people are extremely helpful and fair. Efforts to get to the top are likely to succeed. Business ventures involving publications, recordings, and other communications media are likely to be lucrative. Happy for social activities, especially if it can lead to romance.

22. TUESDAY. Good. Things seem to be going very well for you at the moment and there is no reason why there should be any changes in your fortune today. Valuable agreements can be made with friends. This is a good day for going into business partnership with people who are very much on your wavelength when it comes to dealing with artistic jobs. You should be able to get a lot of satisfaction from what is on the agenda for today. Some good luck with mental endeavors will make them more lucrative. You will not have any trouble concentrating on your tasks. New ideas will be coming thick and fast. Romance continues to look happy. Health problems can be improved by more attention to dietary habits.

23. WEDNESDAY. Cooperation. This would appear to be the third in a cycle of "good" days. You seem to be right on top of things at the moment. Be sure that you grasp the opportunities that are offered to you with both hands. Home and family affairs will contain better opportunities for successful attention. Very good day for the Archer who has to operate from their home base. You should be able to get ahead with jobs that you did not have the opportunity to deal with over the weekend. Loved ones will be agreeable. Needful changes can be made in connection with the domestic budget without too much possibility of upsetting others. People behind the scenes will be helpful in real estate affairs.

24. THURSDAY. Fair. As long as impulsive actions are avoided, all will be well today. You must not try to force influential people to act in haste. Although you seem to have been doing pretty well lately, this is not a day when you should try to speed up the tempo at your place of employment. Reliability and stability is what people who have authority over you will be looking for. Someone out of the past may be instrumental in helping those Sagittarians who are looking for better homes or accommodations. Good for entertaining influential people away from the public. Financial plans can be advanced under intimate social conditions.

25. FRIDAY. Disturbing. After a pretty satisfying week to date, you are likely to suffer a number of setbacks this Friday. Perhaps you are expecting too much; in any event, this is going to be a bit of anti-climax for you. Business people are not likely to agree with the decisions that the Archer makes, and this is likely to cause arguments which will require a great deal of self-control. Family relationships are also likely to be lacking in harmony. It will not be easy to relax and unwind and your spouse or partner is probably going to find your tensions rather catching. Romance will be too expensive for what it offers. Remember your diet.

26. SATURDAY. Variable. Speculative ventures that are suggested need to be approached with a great deal of caution. You may have one or two tips passed on to you to take a gamble on a sporting venture. Be sure that if you do take any risks with your hard-earned loot, you can afford to suffer the loss. It might be best not to allow close associates to have too much influence over your financial decisions. The feelings of loved ones will be sensitive and this will increase the possibility of arguments within the home. Club affairs may contain misunderstandings with other members. Personal plans for seeking pleasure may be stimulated by unusual events taking place that you could not possibly have foreseen.

27. SUNDAY. Quiet. You are in need of more rest. Do not take on too many commitments this Sunday. Make it a typical family day. Try to make it up to loved ones if you have been spending a lot of time dealing with outside affairs. This will be a slow-moving Sunday when people will be in a lethargic mood so you will not feel that there is any great pressure placed upon you. Good for giving time to hobbies that you have put to one side for too long. It might be possible to turn what you have always considered a pleasant pastime into a moneymaking concern. Friends will be congenial. Family conferences about shared investments will be beneficial. Gather your energy for the coming week.

28. MONDAY. Disquieting. Don't be too hasty. Important decisions concerning your financial situation must not be taken on impulse. This is not a time to place too much reliability on your intuition. Secret enmity could be working against Sagittarians. Someone who you work with may be jealous of you and be trying to lower you in the eyes of superiors. It would be best not to get involved in petty arguments. Health problems may develop later on in the day and this may mean that your work progress is slowed down. Important documents must be signed with more care. Talk vital issues over with your spouse, or partner, before you make any important decisions about your career.

29. TUESDAY. Deceptive. Arguments could easily develop over cash. Friends and finances should be kept separate. A good friend may come to you with a hard luck story and want you to advance them some money; it would be best to refuse firmly. People may not be able to pay you back as promised and this state of affairs could sour a relationship that you value. You might be having some problems when it comes to concentrating at your place of employment. The main hang-up could be that the jobs that you have to turn your hand to are not stimulating enough. Profits need more protection. Don't invest in any projects where the risk factor is high. False friends can be made. Sagittarians have to be cautious where glamour is emphasized.

30. WEDNESDAY. Varied. Occupational affairs continue to look somewhat unsettled. You might have to deal with personal problems in the early part of the day and this could get you behind schedule. Do not resort to panic measures, however. Take your time with jobs that require special attention to detail. No changes should be made in types or places of work. Do not throw away your present position just because you are promised something at a later date. You must be more security minded or you could end up losing ground and falling back on your reserves. Co-workers are contrary and this may turn you off at the office or shop in which you work. Later in the day you will have more fun. Get out and do something that cheers you up with family members or close friends.

31. THURSDAY. Improving. Mixed trends are indicated for the last day of the month of October. You will be looking back over the last few weeks and trying to balance the books. You will come to the decision that you must take some definite steps to cut back on your spending. With the winter months approaching, you must try to put more cash in the bank to meet the additional bills that you are going to be called upon to pay. Friendship continues to be important. It might be a good idea for you and your spouse, or partner, to get out for a short trip with some mutual friends. Useful agreements can be made with relatives that could lessen your domestic duties. Secret alliances and transactions with daily business associates should be shunned however. Go over documents that you are asked to sign; keep your eyes open for incorrect details.

NOVEMBER

1. FRIDAY. Good. An especially happy day for associating with friends, including those that you have not seen for some time. You should be able to meet up with people who mean a great deal to you whom you have not seen because of family obligations and pressures of work. The accent would appear to be on pleasure rather more than business on this first day of November. Romance will be important to you as well; agreements can be consummated with loved ones. Good for dating and seeking pleasure and entertainment with a difference. Interesting people can be met by becoming members of clubs and societies. Hopes and wishes never revealed to others can be brought closer to fulfillment.

2. SATURDAY. Disquieting. People may not live up to their word. This is one of those days when you will really have to rely on yourself if you are going to get anywhere in your career. This is a more hazardous day for financial activities. You want to be wary about being drawn into investment in risky ventures. People will be out to talk you into taking chances with your savings. Don't be a sucker for get-rich-quick schemes. Spending on personal items must be kept within reasonable bounds. Don't throw away money on luxury items that are really beyond the reach of your pocket. People behind the scenes will be helpful to attempts to solve mysteries; efforts may lead to hidden assets being discovered.

3. SUNDAY. Sluggish. There will be quite a lot to ponder today. Problems of the past will have to be discussed with members of your family. Financial affairs need looking into in greater depth. You should listen to your spouse, or partner, who is likely to have some pretty good ideas about the best way to economize. It would appear that you are more guilty than other members of your family with regard to giving in to extravagant tendencies of late. This will not be a particularly eventful day from the social point of view, but any activities that you get involved in with friends should be pleasant enough. Time can profitably be used bringing taxation and insurance matters up to date.

4. MONDAY. Fortunate. Energy put into group affairs will not be wasted. Good day for drumming up support from people who are in a position to help you progress in your career. Business and pleasure can be mixed satisfactorily. Sagittarians can increase their sphere of influence. Superiors will be helpful and your creative ideas have a good chance of receiving backing that will take the form of more than simply verbal promises. Mental alertness is vital to the success of this day. Old debts or kindnesses can be repaid. New acquaintances can be made and will prove to become staunch and loyal friends in the future. Elders will be more cooperative.

5. TUESDAY. Unsettling. Arguments could develop with relatives and things will become heavy. You want to steer well clear of discussing subjects with other members of your family who hold widely differing views from you; be especially careful with brothers and sisters. Keep your more radical opinions to yourself. Arguments could lead to bad blood. People at a distance will be difficult to please. It might be best to postpone any plans that you had for making trips, especially if they were going to be trips for pleasure. Secret activities involving financial deals should be shunned. Keep all of your monetary dealings strictly open and aboveboard. Good for dealing with professional people, especially related to advertising and publicity.

6. WEDNESDAY. Changeable. Professional people will continue to be helpful. Interesting day for Sagittarians who are trying to make a name for themselves in the field of entertainment. Romance will be happy. Social activities could lead to meetings with members of the opposite sex who you find most attractive. Especially good for associating with people from the creative and the beauty world. Friendships can be established which will be of value to you. This is not a good day for making any changes in your relationship with people behind the scenes, however. Don't do anything to increase the possibility of loss through speculation.

7. THURSDAY. Caution. It might be a little difficult for you to get into high gear today. You will probably find that you have lapses in concentration during the early morning period. You must watch out for the possibility of errors in paperwork, especially connected with accounting. It would appear that there are a number of personal problems that are weighing rather heavily on your mind. Thinking can be faulty with regard to career decisions, so no important ones should be made until you have given yourself more time to ponder on the options that are open to you. Beware of talking about people behind their backs; gossip can create hostility. Relatives will not be likely to grant favors.

8. FRIDAY. Positive. Bankers will be more inclined to help you. Have a chat with people who look after your financial affairs. They may be able to offer you wise advice on the best way to increase income from capital that is standing idle. You want to seek out people who are experts in dealing with your money. Business affairs involving publications, transport, and communications can be made more profitable. Good day for travel in connection with your job. Your energy and drive will create an excellent impression on those who can help you further yourself. Happy reunions are possible with friends who have been working or residing in distant parts for some time. The mail can bring you good news.

9. SATURDAY. Promising. You seem to be in the middle of a rather promising period. You should be going from strength to strength this Saturday. Today could see the successful culmination of many of the things that you have been attempting to achieve in the week that is about to end. Energetic friends will have lots of interesting ideas that will make this day rather strenuous, but you will be eager to keep on the go. You appear to have quite a lot of excess energy to burn up at the moment. Business activities will continue to offer ample opportunities for additional profits being made. Good for reforming and crusading attempts.

10. SUNDAY. Fine. Another tip-top day. You will find that the atmosphere at home is pleasant, and this should mean that you will be able to do pretty well as you please. Good for making up to loved ones who you have not seen too much of recently owing to outside pressures. Drop in on older relatives. Trips to visit people who may be feeling down in the dumps would certainly be very much appreciated. Romantic attractions can develop with people behind the scenes. Looks as if the Archer will be lucky in love today. Loved ones will be helpful to your financial plans, possibly through people that they have met in the past. Health expenses can be reduced. You should be feeling much fitter in yourself.

11. MONDAY. Improving. Beware of gossip. Keep out of groups who are talking about people who you have some sort of loyalty and responsibility to. You do not want to get the reputation that you are not a true friend. This is one of those days when certain people who you come into contact with will be in a particularly malicious and nasty mood. It would be best to keep your opinions to yourself. People behind the scenes will be watching your progress at work and this is not a period when you can afford to slack off. Promises must not be made unless you are pretty sure you can keep them. More energy put into business affairs can lead to additional profits, but it must be directed wisely.

12. TUESDAY. Good. Don't forget that there is not all that far to go till Christmas. This is the right time to have a conference with members of your family and make attempts to find ways to put more cash to one side for the additional expenditures that you will be responsible for. You will find that loved ones will be agreeable to your schemes for building up your reserves by making cutbacks in unnecessary expenditures. Especially good day for quietly manipulating events from behind the scenes. This will help you prepare for launching of operations that you are anxious to get underway pretty soon, possibly even tomorrow. Background efforts made today have more chance of producing the desired results, so don't postpone your plans.

13. WEDNESDAY. Improving. There are lots of new projects that you want to get involved with. This can be a useful day for making progress so long as you do not attempt to do too much too soon. Personal objectives may be easier to reach than business ones. Sagittarians who have recently been introduced to someone who they feel attracted to may be able to fix up a date in the near future. Leaders in business and industry who are born under the sign of the Archer will find this a good day for discussing future plans with colleagues. Get to know your work force. Do not lose touch with grass roots feelings in the ofice or on the shop floor. Secret love affairs can be happy but have to be handled with greater discretion; such attractions can be initiated.

14. THURSDAY. Quiet. Looks as if you had a pretty hectic start to the week. Although you will not have much chance to increase profits to any significant extent, you will be somewhat relieved that you can take life a little easier. If you have been feeling under considerable strain and a little run down, then it would be a good idea to pop in and see your doctor just to have a routine checkup. This day is too slow for handling any important personal affairs but it can be useful for going over plans and making sure that details have not been neglected. Possibly a day for waiting patiently, not trying to force unnecessary speed.

15. FRIDAY. Mixed. Friends must not be allowed to exert any influence whatsoever on the way you handle your business. All decisions connected with your career must be yours and yours alone. It would seem that you need more time to decide which course to take as far as a job situation is concerned. Do not make that Sagittarian mistake of rushing in feet first. Suggestions of friends may be overly speculative and could lead to loss. Arguments can develop with loved ones over money. People may feel that you have been too extravagant with yourself of late. Good day for financial wheeling and dealing behind the scenes. You may be able to win the influential backing of superiors who like to remain anonymous.

16. SATURDAY. Cooperation. A starred day for financial moves. Looks as if you are thinking a good deal more straightforwardly about money matters now. Once you have decided which direction you wish to go in, allow no one and nothing to dissuade you. People will be cooperative and helpful. Sagittarians will be just where they like to be: in the driver's seat and calling the shots. Any cash moves which rely a great deal on secrecy are likely to have a successful outcome. Debts that have been outstanding for some time could well be repaid today; if not in full, then a reasonable amount certainly. Good for attempts to discipline yourself and to break any bad habits. You will be in a strong-willed and determined mood and will not brook delaying tactics.

17. SUNDAY. Disquieting. Your energy may have drained away from you and this could cause you to be short with your loved ones. You must watch that temper of yours. Do not pick on your spouse or partner; they may be in an emotional mood and not strong enough to take it. Have more consideration for the desires of others rather than trying to get your own way all the time. Any contacts that you have with relatives are likely to lead to misunderstandings. There could be rows breaking out with in-laws. Sagittarian women in particular must be very careful that they do not alienate someone whose help and assistance they may well need at a later date. Secret affairs should be avoided.

18. MONDAY. Good. Useful agreements will be easier to negotiate. After what appears to have been a somewhat trying Sunday, you will be pleased to get back into the swing of things. Office jobs will be more stimulating and you should be able to brighten up routine tasks with the help of inventive associates. Time should be given to writing and to mental pursuits. You should make more use of your natural talents in your spare time. Relatives who have been opposing you are now much more likely to be cooperative. Contacts with neighbors to discuss community affairs will be more rewarding. You may be feeling much more public spirited. Unexpected meetings with people from the past may give you pleasure.

19. TUESDAY. Varied. People with whom you are attempting to have perfectly open and honest dealings are likely to be suspicious of your motives. It will be hard to persuade associates in other locales that you are in fact a person of your word. It might not be enough to make verbal agreements, contracts may have to be drawn up as an act of good faith. Secret enmity has to be guarded against. Someone may have been attempting to sabotage your efforts. Watch out for competitors who would think nothing of going in for dirty tricks. Important decisions with regard to personal family issues would be best postponed. Health problems will delay you. Prospects for having a good time look brighter later on.

20. WEDNESDAY. Fair. Good day for Sagittarians to advance romantic hopes. Call up someone who you have only recently met but fancy strongly. You are likely to discover that your feelings of passion are reciprocated. Intimate meetings will go off very well. You will be in good form and people will be impressed by your boundless energy and your sense of humor. Just be sure that you do not get too heavy too soon in new liaisons. Good for introducing people who you care about to the folks. Friends will be energetically helpful in supporting your personal plans. Surprises should not be sprung on older relatives however. Be gentle when you are talking over your future ambitions with parents.

21. THURSDAY. Good. Probably one of the best days that you have experienced for quite awhile, especially if you are attempting to be of assistance to those less fortunate than yourself. You will feel a sense of well being if you can bring pleasure to people who have been having a particularly rough time of it of late. You may be able to do quite a lot to help a member of the younger generation who is trying to make something of their lives; they will be grateful for your concern and the benefits that you can offer them from your own experiences. Influential people will be prepared to pull a few strings for you behind the scenes which could lead to an increase in profits. Secret enmity can be brought out into the open and dealt with once and for all.

22. FRIDAY. Changeable. Promising day for efforts to make advances with creative work. The best way to brighten up jobs that have lost their sparkle is to bring your artistic talents into play. Superiors will be impressed by your inventiveness. You should be able to complete some of your chores in record time and this will give you the opportunity to deal with personal issues that have been weighing you down in connection with household affairs. Words can be used with good effect when trying to get your own way with important people. No attempts should be made to contact government officials behind the scenes. Favors will not be granted that would not be strictly open and aboveboard.

23. SATURDAY. Superb. Another favorable day for continuing in your efforts to make improvements in creative enterprises. Your imagination will be working overtime. You can perhaps find ways to turn hobbies into paying concerns. It will be easier to bring influence to bear on those who are in a position to offer you financial assistance. You will be more in the mood for work than for pleasure seeking in the earlier part of the day. Unforeseen events later on can be helpful to personal plans and make your quest for entertainment with a difference a possibility. Romance will be pleasant, but perhaps not quite as exciting as you may have been hoping for. Happy for married Sagittarians who spend more time with spouse and children.

24. SUNDAY. Ordinary. Although you might not be in the mood for it, Sagittarians who do have to go out to earn a living today should be well pleased at the extra cash that they are able to earn for their efforts. There may be better jobs available to you, and the weekend bonus payments will be too much of an incentive to turn them down. This is not a day when you should indulge in secret activities, however, either in the business or in the personal side of your life. Play it straight with people who you are romantically involved with. Do not build up their hopes and expectations if you have cooled towards them. Good for discussing financial problems with family members who can be helpful.

25. MONDAY. Guarded. Workmates are likely to be contrary. This is not the best of days for getting along with people who you have to work beside. Keep to yourself as much as possible. Be alive to the dangers of accidents due to negligence. Do not allow your mind to wander while on the job. Sagittarians may find their independent natures prevent them from making necessary compromises so that employment conditions will remain unsettled for most of the day. Better day for those who are doing business outside the office; personal efforts can be helpful towards making transactions more profitable. Rest up for a challenging week.

26. TUESDAY. Disquieting. Friends may be seeking your advice, but unless you feel confident you can give them sound counsel, be wary of telling them what to do. Otherwise you may find later that they're blaming you for their problems. Frankly, it would be wiser not to involve yourself at all in what does not concern you. Romantic attachments contain the possibility of some unhappiness. Sagittarians who were looking forward to dating tonight may be let down without a very good excuse being offered. Employment affairs continue to be sensitive. Pets may be pining and need more love and care. Make plans now for any family get-togethers.

27. WEDNESDAY. Disturbing. The opposition of your partner to your plans is likely to upset your applecart this midweek day. It will be annoying to you that loved ones seem unwilling to help you to make the cutbacks in expenditures that you feel are so vital if you are going to keep your head above water. Be on your guard with neighbors. It will be unwise to air your opinions too freely to them, especially if they concern mutual acquaintances. Personal plans may come to a full stop. You will be expected to spend more time at home if you want to avoid a full-scale fight. There can also be difficulties with influential people who are likely to remain contrary. Control your temper or you will only increase tension.

28. THURSDAY. Good. Good day for getting in touch with relatives. You should be able to get sensible advice from people whose experience you should be willing to learn from. Friends will be helpful when it comes to assisting you in smoothing over differences that have taken place within the home between you and your spouse, or partner. Might be a nice idea to arrange some special treat this evening. Entertainment with a difference need not cost a great deal of money. Club activities will be helpful to business as well as giving you a bit of fun. Influential people will be more inclined to sign important documents that you want them to become a party to. Enjoy your family or friends and be thankful for them.

29. FRIDAY. Deceptive. Other matters having been dealt with, you can turn to odd jobs, and those various other things you've been leaving aside. Someone may be eager to pass on "inside information" about money matters. It's likely to be misleading information so check with professional people who should be in the know before you act upon it. It might be best to avoid all speculation no matter how tempted you are to take a chance in order to make a quick buck. People will be unpredictable. It is not a good idea to plan too far ahead. Joint owners of funds and resources are likely to create confusion. Tax troubles can easily be made worse.

30. SATURDAY. Splendid. Undoubtedly a great ending to the month of November for you, so don't waste it. Good for business trips and for closing deals that you do not want to have to ponder over the weekend. You will be able to put important new projects into practice sooner than you expected during the month of December, too. Good for making arrangements with friends. The only thing for which this day is not auspicious is trying to overcome obstacles put in your path, probably by an elder. Think about old-age security and put more of your earnings into pension funds. Needful changes can be made in financial plans without upsetting close family members. People behind the scenes can be helpful.

DECEMBER

1. SUNDAY. Good. You start the first day of the last month of the year in fine shape. Looks as if you have set yourself many challenges which you feel confident you can fulfill. This is a pleasant rest day. A time for being with loved ones and for giving them more of your time and attention. Romance can be started behind the scenes for those of you who have to work. Favorable for discussions with other owners of funds on ways to increase profits on cash that you have invested. Influential people will be accommodating. Health difficulties that have been a worry for you are not likely to be quite so troublesome.

2. MONDAY. Mixed. Personal plans can be carried out. You will enjoy giving attention to matters having to do with your happiness and the well-being of the people who are closest to you. Communicating with people at or from distances will be helpful; you can probably save yourself quite a lot of expense by getting in touch with them over the telephone or through the mail. Influential people will be prepared to give you the benefit of their knowledge. Heed the advice of superiors even if it requires more self-discipline for you to follow them. Health may need some attention. Make sure that your diet is giving you all the vitamins that you require. Get plenty of rest and exercise if you need it. Make a dent in holiday shopping.

3. TUESDAY. Special. A happy day for romance. Get in touch with someone who you have been thinking about quite a lot. It is up to you to take the initiative where matters of the heart are concerned. Warm feelings that you have for a member of the opposite sex are likely to be reciprocated. Sagittarians will be feeling much more secure and confident. People will be eager to have the pleasure of your lively company. Personal magnetism will be high. You should also be able to make good progress in your job. The day is starred for Sagittarians whose work involves them in acting or other forms of media entertainment. Friends will be enthusiastically cooperative. Good for contacts with professors or colleges. Study programs can be advanced.

4. WEDNESDAY. Disquieting. It will not be easy for you to settle down. Concentration will be difficult to attain and maintain. Perhaps you have set targets for yourself that are too high. Do not take on additional workloads that would mean you have to brush over details. Differences will develop with loved ones over money. You must try to keep a check on the extravagant side of your nature. This is a time of the year when you should be trying harder to put more cash to one side. Business transactions can be helped through more secrecy. You will find that it profits you to operate away from public scrutiny. Some charity activity may be rewarding for you. The way to shake off the blues is to go to the assistance of those less fortunate than yourself.

5. THURSDAY. Fair. This day will be useful for negotiating agreements that require a certain amount of secrecy. Talks that you have behind closed doors are likely to bear fruit. You will be able to reach agreement with colleagues who you know from past experience are hard bargainers. Sagittarians must keep a tight rein on the impulsive side of their natures however. Do not allow yourself to be bulldozed into making decisions that you might have cause to regret at a later date. People with powerful personalities must not be allowed to have too great an influence over you. Some good luck can come through influential people including public officials. Personal effort will be important to the success of this day.

6. FRIDAY. Deceptive. A sensitive time for financial matters. You will have to watch your step with cash. Do not lay out more than you can honestly afford in order to purchase luxury goods or articles for home or for your personal use. Pay outstanding bills. Do not keep people waiting too long who you owe money to. Misunderstandings can easily occur, especially with friends. Check any arrangements that you have made to see close associates. Good day for romance. The Sagittarian personality will be more attractive than ever to members of the opposite sex. Business profits should be conserved and not reinvested. This is not a day for speculation.

7. SATURDAY. Good. An excellent ending to the first week of December appears to be in store for you. You will have more energy at your disposal. For Sagittarians who have to work, this looks like being a particularly promising day. Influential people will be extremely pleased with your recent efforts and it may well be that some additional cash incentives will be dangled before you. Go all out to prove your worth to people who are in a position to help you to climb higher up the ladder of success. Relatives will be helpful. New friends can be made. Social activities that bring you into contact with people from different walks of life are likely to appeal.

8. SUNDAY. Settled. A fortunate day for doing a bit of business on the side. You will be able to have valuable conferences with people who you did not have the opportunity to get in touch with during the working week. There is not likely to be any additional pressure placed upon you by loved ones. You will probably want to do a favor for an older relative who has shown you particular kindness in the past. Associates will be congenial if you have to go out to work. There are not likely to be any difficult situations to cope with at your place of employment. The use of more imagination will be helpful to financial problems. Make more of an effort to recover old debts. People in hospitals or in difficult circumstances will arouse the compassion of Sagittarians.

9. MONDAY. Disquieting. It will not be easy to settle down to jobs of a routine nature. This is likely to be a particularly trying time for the Sagittarian office or shop worker. Health problems are another factor that could cause holdups. You may be delayed from carrying out your chores because there are staff shortages or perhaps your own physical well-being is not up to par. Risks must not be taken when handling tools or machinery. Take care when driving too. Do not break any highway laws in any way when you are behind the wheel or you could find yourself on the wrong side of the law. Sagittarians have to avoid being tactless or blunt. Promises should not be made which cannot be kept.

10. TUESDAY. Unsettled. Sagittarians will probably be in a more subdued mood. You are likely to be thinking about past mistakes and doing what you can not to repeat them. This would appear to be a better day for planning than for taking action. It would be folly to rush into speculative projects before you have had the opportunity to examine them from all angles. Ideas that friends come up with for making easy money will be too farfetched and impractical. Looks as if you will be having some frank discussions with loved ones in an attempt to clear the air at home. Do not allow discontent to lead to recklessness with money. Do not squander your hard-earned cash through seeking momentary pleasure. Influential people and the promises that they make cannot be depended upon.

11. WEDNESDAY. Fair. A restless sort of a day appears to be in store for you unless you make more of an effort to channel your energies in a constructive manner. Get a schedule organized and stick to it. There may be distractions at your place of employment but you must not allow these to get under your skin. Take care on the roads. Do not drive too fast. Obey the speed limit and watch out also for the carelessness of other drivers. Reunions are possible with relatives who have been away, possibly out of the country. Any personal plans that you have the opportunity to carry out in the latter part of the day have more chance of producing good results.

12. THURSDAY. Strenuous. Don't overwork yourself. You could be pushing too hard. Pace yourself for a full day's work as the pressures on you are likely to increase from midafternoon onwards. You may even have to work past your usual quitting time. Rush jobs may come up that have to be dealt with then and there. Conditions are deceptive for financial affairs. With the expensive festive season upon you, you must be cautious that you do not spend extravagantly. Sagittarians should be doing more to save up for special presents for loved ones. Good later on for activities with friends, especially if clubs are involved. You will certainly want to unwind and forget all about career issues.

13. FRIDAY. Quiet. Superstitiously minded Sagittarians have no need to be concerned about this particular Friday the thirteenth. This day looks as if it is going to be marked by its lack of activity. This will not be such a hazardous period for finances. Look out for bargains in the shops. You will have more time to give consideration to the presents that you should get for people who you always have problems in buying for. Domestic Sagittarians should be able to get ahead with the household chores before the weekend. Good time for catching up with routine odd jobs. Sagittarians will be less inclined to throw their money around extravagantly. Prepare your Christmas budget. Try to work out just how much you are going to need to spend on food and drink this festive season.

14. SATURDAY. So-so. Friends must not be allowed to have too great an influence on the financial decisions that you make.

When it comes to money you must work out problems for yourself. The advice that is offered by close associates about savings may be meant in a spirit of goodwill, but what they have to say is unlikely to fit your personal situation. No major commitments should be made affecting business profits. Group activities are likely to be a bit of an anticlimax. Going out on jaunts may not come up to your expectations. Sporting activities may be a letdown. A person or a team you support may not play as well as you had anticipated. Better later on for attending to correspondence or making short trips. The health of an older relative should be improving now.

15. SUNDAY. Good. A happy day, especially for the Sagittarian parent. Children will be a source of great pleasure for you. You will feel that you are closer to your loved ones than has been the case for some time. There may also be opportunities to do a bit of business, though this might involve making a short trip. People who you visit will be obliging and some valuable deals may be set up that will mean more cash in your pocket before Christmas. Your spouse, or partner, will be affectionate and cooperative. Good for doing odd jobs in and around the house that require more than one pair of hands. Happy for romantic ventures. Unforeseen happenings can bring something very special to your day.

16. MONDAY. Fair. Go all out to enlist the goodwill and support of an influential person. You should discover that superiors will be only too pleased to be of assistance to you. Do not be afraid to seek advice if you are not one hundred percent certain about the best way to deal with a new job. Important documents can be signed. Now is the time to enter into contractual agreements that will ensure security next year. It would seem to be pointless to attempt to hold out for better terms as it is unlikely that you would be able to improve on offers that have already been made. Sagittarians have to guard against becoming depressed; problems may not be as difficult as they first appear. Care must be taken to guard against catching coughs or colds.

17. TUESDAY. Quiet. One of those days which is not likely to offer any interruptions. You should be able to get on with your work without having the interference of people nosing about and looking over your shoulder. It must also be said that there are unlikely to be any stimulating things to do from the pleasure seeking angle. It would be best to keep yourself meaningfully occupied within the home if you do have some spare time on your hands. If you go out in order to seek kicks, you are likely to spend more cash than you can afford. This is not an active enough day to attempt to make any new starts with business ventures, but unimportant affairs which are outstanding can probably be brought to a close.

18. WEDNESDAY. Disquieting. Calm down. You seem to be in a tense and nervous state. Do not get yourself too worked up. You could be letting your imagination run away with you and make mountains out of molehills. Transactions involving homes or land and its products have to be handled with more caution. Sagittarians must avoid being overly dominant with loved ones. Allow members of your family to make decisions that they will have to be ultimately responsible for. The cooperation of influential people may not be so easy to get as you thought. It might be best to wait for a more favorable period before you ask for any special favors. Unexpected happenings this evening can help to make romantic affairs more interesting; break-ups are also possible.

19. THURSDAY. Improving. Speculation should be avoided. This is certainly not a time of the year when you should be taking risks with your cash. Do not allow yourself to be easily led by friends who have a strong gambling streak in their nature. The tips that they pass on to you are not likely to reap dividends. All financial affairs contain the possibility of deception this Thursday. Agreements that you thought you were very close to reaching may be delayed. Good for working on creative enterprises that do not require any outside assistance. Romantic affairs may be getting a bit more serious; but spending on glamorous outings can be misunderstood and create unhappiness.

20. FRIDAY. Good. Probably the most interesting and exciting day of the week so far. You should be getting well into the spirit of the festive season. You will have more energy at your disposal and this should make it possible for you to get ahead with your Christmas shopping. Bargains can be found in the big department stores for people who you always have difficulty in buying for. Creative and mental projects can be made more successful; good for efforts to obtain the help and support of influential people that would enable you to expand existing enterprises. Relatives will not be making so many demands upon you. Correspondence is likely to bring you some good news. Unexpected events are likely to work in the favor of Sagittarians.

21. SATURDAY. Happy. You will have plenty of energy today and that will be just as well. There will be lots of last-minute shopping to get in. Loved ones will be easy to get along with. This is a pleasant day for teamwork on all levels. Every effort should be made to fulfill personal plans and desires that you may not have time for over Christmas. People generally will be more likely to cater to the wishes of the Archer. Romance would appear to be perking up more than has been the case for some time now. This day is starred for the Sagittarian in love. Activities with children will give pleasure. Imagination will be livelier and will be helpful to creative enterprises.

22. SUNDAY. Quiet. Take it easy. It is important that Sagittarians build up their inner reserves of strength this Sunday. Relax and unwind. It would seem that you will get more satisfaction by sticking to local surroundings. Trips that would take you to unfamiliar territory are unlikely to be necessary or advisable. Useful for working in and around the home and for putting up the Christmas tree and similar decorations. Check the list of people who always remember you at this time of the year and make sure that you have sent a Christmas card to them. Good day for getting in touch with people who are going abroad in the next day or two. Sagittarians should find that they are in the mood to complete numerous odd jobs that they have postponed too often.

23. MONDAY. Lazy. This will not be a particularly active or stimulating start to the work week. As Christmas is so soon, it would seem that conditions at your place of employment will be far too slow-moving to contemplate making any new starts. It would be best to try to wind up routine affairs. Deal with jobs now that you do not want to have hanging over your head during the next few days. People will be pleasant enough but anxious to knock off from the office or family early if they possibly can. Conditions will lack force generally. It should be possible to keep distant operations on the move over the telephone or through writing letters. This is not the right time for setting out on any long journeys.

24. TUESDAY. Disquieting. Don't get in a flap. Take life at a calm and steady pace. Spouses, or partners, will be contrary so that cooperation will be difficult to obtain. The contrariness of others could set back your personal plans. Some worry is likely over health. You may not be feeling up to snuff. If it is not your own physical condition that is giving you cause for concern, then it will be that of a close associate. Favorable agreements will be difficult to consummate. It would be best not to try to rush contracts through before Christmas. Legal action should be deferred. Delays connected with court cases are likely to last longer than you would have anticipated.

25. WEDNESDAY. Merry Christmas! Don't get overexcited. Tact and patience will be required with loved ones. You may have plenty of motivation at your disposal, but you should have a little more consideration for loved ones and members of your family who may not be feeling on top of things. Don't be too pushy. There could be arguments with your spouse, or partner. Short trips will work out better than long journeys. Conditions in distant parts are likely to be somewhat deceptive. No financial commitments should be made. Don't get embroiled in business discussions this Christmas day. Best to stick to seeking pleasure in simple ways.

26. THURSDAY. Disquieting. You will be getting wind of much that has been kept quiet, as people will be confiding secrets to you. However, if they are quizzing you about your own affairs, best to be reticent until you can accurately gauge their motives. Someone you're trying to track down may be very elusive today, and if you're trying to pin people down to hard and fast commitments you may find they are unwilling or unable to make definite promises. It's one of those days when much may be attempted but too little accomplished. The opposition of your partner or spouse could make it difficult for you to fulfill your pleasure plans. Sagittarians can be flirtatious and this will only upset loved ones even more. This is not a day for proposing marriage.

27. FRIDAY. Promising. People behind the scenes will show a greater willingness to be of assistance to you. Sagittarians may not have had quite such an enjoyable time this Christmas as they usually do. You will be quite pleased that the festive season is over and you can get back into the swing of your regular job. Do what you can to make the future look more secure for you and yours. Hidden assets can be discovered. Make sure that any cash that you have on deposit is earning you the best possible interest. A good day for getting to the bottom of mysteries, possibly associated with people or events in the past. Delays can now be overcome with energy and determination.

28. SATURDAY. Good. Another excellent day. You seem to be ending the week in quite a burst. Needful changes can be made in the way you organize your financial affairs. Look at your present monetary policy; surely there are ways you can cut down on unnecessary spending. You should find that influential people are a good deal more helpful. Plans can be made for improving your prospects of promotion in the New Year. Operate from behind the scenes. Excellent day for gaining information from people who like to maintain a low profile. Secrecy is likely to be particularly important to all that you undertake. Health can probably be improved without having to lay out any more money.

29. SUNDAY. Mixed. Favorable business opportunities may arise from Sunday activities. There could be good opportunities opening up to you for getting in touch with people who were not available over the Christmas period. Sagittarians do have to be a little wary of making any hasty moves or decisions. Better time for discussions than for making any definite and legally binding contracts. Seek information that you can store away for use in the New Year. Speeding has to be avoided. Do not be in too much of a hurry. Although this is a Sunday, there could well be police traps around for people who go over the limit that has been set by the law. Speed and carelessness spell disaster.

30. MONDAY. Doubtful. Appearances are not to be trusted today; situations are not quite what they seem, so you should keep an open mind about what's going on. What you were hoping would come to a boil in working surroundings will be left simmering. Be careful not to let your imagination run away with you. It's a time to keep your head out of the clouds and your feet firmly on the ground. Arguments could develop with distant people. Contacts with professors or colleges are not likely to be very satisfactory. You may have the chance to discuss an exciting new project for the New Year. Friends and their company will cheer you up this evening and you will feel more like celebrating tomorrow.

31. TUESDAY. Good. This will not be a particularly strenuous ending to the New Year. Still and all, this should be a pleasant enough day. There may be opportunities to involve yourself with glamorous people or situations, especially if you are going to hit the high spots and celebrate in a rather special way. Go along with the ideas of your close associates; they may not have too much appeal at first, but what they suggest in the way of pleasure-seeking is likely to be your best bet. Be alert for business opportunities. You may have the chance to make a little money through taking a calculated risk. Colleagues may come up with some worthwhile propositions.